MW00930453

Pharmacy School Confidential
An Insider's Guide to Getting in, Getting out, and Getting the Most from the Experience

Jennifer G Schnellmann, PhD

Pharmacy School Confidential

Copyright © 2013, 2014, 2015, 2016 by JG Schnellmann

All rights reserved. No part of this book may be reproduced or transmitted in any form or any manner, electronic or mechanical, including photocopying or recording, or by any information storage and retrieval system, without permission in writing from the author.

ISBN-13: 978-1484159460

ISBN-10: 1484159462

INTRODUCTION AND PURPOSE

This book is for anyone actively pursuing enrollment in a school of pharmacy, but it applies to currently enrolled students, too as it offers hard-to-find details to sharpen your sense of what is important to pharmacy school faculty. Such knowledge can smooth your transition into professional school, perhaps increase your scholastic performance, and ultimately help you land the perfect job in your field.

During my tenure on the faculty of an accredited, 4-year public college of pharmacy in the south, I have had the fascinating role of interviewing prospective applicants, seeing first-year students on "day 1" of class, and watching graduates leave after commencement...and a smidgen of everything in between.[*] In the college, I teach, listen, and learn from our approximately 200 matriculating students each year. Serving as a first-year student mentor gave me eye-opening insight about the minute details of students' adjustment to pharmacy school and how this affects their personal behaviors and scholastic performance. My service on the college's professional education committee allowed me to see how courses integrate to provide an education worthy of a PharmD. Finally, my work with the admissions committee informed me about student hurdles for entry into pharmacy school.

Information is power and *inside information* is the true coin of the realm. To this end, this book provides an intriguing glimpse into the professional school educational system that few see "behind the scenes". Specifically, I demystify the admissions process and deconstruct the first, and often most demanding, year of the program, concluding with information about the remaining years and beyond. Because students seldom receive such direct, honest feedback about faculty, a generous characterization of the pharmacy school instructor is given, along with expectations and pet peeves. Facts about course materials and testing, which are notoriously difficult to obtain, are included too. Sources used for the book are chiefly peer-reviewed scientific publications and a few personal observations. An index allows quick relocation of specific sections, and the bibliography contains all cited sources.

Every pharmacy student begins school with high hopes and grand plans, seeking the most for his educational dollar. Graduates want the scientific knowledge and clinical skills to be perfectly poised as highly desirable potential employees, enjoying multiple job offers. Hopefully, this book will assist students to maximize their return on their relatively brief time spent in professional training.

Disclaimer: Information within does not guarantee admission or success in pharmacy school but rather provides an "insider's view" of successful applications and habits of high-achieving students.

TABLE OF CONTENTS

CHAPTER 1   1

Contemplating a Career in Pharmacy   1

   Motivation   2

   Pre-professional Experience   5

   Educating the Pharmacist   7

   Degree Details   9

   PharmD "Plus One"   11

   Choosing a Program   12

   Program Tuition and Fees   13

   Top of the Heap   15

   Potential Classmates   19

CHAPTER 2   21

Applying to Pharmacy School   21

   Criteria for Going   21

   Creating Student Advantages   25

   The PCAT   28

   The Application Process   29

   The Interview   30

   Letters of Recommendation   35

   The Personal Statement or Essay   36

   The Acceptance Process   39

CHAPTER 3   41

Making it through the Professional Program   41

   Textbooks   42

   Does Working "Work"?   43

   In the Know   44

   Coursework   45

   Attendance   47

   During Lecture   47

Distance Education 49

Lecture Recordings 50

Honor 53

Professionalism 55

The Internet and Social Media 59

Student Entitlement 60

Self-Awareness 62

Student Abilities 65

Student Disabilities 66

CHAPTER 4 .... **69**

The "Inner workings" of the Professional Pharmacy Program ... 69

The Players: Deans, Chairs, Faculty, and Staff 69

Communication with Faculty 74

Faculty Duties 77

Resolving Problems 79

Class Structure 81

Course Materials 86

CHAPTER 5 .... **90**

Exams and Student Evaluation Tools 90

Online Testing 91

Audience Response Devices or "Clickers" 93

Testing Preparedness 95

Test Review 98

"Testing" the Test 98

Making the Grade 102

Grade Modifications 103

Failing 107

Leave of Absence 108

Attrition 109

CHAPTER 6 .... **110**

The First Year 110

Course Descriptions 111

Expectations 115

Activities 117

Between Years 118

The Significance of the White Coat 120

CHAPTER 7 **122**

The Second Year 122

Course Descriptions 123

Expectations 125

Activities 127

CHAPTER 8 **128**

The Third Year 128

Course Descriptions 129

Expectations 132

Activities 133

CHAPTER 9 **135**

The Final Year 135

Course Descriptions 136

Expectations 136

Activities 139

CHAPTER 10 **145**

Post-Graduation 145

Why To Do It? 147

How To DO It? 148

The PGY1 Experience 150

The PGY2 Experience 151

Stipends 152

CHAPTER 11 **154**

Putting Your Degree to Use 154

Changing Roles of the Pharmacist 154

Who's the Boss? 158

Working with the Public	*158*
Working with Other Healthcare Professionals	*160*
Major Laws and Rules Governing Healthcare	*163*
The Pharmacy Workforce	*166*
CHAPTER 12	**176**
In the Trenches	*176*
Comments from Current Pharmacists	*176*
Conclusion	*179*
Bibliography	*181*
Index	*206*
Appendix I: US Colleges of Pharmacy	*216*
Appendix II: Pre-Requisites for US Colleges of Pharmacy	*224*
Appendix III: Professional Organizations for Pharmacy Students	*232*
Appendix IV: Answers to Practice Questions	*238*
Appendix V: Top 200 Drugs by Prescription Sales	*240*
Author Information	*245*

CHAPTER I

CONTEMPLATING A CAREER IN PHARMACY

When college students are queried about their future career choices, they often suggest professions that they believe will lead to a particular lifestyle they may have imagined for themselves. For example, some students will reply to job-related questions by suggesting career choices that are tied to secure incomes. Other students contemplate a specific career for the flexible hours it may offer. Still others may consider professions with significant public visibility and lasting social meaning.

Interestingly, the profession of pharmacy is an answer that addresses all of these career motivations. Thus, hundreds of students *do* respond with "I want to be a pharmacist!" when asked, "What are you going to do with your life?"

However, often, *past this point of information*, little more is said. Overwhelmingly, when students who are interested in a pharmacy career are asked, "Why do you want to be a pharmacist?" they provide generic answers which suggest that their career choice was more spontaneous than well-considered.

How can this be true?

Let me explain...

MOTIVATION

Although students can and do readily profess to be interested in a career in pharmacy, they almost always have one of two answers to rationalize their interest or enthusiasm for the profession. Specifically, they report, "I want to help people", or "I like science". Both of these responses are uninspiring, vague, and insufficient.

For example, at its essence, "helping people" can take many forms, from driving a sanitation department truck to teaching in a rural public school. Volunteering to shelve books at the local library or mentoring disadvantaged youth through a city program is also a form of "helping people". Therefore, the answer that "helping people" motivates the student to seek a career in pharmacy is not particularly specific.

The next response—that the student "likes science"—is common, too. While such scholastic enthusiasm is essential, it is insufficient to sustain a student through a four-year educational pursuit that actually is *not* totally comprised of science. Indeed, although professional pharmacy training is based on science, it also includes math, writing, and significant analytical, clinical, and communication skills. Therefore, such a rigorous course of study will demand so much more than just "liking science".

So, let's agree that "helping people" and "liking science" are weak rationales for entering pharmacy school. Then, we can suggest that the *ideal* pre-professional student (read: the one you want to be) will have contemplated much more than this. To inspire such contemplation, two series of thought-provoking questions are listed below. The questions are crafted to allow students who are interested in pharmacy to sort or assimilate meaningful ideas, and perhaps gain some practice in articulating their true motivation to study pharmacy.

Note that the questions posed in the list fall into two categories, the "feel-good" queries and the "gut-check" questions. These two inquiry clusters are purposeful. Anyone can answer a question that promotes warm feelings and thoughts of security, self-importance, and well-being. These are easy. However, more concentration and self-study are needed to address reality-focused questions about a career in pharmacy. In fact, students may have never considered the less desirable aspects of the career, an unfortunate oversight because few jobs are flawlessly sublime.

R_x **" The "gut-check" questions are harder to contemplate, but this does not negate your obligation to consider them seriously. Answers to these questions are probably more true gauges of your aptitude for pharmacy as a life-long profession. "**

Here are the "feel-good" questions that can stimulate more novel responses about personal professional motivation:

- Do you want to help patients?
- Are you interested in understanding the mechanisms of action of hundreds of drugs?
- Would you feel empowered if you prevented a dangerous drug interaction in a patient?
- Would you feel knowledgeable if you helped a physician find the best drug formulation for his patient?
- Do you want to contribute to the health and welfare of your community in a meaningful way?
- Do you want to interact with multiple tiers of society, from the well-educated to the functionally illiterate?
- Would you like to run your own business?
- Would you enjoy a visible public presence in your community?

The "gut-check" questions are harder to contemplate, but this does not negate your obligation to consider them seriously. Answers to these questions are probably more true gauges of your aptitude for pharmacy as a life-long profession.

- Are you willing to reason with unreasonable people?
- Are you willing to defend your authority and profession against the occasional arrogant physician?
- Are you willing to explain (again) to a patient that having insurance drug coverage does not mean that the drugs are free?
- Do you have the patience to be put on hold when calling a physician...only to have her staff forget that you are waiting on the phone?

- Are you willing to report colleagues who abuse drugs or divert pharmacy merchandise?
- Are you willing to work in a retail setting, potentially filling hundreds of prescriptions a day, with no break?
- Are you willing to counsel patients about medications that would be unnecessary if these patients would simply get rid of a few bad habits?
- Are you willing to work in a hospital to train students?
- Can you conceive of being responsible for getting each prescription right, every time, for every patient?

All "potential pharmacists" should explore their deepest motivation for this career choice. In fact, answers to more provocative questions posed here could reveal more about their true intentions and desires with respect to this profession. As any employed adult can tell you, many days the only joy you experience on the job is the very joy you brought to work that morning.

Also, many students who have not had much real work experience may fantasize about the idea of being a busy pharmacist, but because daydreams allow us to experience excitement, joy, or pride without risking anything or actually suffering through the hard work, the reality of four years of pharmacy school is often a supreme disappointment or worse, the job is unfulfilling because expectations were poorly managed or very misinformed.

❝ Often pharmacy school applicants are not really interested in pharmacy. They are applying to the program as a 'Plan B' if they do not get accepted to medical school, and the admissions committee interviewers know it. Why settle for an occupation that was not your first choice? You can easily fail at something you don't love, so why not try something you do?❞

At a minimum, pharmacy school applicants should know something about current medications, how they are used, and what are the most common drugs prescribed. A list of the 2015 Top 200 prescribed drugs will help those who have not begun to research medications and how they work (mechanisms of action). Applicants who are familiar with many drugs and their indications (uses) should attempt to read the scientific literature (pubmed.com) to get a feel for how drug studies are reported.

Becoming familiar with the scientific and clinical literature will expose students to the highly specific and technical language used to describe patient populations, medication management, and pharmacy as a profession. Better applicants will read more broadly to learn how health care professionals create teams for patient care. Even though these exercises are common sense activities for someone professing to be interested enough in a field to actually enroll in a program of study, many students appear each year with zero idea of what types of drugs are available and how they might be used. This suggests to faculty that their interest is superficial or that these students are not curious about their chosen future field.

PRE-PROFESSIONAL EXPERIENCE

Because no one without first professional pharmacy credentials (the doctor of pharmacy degree, or the "PharmD") and the associated licensure can actually practice pharmacy, students can never be entirely sure if they are interested in a pharmacy career. How can you know anything about something you have never done?

To address this very question, students often gain the limited experience available to non-degree-holding, non-licensed individuals by accepting jobs in local pharmacies as cashiers, shelf-stockers, or assistants. Other pro-active students will take the extra step to become a certified pharmacy technician, which allows them more involvement in the profession.

To work as a pharmacy technician, the student only needs a high school education or a General Educational Development* certificate (referred to as "the GED"). Also, the student must have no felony record, and age-requirements may apply. Such training necessities will vary from state-to-state. Students seeking a technician certificate may choose to complete a formal educational program through a local community college or technical school. In these programs, the students receive approximately 240 hours of classroom instruction to earn certification. In some states, this avenue may be the only way to obtain such training. Community and technical schools are appropriate for seeking technical credentials, but, as you will read later, these schools are not as favorably viewed for meeting pre-pharmacy core requirements at this time.

Also, technician certification can be acquired from on-the-job-training, which may be referred to as an "externship".[1-3] An externship is an employer-sponsored, paid training experience which must also meet specific requirements, similar to its formal training counterparts. For example, minimal criteria for technician externship programs in retail chain drugstores

---

*The GED is not the same as a high school diploma and was not meant to be.

may include accreditation through the American Society of Health-System Pharmacists (ASHP).

Irrespective of whether the student participates in a program in a community college or gains the necessary experience on the job, once the technician has sufficient training, he will register with the state board of pharmacy. A *national* certification for technicians exists, as well. The National Pharmacy Technician Board Certification exam, which can be required in some states *before* a student seeks state certification, compels mandatory continuing technical education and a renewal of this national certification every two years.

❝ A pharmacy school applicant who confesses to never having spoken with a pharmacist prior to applying to pharmacy school cause faculty who interview him to question the legitimacy of the student's application. If you cannot acquire experience, at least talk to a pharmacist!❞

Even with proper credentials, a pharmacy technician may be permitted only limited duties in most pharmacies.[4] For instance, the technician may count drug dosage forms such as tablets or capsules, enter prescriptions into a computer database, type drug labels, and prepare IVs, including those needed for chemotherapy treatments.[4-6] However, in most pharmacies, a technician may not counsel patients about their therapy. The technician is not qualified to do so, no matter how many conversations he has overheard between the pharmacist and patients.

This clear restriction from patient counseling has practical and legal implications, and it separates the duties of the supervising pharmacist (who has a degree, a license, and experience) from the student who may have only passed a certification exam. Rarely, even in the face of these facts of law and prudence, some privately owned retail pharmacies may tolerate more technician involvement. For instance, if the lead or supervising pharmacist simply cannot handle the patient volume, technicians may be given more responsibility.[4]

In the end, the supervising pharmacist is legally and ethically (read: completely) responsible for the technician's actions and must formally sign off on many of the technician's tasks, such as confirming drug dosages. This check-and-balance system ensures patient safety while allowing the technician the freedom to assist the pharmacist with less patient-critical duties. Other safety features built into the pharmacy profession include limitations on the number of technicians that one pharmacist can supervise during a work day.

> **R_X** **66** *...The requirement of a first professional doctoral degree to practice pharmacy demonstrates that pharmacists are trained in the fashion of dentists, physicians, and veterinarians, to name a few professional degree recipients...(and) other healthcare professionals are confronted with the reality that they will be collaborating with rigorously and equivalently trained pharmacists who have earned the respected (and appropriate) title of "Dr".* **99**

Some students will be unable to find paid employment in a pharmacy, so they may choose to shadow a pharmacist during a typical work day. Shadowing is a special un-paid opportunity that may last one day or more, but this activity has inherent restrictions: if you are not helping to get the job done, you are probably in the way of those who are.

Whether you work in a pharmacy as an employee, a volunteer, or as a state- or nationally-registered technician, seeking acceptance to a pharmacy program will almost always require some type of experience in a pharmacy setting. Also, whether you find experiential opportunities in a pharmacy or not, talking to someone in the field is an absolute must.

Most students who have a real initial interest in pursuing a PharmD will have spoken with an actual pharmacist prior to investigating a professional program. Also, some applicants have a parent or other family member who works in the field, so their exposure to this profession is personal and could be life-long. Talking to different types of pharmacists, especially those who are at various stages of their career, is enormously helpful. These conversations may provide initial guidance for the student, allowing him to form preliminary and informed opinions about the potential enjoyment of a course of study in pharmacy and whether the job will be a worthwhile pursuit.

EDUCATING THE PHARMACIST

Pharmacists who have been in the profession for several decades may be willing to share stories about how their field has changed and how a pharmacy education has evolved. For example, seasoned pharmacists may recall that, in the past, a pharmacist acquired a Bachelor's of Science (BS) in Pharmacy to practice pharmacy. This degree was obtained in a 4- or 5-year professional undergraduate program.

PharmDs were also offered in the US, but these were distinguished from the undergraduate first professional degree. Thus, pharmacists with a BS in Pharmacy were given the professional designation of "BSPharm". The separate designation, "RPh", recognizes a pharmacist who has registered with the state to practice pharmacy. These unique titles reflect that the pharmacist possesses the necessary undergraduate training and the successful passage of board exams, state licensure requirements, and pharmacy law exams.

In 1990, the PharmD was declared by the American Association of Colleges of Pharmacy (AACP) as the first professional degree for all US pharmacists, and this diploma became the standard degree offered by each US accredited college of pharmacy. Pharmacists who have been on the job well before 1990 may appreciate the degree "upgrade", but others may question its necessity, even now, when significant credentialing is required for most patient-centered occupations. Rest assured (and this will be re-iterated again), that this degree change was intentional. The PharmD, or the doctoral-level designation of the first professional pharmacy degree, was meant to reflect the increasing amount of information required for pharmacists to practice their specialty.

Also, the requirement of a first professional doctoral degree to practice pharmacy demonstrates that pharmacists are trained in the fashion of dentists, physicians, and veterinarians, to name a few professional degree recipients. Of course this also means that other healthcare professionals are confronted with the reality that they will be collaborating with rigorously and equivalently trained pharmacists who have earned the respected (and appropriate) title of "Dr." See the "**Degree Tree**", **Figure 1**

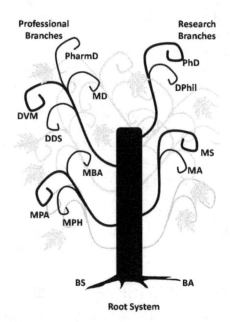

Figure 1. Stratification of US Degrees

to understand what this means in the greater scheme of overall education. The metamorphosis of the pharmacy degree still causes furrowed brows in a few (but thankfully shrinking) physician populations. More information about these amusing turf wars is described later.

DEGREE DETAILS

Although the PharmD as a professional requirement has been previously explained, some students admit to having confusion over the terms "graduate school" and "professional school". There is a difference between the two paths. Graduate programs exist to prepare the student to contribute to the knowledge in his field; professional school programs prepare the student for practical application of his knowledge.

The short-hand version is this: graduate programs prepare you to study; professional programs prepare you to work. Such unique purposes of each program point to differences with respect to program content and student expectations.

Thus, a pharmacy student who remarks that he is in "graduate school" is referring to another educational pathway. He may tell people he is enrolled in a "graduate level professional program", or she may tell her family that she is "seeking a professional doctoral degree" (or a "first professional degree"), and both of these statements are accurate. However, both students mentioned above are only actually enrolled in graduate school if each is seeking a PharmD/PhD (dual degree). More information about dual-degree pathways is described later.

Additional graduate *vs.* professional school distinctions include the specific degrees awarded in each program. The only graduate degrees available are the Masters of Science, Philosophy, or Arts and the Doctor of Philosophy (PhD or DPhil).

A Master's degree could be considered a terminal degree in a particular field if it is the highest obtainable degree in that area. For example, in architecture, the Master Architect degree is the terminal degree in that discipline. Otherwise, the PhD is the highest degree awarded in the US. Other professional degrees, and their relationships with one another, are depicted in the **Degree Tree (Figure 1)**.

Another concept that often confuses pharmacy students is the term "PharmD candidate". You may see this term in the signature line of e-mails from your friends who are in pharmacy school. This term is explained below in great detail to help the student understand its proper usage. The origin of the label "candidate" came from graduate programs. Specifically—for example, to earn a PhD in biochemistry—the student may take two years of classes, after which he will be given a *candidacy exam*. This exam is usually comprised of a written component and an oral portion.

Written candidacy exams require answering essay-type questions for 8–10 hours each day over two days, or they may be open-ended with respect to time (they go for as long as the student can write). The oral candidacy component may be a presentation that the student gives to the department, or it may be a question-and-answer session that lasts several hours. During oral exams, any question can be asked by any faculty member (within or outside of the department). Questions may be specific or general, and the exam ends when the faculty proctoring the exam are satisfied that the student possess sufficient expertise. Additional requirements may include presentation of an original research proposal.

If both the oral *and* written exams receive a passing grade (better than a "C"), then the student is a "candidate for the PhD". This example emphasizes that candidacy is an invitational concept; the student cannot be a candidate until passing the candidacy exam. Then, after several years of research and an original contribution to the field, the candidate will defend an original dissertation publicly under the guidance of a dissertation committee. The PhD then will (or will not) be awarded at the end of this effort based the recommendation of the dissertation committee. Approximately 10% of PhD candidates in the life sciences defend their dissertation in 4 years, and rare students complete one in less than this time (fewer than 5% of students).[7]

In professional school, an entirely different process occurs. Students in the first year may define themselves as candidates because they have passed the Pharmacy College Admission Test (PCAT), which is analogous to the graduate students' Graduate Record Exam (GRE). Thus, pharmacy students may consider candidacy to have been granted when the student met the entry requirements to enroll in pharmacy school. Then, the student may consider himself to be a "candidate" during the four years leading up to graduation, after which the North American Pharmacy Licensure Exam (NaPLEX) and related pharmacy law exams may be undertaken.

However, an analysis of common professional training nomenclature across programs suggests that dental students call themselves "dental students". Also, medical students refer to themselves as "first years", "second years", or "medical students", and so on. Thus, establishing a separate and confusing term for similarly trained, first professional pharmacy degrees is not be necessary and it is actually in accurate: there is no real for formal juncture at which a pharmacy student becomes a candidate, and the use of the term is likely inflated. Nevertheless, the idea that you are a "pharmacy student" is sufficiently impressive to anyone who appreciates the goals you are setting for yourself.

PHARMD "PLUS ONE"

Earning a PharmD in tandem with a graduate degree is becoming more common. Studies suggest that dual-degrees increase the prospects for employment of future PharmDs.[8] Some dual-degree combinations are described below, but these do not represent every available offering. Of course, to enter a dual-degree program, the student must meet the entrance requirements for both programs.[8-12]

- *PharmD/PhD*

The PharmD/PhD track accepts a small number of high-achieving students who want a terminal research degree (PhD) along with a first professional degree. These degree paths may take 7–8 years to complete entirely.[10, 12] Some of your pharmacy school classmates may be working toward a PhD, researching a scientific topic of interest to them. To finish the PhD, the student must complete a dissertation and offer an original contribution to the field of science as described in the previous candidacy/graduate school description. A post-doctoral fellowship (2–5 years) is optional, and its necessity may depend on the student's longitudinal interests.[13]

- *PharmD/MBA*

Students who want more education in business through the Masters of Business Administration degree may choose this approach.[13] Schools vary in the structure of their programs, allowing some students to begin an MBA as early as the first year of pharmacy school. PharmD/MBAs are perfectly poised for management positions, and these graduates offer a host of unique perspectives about business, finance, and pharmacy.[9, 13-14]

- **PharmD/MHA**

A Master's of Health Administration is acquired along with a PharmD in this track. Students interested in leading hospitals or healthcare systems may choose this degree combination.[11] Every healthcare system requires well-educated leaders, so if you love regulations and policies, and you have outstanding management skills, this is the track for you.[11]

- **PharmD/MPH**

This program combines pharmacy education with a Master's of Public Health, which can be focused on topics that range from pharmacotherapy to disease prevention and medication safety, for example. Graduates of this dual-degree program may work in government agencies, health departments, not-for-profit organizations, and private-sector jobs such as the pharmaceutical industry. They may also work in the health insurance industry. This degree combination will open unexpected and exciting doors for newly graduated PharmDs.

- **PharmD/MSCR**

Students who want training in clinical research by way of the Masters of Science in Clinical Research along with a pharmacy degree may choose this program. This track may appeal to a student who is interested in leading clinical drug trials, an area that requires specifically trained investigators. The absolute sensibility of a PharmD/MSCR leading clinical trials instead of physicians (who typically lead such) is marvelous. Pharmacists with clinical research training will be valuable additions to the drug trial workforce.

- **Other Degree Combinations**

Other dual-degree programs exist, such as PharmDs coupled with Master's in Public Administration or Economics, or even a *Juris* Doctor (terminal law degree).[14] Descriptions of these degree programs can be found on campus web pages. Also, students should ask about degree combinations that interest them, even if no formal program exists at that time. Enthusiastic and supportive faculty love innovative ideas and may be able to help you achieve a unique educational path that you develop for your own goals, so ask!

CHOOSING A PROGRAM

If you are interested in applying to pharmacy school, but you have not chosen a program at this time, by 2016, 138 schools of pharmacy are predicted to be operating in the US. Such an abundance of choices should offer multiple options for anyone who seeks a pharmacy degree.[15] **Figure 2** depicts the locations of US schools of pharmacy, and **Appendix I** offers a current listing of colleges of pharmacy along with their affiliated university (if

Figure 2. Distribution of US Schools of Pharmacy.

they have one).

Roughly half of US pharmacy schools are private institutions. Differences between public and private schools are typically based on program-funding sources.

For example, public schools may have been established by the state and funded by the legislature, which contributes to some costs of school infrastructure and operations. Tuition is also a major source of revenue. In recent times, state school funding has incrementally but continually decreased and less legislative support to public schools of pharmacy is a trend that may continue. Even with budget shortfalls and deductions, tuition for students at state colleges can be, but is not always, lower than tuition for private schools.

In contrast, private schools may not receive state funding toward the costs of running these schools. Thus, student tuition and private contributions, such as gifts or endowments from industry or alumni, may support the institution. Another difference between private and public pharmacy schools can be class and campus size. Public campuses tend to be larger, and the classes hold more students. In private schools, classes are usually smaller, reflecting the overall proportion of the campus. Also, private schools can change their status to become public campuses, but this is rare.

PROGRAM TUITION AND FEES

An important factor for many students who select a college of pharmacy is affordability. Whether the school is private or public, as of 2013, tuition is high. See **Figure 3** for a representation of current tuition across US pharmacy schools.[16] The price of a pharmacy education is not tied to its quality; many factors go into creating tuition rates. Thus, if the thought of paying down a several-hundred-thousand-dollar loan makes your stomach lurch, consider price carefully.

Also, whether you choose private or public, out-of-state tuition for pharmacy colleges is usually higher than in-state tuition. Non-residents pay a premium to attend.

This appears to reward students for staying within their state, preserving

- $10,000 or less
- $10,001-$20,000
- $20,001-$30,000
- $30,001 or more

Figure 3. In-state Pharmacy School Tuition across the US.

whatever "brain trust" the state possesses in the form of intellectual capital. However, it is obvious to the most casual observer that out-of-state students are often choice candidates for professional programs simply for the extra cash they bring to the school; although, no one will say this to an applicant. In short, bills must be paid to run the school, so money is necessary, and more money is better.

Our-of-state students with time on their hands can relocate to the state where the program exists, find a job, and establish resident status after a specific period of time (this varies by school) to take advantage of in-state tuition discounts. Smart and forward-thinking students may choose an undergraduate school in the desired location, obtaining in-state status by graduating from a college within the state boundary. Either way you choose to approach professional school, whether you seek an in-state institution or one that is across the country, you are never too young to begin planning a strategy to maximize your life's return for the investment of your intellect and talent.

Tuition is designed to pay for the administration of and instruction within the pharmacy program, supporting college faculty and staff for example. Room and board payments cover residence and dining options, which are typical for undergraduate colleges but unusual amenities in professional school. They are only mentioned here for completeness of information. Students often see the terms "tuition, room, and board" used together, so an explanation of each might be helpful to some.

Other fees that catch students unaware could be application fees, seat fees, matriculation fees, re-admission fees, student activity fees, laboratory materials fees, course packet fees, and more. Seat fees are charged to students who are accepted into the college for the purpose of guaranteeing a "seat" or placement in the first year class. Usually these fees are subtracted from tuition when the student enrolls, so the fee is rather like paying forward a portion of tuition in the form of "earnest money" prior to matriculation. Seat fees (also called seat confirmation/reservation fees or seat deposits) are non-refundable for most schools, and they may vary dramatically from school to school. Thus, students who are accepted and have paid the fee, but then choose to attend college elsewhere, lose this money to the school which accepted them.

Matriculation fees are charged to support costs associated with college admissions and student orientation. Matriculation fees may be paid at particular intervals or they may be charged for each credit hour in which the student is enrolled. Matriculation funds can also be used to cover costs of student transcripts and services offered to new students. Application fees may also cover these costs and substitute for matriculation charges at some colleges of pharmacy.

Technology or education delivery fees can be assessed each semester for all students who use online courses or technological applications and services. These fees may cover computers used on campus (aside from the students' personal computers), such as computer centers or laboratories, educational network or distance education services, and other telecommunication services. Some colleges of pharmacy loan laptops to students instead of requiring students to purchase their own computers, so technology fees may go toward funding this generous program.

Building/infrastructure/capital/equipment fees may be required of students enrolling in colleges of pharmacy, and these may be state-mandated collections to pay for campus construction. Additional fees may be charged to the student for the purpose of funding student union operations; educational, cultural, and student governmental activities; or athletic activities. Sometimes, these efforts are supported through student activity or recreational fees. Student service fees may fund career guidance, behavioral counseling, or miscellaneous health services. Finally, laboratory fees and white coat charges may be assessed to incoming students, and these are self-explanatory.

TOP OF THE HEAP

Students are always intrigued by the idea of attending the "best" pharmacy school, but they are often stumped for an answer when asked to define what this means. Most US university research faculty consider research dollars from the National Institutes of Health (NIH) to be a major criterion for ranking pharmacy schools in the US. Such faculty members know that having this type of research money means that the college is engaged in advancing science and has employed scientists who are successful at obtaining funding for their work. Also, schools with highly visible research programs tend to attract other outstanding professors, perpetuating the excellence forward.

Of course, having a bevy of Nobel-Prize-worthy scientists or clinicians at your college of pharmacy may have nothing to do with the school's ability to effectively teach you. Some of the best scientists and clinicians may be the worst instructors. Also, many top-notch faculty may find themselves "too busy" to teach, so they use teaching assistants to accomplish the educational missions of the college. Nevertheless, savvy students should have an awareness of how pharmacy schools compare with respect to NIH research awards, and these are listed below, in descending rank order.[17] This order is fairly consistent from year to year: top schools tend to retain their formula for success.

1. University of California San Francisco
2. University of Kansas Lawrence
3. University of North Carolina Chapel Hill
4. University of California San Diego
5. University of Washington
6. University of Utah
7. University of Colorado Denver
8. University of Michigan at Ann Arbor
9. Northeastern University
10. University of Illinois at Chicago

So, having the most research money from NIH is a distinguishing feature of a college of pharmacy for sure (if it has a ranking at all), but this may not be indicative of program rigor or whether a student will be a good fit for that school. Perhaps, the more important question to consider when choosing a program is what *you* think about it. Do you like the city where the school is located? Can you get around town easily and afford the cost of living? Surprisingly, choosing a school based on where you want to live and work after obtaining your degree might not be the best immediate plan. This will depend mightily on the job you want at the end of your training.

Thus, students should be familiar with institutional hiring trends in pharmacy in their ultimate desired location. It is never too late to be aware of where you want to work after you finish school, especially for the dual-degree graduate. For instance, if you graduate with a PharmD/PhD, you may be tacitly restricted from working where you obtained your degree. Scientific research positions for PharmD/PhDs may be preferentially given to graduates from *outside* the campus environment. The rationale for this is that research thrives on fresh ideas from people who have been trained elsewhere. Researchers who hire their own graduates are engaging in what the scientific community refers to as "intellectual inbreeding".

℞ **" A question rarely asked (but should be) by pharmacy school applicants is whether the program to which they are applying is affiliated with a teaching hospital or an academic medical center. "**

In contrast, a student with a PharmD may enjoy more flexible options, and she may be a very desirable hire for the university from which she graduated. Thus, students should know the culture of their college and the relative trends of the employment area where they eventually want to be. Inquiries about employment options are suitable questions at any stage of your pharmacy education because "hiring attitudes" are often unspoken institutional philosophies.

Thus, ask where current faculty completed their degrees when you interview, or go online to investigate the pedigrees of successful faculty within the department. If virtually all of your instructors obtained their degrees from the university which employs them, then you are probably safe in assuming that the university hires its own products.

If your program has a culture of not hiring its own graduates, knowing this early will enable you to plan your future more effectively. Perhaps you can attend school in your *second* favorite location with the intention of practicing pharmacy in your absolute favorite location (for example, you may choose a school in the Midwest and then practice pharmacy on the East Coast or *vice versa*).

Dream big and expand your thinking in this regard. Irrespective of the region where you wish to attend school, ask yourself: "Does the program curriculum seem strong but responsive to changes in pharmacy education?" Also reflect on these ideas: "Does the program offer the electives needed for a residency?" or "Does this school offer classes that I cannot find elsewhere?" or "Would I enjoy research in addition to my clinical training?" Examine school websites closely to obtain descriptions of courses as well as the surrounding city environment.

If, after addressing these important questions, you are still unsure about the caliber of your potential program, *US News and World Report* annually ranks institutions of higher learning, including pharmacy schools. This ranking is different from the NIH hierarchy. The methodology of *US News and World Report* for ranking schools of pharmacy is based on assessments sent to pharmacy college deans and faculty.

Respondents rate the academic quality of their own program. Thus, this report is inherently biased, and data outcomes are highly dependent on the number of surveys being returned. Despite the less rigorous compilation techniques, students are still interested in this information. Thus, below are the *US News and World Report* rankings of US schools of pharmacy for 2012, which was the last time these were ranked.[18]

1. University of California San Francisco
2. University of North Carolina Chapel Hill
3. University of Minnesota
4. University of Texas Austin
5. University of Kentucky/University of Wisconsin Madison*
7. Ohio State University/Purdue University/University of Michigan at Ann Arbor**
10. University of Arizona/University of Southern California/University of Utah***

A question that students rarely ask (but should) about pharmacy school is whether their program of interest is affiliated with a teaching hospital or an academic medical center. The answer to this question will profoundly influence the education you receive in a professional program. At this time, 49 pharmacy programs are affiliated with teaching hospitals/academic medical centers, either on the same campus as the pharmacy program or sufficiently near the campus to provide access to patients and clinical instructors.[16] Such an environment for training is so important that some schools promote clinical patient contact hours as evidence of the excellence of their program[19]

Attending a pharmacy school with no immediate access to a teaching hospital may pose distinct disadvantages in clinical training, and schools in this predicament may send their students to private or non-teaching hospitals outside the campus to rectify this training gap. However, students should know that private hospitals and clinics may not permit students to interact with their patients due to considerations of confidentiality (See **Chapter 2, §The Interview**, footnote and **Chapter 11 §Major Laws and Rules Governing Healthcare**) and patient preferences: literally, private hospital patients may prohibit students from "practicing" on them.[20-23]

A student who completes pharmacy school having had little or no interaction with actual patients has an immediate experiential deficit compared to PharmD graduates from programs that are united with hospitals of instruction. The argument that patient interactions can be obtained on the job, thereby eliminating any long-lasting educational disparities, may be true for a few students.

Tied for the ranking, but representing #5 and #6
**Tied for the ranking, but representing #7, #8, #9*
***Tied for the ranking of #10*

However, the PharmD who has not been involved in a hospital experience may not have interpreted actual laboratory data, witnessed real-time medication management therapy, interacted intensely with nurses or physicians, or observed the very diseases and symptoms his profession is poised to treat. These are important considerations in light of the fact that current physicians regard themselves as better medication management specialists than pharmacists, a fact that will have future implications on expanding pharmacists privileges in healthcare.[24]

POTENTIAL CLASSMATES

Applications to pharmacy school each year number in the hundreds of thousands nationwide.[25-29] Women comprise the majority of pharmacy school applicants at the present time, and general enrollment for both genders in colleges of pharmacy has increased about 4% each year since 2001.[15] That women are enrolling in professional school in greater numbers indicates that the previous gender stereotyping of women is being overcome. Not long ago, men were perceived as being more potentially successful at managing a career in pharmacy because they were perceived to have greater time to commit to the profession.[30]

Your classmates may be of a variety of ages, as well. Students in pharmacy school may be as young as 18 years-of-age, or they may be in their 50s, returning to school to find a new challenge or more job security.[31] Racial and ethnic profiles of students vary, too. For example, in the past few years, enrollments into schools of pharmacy were roughly 35% White and 35% Asian.[25] African-American students comprised about 10% of US enrollment nationwide, and various other nationalities were represented by more than 13% of the students entering pharmacy school.[25]

Because roughly half of the current students who enroll in pharmacy school possess a 4-year degree of some sort, students with such a degree may assume that their classmates will be likewise credentialed.[25] However, depending on the program requirements, students holding Bachelor's degrees may share classes with students who have completed only the basic requirements to gain admission (See **Chapter 2** for more details).

This might translate into a palpable difference in attitude or maturity. Younger professional students often behave much differently than students who have endured four years of undergraduate study. For example, less mature students may initially talk during the lecture, complain more vocally about grades, or routinely skip class to pursue personal enthusiasms (**§Attendance, Chapter 3**). This comment does not describe all "young" students; but, trends do exist, and faculty can detect the overall "age" of the class by behavior, often with superior reliability.

In defense of a younger student population, these unprofessional behaviors may arise because less experienced students may not perceive the shift in expectations between both educational programs. Thus, they may retain behaviors permissible in undergraduate school but frowned upon in pharmacy school. Ideally, students who only finish the minimal requirements to enter professional school will quickly recognize that they are transitioning into a vastly different experience that will be rigorous and unrelenting for several years. Then, (again, ideally) their behaviors will reflect this realization.

CHAPTER 2

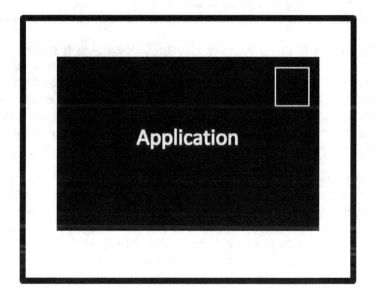

Application

APPLYING TO PHARMACY SCHOOL

Now that we have established that you are indeed interested in a pharmacy career, the time is right for discussing the most direct route to obtaining that PharmD.

CRITERIA FOR GOING

Although the PharmD is essentially the same across the US, the approaches to enter pharmacy programs are varied. For instance, some colleges of pharmacy will permit students to enter the PharmD program after two years of college during which they complete only specific prerequisites; hence, this should explain the comments about younger students in the preceding chapter. Required courses to apply for pharmacy school may be comprised of 60 to 80 hours of college credit and may cover typical science-major core components such as chemistry, mathematics, and biology.[32-33]

66 *Students who enter pharmacy school after completing only the prerequisites (read: they earn no degree) are gambling heavily. Students who leave the program (due to illness, family crisis, pregnancy, program dissatisfaction, etc.), may do so with loans to repay and no four-year degree as 'fallback insurance.'* 99

Some colleges of pharmacy have so many prerequisites that students need more than two years to complete the undergraduate classes, either due to course sequencing issues or overall class-load mathematics: there are too many hours to complete in two years. Some US schools of pharmacy allow enrollment into the PharmD program only after the applicant has earned a 4-year Bachelor's degree (and a few applicants to pharmacy school may have a Master's degree or more).

To learn what prerequisites are needed for all US colleges of Pharmacy, turn to Appendix II to see a list that focuses on science-specific details. For instance, not every school of pharmacy requires biochemistry, but you may want to take this class anyway so that you do not feel overwhelmed when you encounter it in pharmacy school. Remember, you want to have every advantage. Just because a class is not required *before* pharmacy school does not mean you will not need the information.

While fulfilling professional school requirements in college, students frequently declare that they are "pre-pharmacy" or "pre-med" majors. Interestingly, this is incorrect: "pre-med" and "pre-pharmacy" are not majors; rather, they are college advisory tracks, "intentions", or pathways to professional school. Some schools may refer to this pathway as "pre-pharmacy studies," but the bottom line is that a degree is not awarded in "pre-pharmacy".

Thus, students may choose to pursue a science or non-science major, even if she is self-described as "pre-pharmacy" because majoring in science is not required to enter pharmacy school. However, a biology, biochemistry, or chemistry major may be the most expedient way to fulfill pharmacy school requirements.

For example, an analysis of pharmacy college requirements suggests that necessary classes tend to include most of the following: organic chemistry I, II; biology I, II; anatomy and physiology I, II; biochemistry; microbiology; statistics; physics; immunology; cell biology, some type of composition or writing course; an economics course; and calculus.[33-35] These are typical curricula for science majors, which should explain the trend for future pharmacy students to major in biology, chemistry, or biochemistry. Some pre-pharmacy course requirements also include ethics, genetics, public speaking, and a religious studies course.[33]

A foreign language may not be required for many colleges of pharmacy, because the expectation is that two years or more of a foreign language were completed in high school to satisfy undergraduate entry requirements. Interestingly, some professional programs offer a specific foreign language elective, usually medical Spanish, for students who may practice in an area with a significant Hispanic population.[36-38]

Other than knowing what prerequisites are needed for pharmacy school, students should ask current pharmacy students what *non-required* courses they thought to be "essential" for their pharmacy program. You may find that, for example, biochemistry is not *required*, but that taking it in undergraduate school makes the difference between earning an "A" for the course (because biochemistry for pharmacy may be similar) or a being saddled with a soul-destroying "D" (because you could not master the sheer volume of content while taking other professional courses).

Whether you only complete the necessary requirements to enter pharmacy school or whether you finish a 4-year degree in science or another discipline, typical choices for pharmacy school are 4-year professional programs which may offer a 1- or 2-year post-graduate practical experience. Other trends in pharmacy education include 3-year programs which require some pre-professional education for admissions and 6-year programs, which have no pre-pharmacy requirements.

Three-year programs may appear attractive for their ostensible expediency, but their cost can be significantly higher than more traditional programs. Also, the stress experienced by students in those programs may be high.[39] In the 6-year programs, pharmacy school prerequisites are fulfilled in the first two years of the professional program, and then the student seamlessly transitions into the professional aspect of study.[16] At the time of this writing, 10 schools offer 6-year programs, and 12 institutions offer 3-year programs.[16]

Therefore, a commitment to a complete course of study in pharmacy may range from 6 (undergraduate: 2$^+$ years + professional school: 4–6 years) to 10 years (Bachelor's degree: 4⁺ years + professional school: 4–6 years), depending on the student's academic path. This is a tremendous obligation of money and time, so every student should explore all possible career options before choosing *any* professional course of instruction to ensure (as much as possible) a job that is satisfying and secure.

Most students interested in pharmacy school are aware that undergraduate grades are important for acceptance to pharmacy school. However, "expected" and "considered" grade point averages (GPAs) may be different for various programs. For instance, a GPA of 3.2 may be expected for a program applicant, but an applicant with a GPA of 2.5 may be considered by the admissions committee, as is the case for Auburn University's Harrison School of Pharmacy. In contrast, a student applying to Ohio Northern University's Raabe College of Pharmacy will be expected to have a GPA of 3.75, and applicants with GPAs below 3.0 may not be considered.[33]

The minimum published GPA considered by any US school of pharmacy at this time is a 2.5; the highest minimal GPA requirement is a 3.75,[33] and these GPA values are based on a traditional 4.0 scale. If your college does not use a 4.0 system, **Table 1** (next page) can be used to help you "normalize" your class averages to this scale to estimate your competitiveness.

Also, students should be aware that not all GPAs are created equal. Undergraduate cumulative GPAs typically account for all science, non-science, and math grades. Science or subject GPAs may include biochemistry, biology, inorganic chemistry, math, microbiology, organic chemistry, and other science classes. Also, the science GPA may include physics and any social sciences (sociology, psychology, etc.).

Table 1—The 4.0 Grading Scale		
Letter	Percent	Value
A+	97–100	4.0
A	93–96	4.0
A-	90–92	3.7
B+	87–89	3.3
B	83–86	3.0
B-	80–82	2.7
C+	77–79	2.3
C	73–76	2.0
C-	70–72	1.7
D+	67–69	1.3
D	65–66	1.0
E/F	Below 65	0.0

Some programs refer to all prerequisite math and science course grades as components of the "key GPA". Also, schools of pharmacy may evaluate each college or university GPA individually for students who attended more than one college (this is becoming more common as technical/community colleges are increasing in visibility). Finally, some schools may "weigh" GPAs from upper-tier undergraduate programs more heavily than grades earned from mid- to lower-tier colleges.

Thus, an "A" from Dartmouth might "count more" than an "A" from Arkansas State University. This may be immediately offensive to some students, but nothing has changed with respect to this trend...the only difference is that, now, you are aware of this practice. Policies or practices such as these exist to reward students in more rigorous programs.

Although students can argue that this is unfair and only confers even more advantages to those students already experiencing (and/or are able to afford) a top-notch education. There may be some truth to this criticism, but consider another perspective: you may not have been handed a first-class ticket to ride the success train, but there is no crime in leaping for that train from the platform.

Some colleges permit students to retake courses under what may be referred to as a forgiveness policy. Under this policy, students who retake courses in which they made a "C" or lower can substitute on their transcript the better grade from the second attempt at the class. Such permissions for coursework can mislead the student into believing that the pharmacy school admissions committee will only "see" the replacement grades from the repeated course.

Students may be unaware that colleges of pharmacy can re-calculate these "forgiven" grades, using the first-course-attempt grade. Thus, colleges of pharmacy examine both the cumulative GPA and the retention GPA when considering applicants. The cumulative GPA is the grade value of all courses attempted in the undergraduate experience. The retention GPA is calculated from all courses attempted *minus* any repeated or remedial courses.

CREATING STUDENT ADVANTAGES

To cover this topic, a brief digression is necessary.

An emerging trend for young students is to approach college admissions armed to the teeth with early college credit. This is accomplished by taking college courses—often community college classes—in high school. This type of scholastic approach or "dual enrollment" may allow students to enter and complete college studies with undergraduate credits from multiple sources.[40] Students (and their parents) may believe that this confers an advantage for the student, especially for future applications to professional schools. After all, having all of the prerequisites completed at the soonest possible date is good, right?

Well, the answer to that is a qualified "yes" and "no".

Now and then, dually enrolled students find that credits earned at a community college will not transfer to more selective colleges, even if both educational programs are depicted as being similar.[40-41] Therefore, the class may need to be re-taken in a four-year college, especially if the class is a pharmacy school prerequisite. This saves neither money nor time. That would be a negative aspect of this process for acquiring prerequisites.

If the community college credit *does* transfer to a four-year college, the course credit may still be questionable at the level of an application to professional school. Community colleges were initially created to be extensions of the high school experience in the early 1900s, and although some have made visible gains in technology and vocational education, training students at a fraction of the cost and time of a four-year program, a stigma may persist.[42]

R℞ **" ...*Many college and professional school faculty believe that community college classes in the "hard sciences"*— such as cell biology and organic chemistry— frequently lack the rigor of even some high school AP or IB programs.* "**

Specifically, many professional school faculty believe that community college classes in the "hard sciences"* such as genetics, cell biology, and organic chemistry, frequently lack the rigor of even some high school Advanced Placement or International Baccalaureate programs.[41] This is another negative aspect of collecting prerequisites. Thus, the ideal student to engage in this type of "community college dual enrollment" is the high-achieving, high-scoring student in a resource-poor school district. This might be considered the most positive use of dual enrollment for prerequisite attainment.

This comment is not meant to disparage any student who uses a community college for its affordability, location, or convenience. Students do enter pharmacy school with technical or community college diplomas in hand, but these people are a minority. Simply put, the community college experience has not yet achieved the prestige that a four-year undergraduate program

---

*"Hard" science does not mean difficult. Rather, it refers to the quantifiable nature of the field. In contrast, sociology is often referred to as a "soft" science; data in this field are less quantitative and more qualitative. Hard sciences are "basic sciences" because they underpin all other science disciplines.

may offer in the field of science. Of course, this is a moot criticism if the undergraduate school is widely known to be a degree mill such as an online degree program.

In addition to good grades, and being armed with all of the necessary courses for admissions, there may be one more step to apply for pharmacy school. The pharmacy school entrance exam, the PCAT, which was defined previously in **Chapter 1 (§Degree Details)**, may be needed for application and subsequent admissions. However, not all colleges require or consider the PCAT in their admissions decisions. At this time, 30 schools do not require the PCAT for admissions.

These schools are as follows:

- California Northstate University
- California Health Sciences
- Florida A&M University (not reported)
- Lebanese American University
- Manchester College School of Pharmacy
- Massachusetts College of Pharmacy and Health Sciences, Boston
- Ohio Northern University
- Oregon State University
- Purdue University
- St. John's University
- The University of Findlay
- The University of Toledo
- Touro University California
- University of California, San Francisco
- University of the Pacific
- Touro College of Pharmacy, New York
- Idaho State University
- Loma Linda University
- Marshall B Ketchum University School of Pharmacy*
- Massachusetts College of Pharmacy and Health Sciences-Worcester
- West Coast University
- Pacific University Oregon
- South Dakota State University
- South University (Georgia)
- The University of Rhode Island
- Washington State University
- University of California, San Diego
- University of Southern California
- Western University of Health Sciences

*No Accreditation Council for Pharmacy Education Status as of 2015

THE PCAT

Students who are required to have a PCAT score will face an exam that is structured to measure the applicant's skills in science, math, and language, all of which are essential for a successful journey through pharmacy school. The PCAT was created in response to a 1963 survey of schools of pharmacy with had unique admissions requirements for applicants but no unified testing mechanism for evaluating those applicants.[43]

The American Association of Colleges of Pharmacy (AACP) established an advisory panel to work with a testing company (Pearson) to collaborate, develop, and deploy a standardized test. Their efforts culminated in the first PCAT being administered in 1974 to 1,600 pharmacy school applicants. The PCAT is revised periodically to reflect innovations in science or improvements in testing techniques, but the basics of the PCAT remain very similar from year to year.

First, the PCAT has five multiple choice sections: biology, chemistry, reading comprehension, and measurements of verbal and quantitative competencies. The biology section emphasizes basic human biology: genetics, health, and human anatomy and physiology. Plant and non-human (animal) biology are not covered at this time. The chemistry portion of the PCAT includes basic biochemical processes as well as inorganic and organic chemistry from college-level courses.

Reading comprehension is simply that: can you understand a passage you read and answer interpretive questions about that passage? The final sections measure practical verbal and quantitative (mathematical) skills needed for pharmacy. Verbal sections may ask you to compare ideas, contrast thoughts, or create hierarchies of concepts. The quantitative section covers basic math up to (but not beyond) algebra.

The abovementioned PCAT sections are scored on a scale of 200–600. Percentile ranks are given for comparisons of overall PCAT student performance and these scores range from 1–99. Percentiles are not percent scores. Rather, a percentile reflects how a student fared compared to all test takers for that test administration period.

For example, for a student who scores in the 80th percentile, 20% of the test takers in that test deployment window performed better than this particular student. Each school of pharmacy may have a unique cut-off or minimum threshold for what they consider to be a competitive PCAT percentile. For example, one school may accept a minimum PCAT at the 40th percentile (Auburn University) and another may require a minimum percentile score of 80 (University of Connecticut).[32]

A composite score for the PCAT is the average, expressed as a percent, of all scores arising from the multiple-choice subtests described above. Thus, this score is not a comparison of students; it is similar to a test score, reflecting the percent of questions that were answered correctly. In general, a composite score of 70% is good (competitive); a score greater than 80% is better (more competitive); and a score of more than 90% is excellent (most competitive). Some schools of pharmacy will not define a minimum composite score required for applicants, but they will wait until the PCAT test period is closed and use the mean score for that test administration period as a basis for setting a minimum acceptable composite entrance requirement.

Students naturally want to ace the PCAT, and they often question how this test correlates with their future scholarship in a professional program. Studies show that the PCAT may modestly measure a student's first-year performance in pharmacy school, but studies have yet to be published in the peer-reviewed literature to support the hypothesis that a high PCAT score equates with high achievement throughout the entire pharmacy school experience.[44-45] This concept is discussed in a later chapter.

Finally, the PCAT writing sample is reported as a unique score on a scale from 1–6, with higher scores being better. The writing sample is an assessment of your ability to communicate through the written word, which requires a sturdy vocabulary, proper grammar, and intelligible logic. Many students presume that writing will not be important in pharmacy school, but this is incorrect.[46-48]

Students with strong writing skills may read faster and comprehend material better, increasing their effectiveness at studying and retaining information.[48-51] Also, with the ubiquity of texting, Twittering, and other linguistic/communication shortcuts, the ability to write well is a talent that is predicted to simultaneously erode as it becomes more precious.[46-47, 52] Therefore, writing is absolutely necessary for well-educated and highly versatile professionals.

THE APPLICATION PROCESS

Students who apply to pharmacy school will probably do so through the pharmacy college application service (PharmCAS) which is a centralized, online resource serving almost all US colleges of pharmacy. PharmCAS also supplies freeware to colleges so that they can review applications that are processed through this service. Students apply to an average of five pharmacy schools at one time, so this online tool can facilitate multiple applications with one interface.[53]

Students who use PharmCAS fill out the application, submit their personal statement (see §**The Personal Statement or Essay**), and update any additional coursework that they have completed through an "academic update window". Schools which do not use PharmCAS may have applications available through their website, and some PharmCAS schools may require a supplemental application to be completed in addition to the PharmCAS-delivered information.

Students should be aware that PharmCAS evaluates application essays or personal statements using Turnitin®, a web-based plagiarism detector with which students may already be familiar from undergraduate experiences.[54-55] The software does not just compare your essay to all other PharmCAS essays; rather it searches the entire internet for matching text. So, in the event that you are tempted to outsource your essay, remember that Turnitin® checks your work against more than 24 billion web pages, more than 300 million existing student papers, and more than 110,000 pieces of published literature.

Turnitin® then generates a homology report that describes the similarity of the essay with other existing text, expressed as a percent. This homology score is sent to your school of pharmacy, which can examine the essay to investigate the cause of a high similarity score. A score of more than 20% from Turnitin® is considered to be suspect; although, a few high homology scores can be explained.[56]

For instance, a student who quotes a verse from the *Bible* to emphasize a point in the essay may be flagged for plagiarism because this text matches another "document". Similarly, quotes from literature may attract attention along with highly clichéd expressions or overworked phrases which appear in published text. If the school can examine the essay and determine that a legitimate quote is indeed the reason for the similarity, then the essay may be acceptable. More about the personal essay is described later.

THE INTERVIEW

Pharmacy school interviews for applicants are required for accredited colleges.[33] During a student's campus interview, he may be grouped with other applicants to tour the campus and listen to a brief presentation about the program. Afterwards, the student might participate in individual interviews with faculty and students. Faculty who interview applicants for the college will teach classes within the professional program, and students who participate in "Interview Day" are frequently first-, second-, and third-year students. Although little obvious emphasis is placed on the interview, it is quite important.

First, the interview might be the first meaningful interaction between a potential student and the program's current students and faculty, which will provide impressions that can be weighed against the information within the application materials and recommendation letters. Because the interview is so brief (often 30 minutes) and the exchange of information within this time is critical, students should be prepared. Also, no applicant should bring a "guest" to the interview. This seems intuitive and perhaps laughable, but some students have believed it appropriate to bring a parent or boy/girlfriend to a pharmacy school interview. Students who cannot appear at an interview alone send a strong signal that they are not ready for professional school, where independence and self-awareness are *de rigueur*.

Interviewing students may meet with faculty in the presence (or in the absence) of current students. Although interviews are very similar with respect to content (many admissions interviews follow guidelines to ensure that the right information is covered but not repeated) more open or spontaneous interviewers may deviate from the prescribed question format.

For example, perhaps you will be asked something about yourself that is not adequately addressed in your application packet. At this time, you may even be asked to share how you became interested in pharmacy or to relate a tale about your experience as a technician or a pharmacy employee (*remember, you should have some type of experience to share*).

This leads us back to the first part of the book: your motivation for entering pharmacy school—can you articulate it? Now, the answer counts. Be energetic; be conversant; and be *interested* as well as *interesting*. Of note, college students who mention extracurricular undergraduate clubs/activities receive favorable reviews from admissions faculty. In fact, organizational involvement has been reported to modestly predict leadership attributes and skills that translate directly into a life-long professional involvement in pharmacy.[57]

The interviewing faculty will have your application essay, if you were required to prepare one. Thus, repeating your essay content is unnecessary. Instead, mention something that will shed new light on the type of student you will be and the type of pharmacist you are destined to become. Moreover, during an interview, you can explain deficiencies or less-than-stellar grades. Honesty is the best approach here. Faculty have likely heard everything, so little is going to surprise them at this stage of the game. Below are additional pointers for a favorable interview:

- Arrive on time and professionally dressed.
- Thank the student or other faculty who served as an escort to the interviewer's office.
- Answer questions succinctly and with relevant answers.
- Make eye contact and smile at the interviewer.
- Clearly deliver the message that this pursuit of a pharmacy education is a *personal goal*, not an assignment to satisfy a parent or other family member.
- Express enthusiasm for the profession.
- Avoid derogatory remarks about other programs of study or areas of healthcare.
- Avoid criticizing any faculty or students you met previously.
- Be charming and engaging.
- Pause to think before answering questions; allow time to formulate answers to avoid rambling and digression.
- Offer stories or examples about pharmacy experiences with patients, without providing patient names** and without demeaning patients or professionals tangential to those experiences.
- Specify why "that" school is preferred, offering relevant and distinguishing facts about the university/college and program.
- Describe any actions taken to improve acceptance, if this is a subsequent application to the program after an unsuccessful first attempt.
- Have ideas about a specific career trajectory, but be open to alternatives should the curriculum spur other interests.
- Avoid interrupting the interviewer or behaving arrogantly.
- Be gracious and thank the interviewer for his time (faculty and students do this at the expense of getting other things done, as a college service).

Just as the student applicant has recommended behaviors and actions, faculty also have a responsibility for conducting a proper interview. Most interviewers *cannot* do the following:

- Inquire about the student's marital status.
- Ask about religious (or lack of) preferences.
- Ask the applicant his age (this will appear within the application

---

**Patient information must be handled pursuant to the Health Insurance Portability and Accountability Act of 1996 (HIPAA) Privacy and Security Rules as well as the Patient Safety and Quality Improvement Act of 2005 (PSQIA). These laws protect information that can be tied to a specific patient, whether the information is about treatments, procedures, or measures taken to assure patient safety in a clinical setting. Sharing names and details of patients you encounter in a job prior to (or while enrolled in) pharmacy school is illegal.

material or a college graduation date may suggest an age range).

- Provoke the applicant by asking questions about highly controversial ethical or moral issues.
- Suggest that the applicant has been accepted or rejected.
- Suggest that any advice given during the interview must be followed for admittance to the program.
- Read recommendation letters about any applicant to that applicant or any other applicant.
- Speak in a derogatory fashion about other schools or programs, even if the student initiates the conversation about competing programs.
- Speak to other faculty or students about the interview, identify the applicant, or discuss the applicant's status with the parents/family of that applicant.

If a faculty interviewer does ask an improper question, the applicant has a few choices. He can demur by responding that he "would like to think about that answer a little bit more." In contrast, he can take a direct approach and state that he is "uncertain about the relevance of such information." Of course, this is a breach of conduct in the interview and should be reported to the admissions director.

When the rare unprofessional interview does occur, some students presume that reporting the incident will reflect negatively on them. This is false. All students in all programs are encouraged to report real or perceived bad acts by faculty or current professional students. Still, humans make mistakes, and enthusiasm for a candidate may cause someone to stray from the recommended interview decorum, which will (hopefully) obviously differ from blatantly unethical behavior.

In summary, let your interview reflect your enthusiasm and commitment for your chosen path. Show the interviewing faculty (and the students you meet) that you are the type of student they want. After the interview is over, faculty typically communicate impressions of the candidate through online interview software that manages all student applicants for that school. Faculty might write additional comments (or reservations), and these will be shared with the admissions committee, who will weigh these observations along with GPA, PCAT, and other data.

Some comments that have been made about interviewing students are presented below to give the reader an idea of how faculty who are conducting the interview think and what they expect. In general, faculty who have a pharmacy background (PharmD) tend to expect that the student has had some pharmacy experience. They weigh this heavily in the interview process. They also enjoy hearing that the potential pharmacy student understands the rigor of the program they want to undertake and that they grasp the sacrifices that will be necessary to live as a pharmacist. These preferences are evident in the hundreds of comments they provide about interviewing students.

Comments clinical pharmacy faculty have made about interviewing students include these (which have been edited for anonymity):

"Bob is a good student with proven study skills."

"Nancy does not have much direct pharmacy experience."

"I have some concern over Juan's previous science courses. His performance was weak, but he indicated how he planned to improve these grades."

"I doubt that Philip will excel in our program, given the grades she received in her science classes."

"I am concerned about Maria's motivation for attending pharmacy school and her reason for selecting our college."

In contrast, basic science faculty are often interested in the student's academic ability and pre-requisites and they may ask more questions about the student's aptitude for science and whether the student has considered a dual-degree program. Basic science faculty are not pharmacists, so it would be reasonable that they may ask less about the student's preparation for the field of work and more about the student's ability to function in the courses they teach.

Comments basic science faulty have made about students who interviewed for pharmacy school include:

"Tamara asked good questions about the coursework in the first year of the program."

"Wendy seems prepared for the rigor of biochemistry even though she admits that she did not take this course in undergraduate."

"Tran has experience in research and has one publication. He seems suitable for entry into the dual-degree program."

"Josh admitted that he '"wasn't ready' for pharmacy school this time last year. He offered a very personal perspective and I thought this was quite mature."

These ideas are not suggestive that one group of interviewing faculty cares less about student grades or experience, but that each interviewing group has biases or tendencies when making comments about interviews, and these comments often fall into two distinct categories that can be described as stated above.

The admissions committee for a school of pharmacy is not terribly mysterious. It is usually comprised of a few faculty members from both academic and clinical aspects of pharmacy, a Dean or Associate/Assistant Dean of the college, and perhaps some students who are currently enrolled. Each member of the committee has something invested in the committee decisions.

Students want to choose the most agreeable classmates who validate their school's excellence and become hospitable future colleagues. Faculty want to enroll students who are ready to learn and enthusiastic about the program. Deans want outstanding students who become successful alumni, enjoying life-long relationships with the college. Thus, the admissions committee has a common mission that is deployed through unique approaches.

LETTERS OF RECOMMENDATION

Students applying to pharmacy school will need letters of recommendation. Admissions committees want these letters authored by people who are familiar with the character and scholastic aptitude of the student. Usually, neighbors and friends of parents are not qualified for this task. These people, though they may know you socially, cannot necessarily attest to student attributes needed for a PharmD.

Still, students will ask a neighbor for a letter, when the only relationship they have is that the student watered his plants while he was on vacation. Relatives who write letters could attest to the student's scholastic prowess and honor, but these are too personal for committees to evaluate. Faculty assume that any relative would recommend a student based on family history; thus, family letters are too biased.

Some students mistakenly believe that a letter from a congressman or visible political figure will be impressive to pharmacy school faculty. This is a mistake. In fact, such letters often appear a bit shameless, and they could be inflammatory. The admissions committee knows the letter was probably written by an executive assistant, perhaps hastily dictated for typing so that the obligation could be fulfilled.

The majority of professional school applicants lack the social standing to know a political or government official well enough for that public figure to comment on the student's school record. Also, a student is taking a large leap of faith that the faculty who receive the letter from the politician will agree with his politics. So, a letter from a conservative Republican could be considered worthless by a staunchly liberal Democratic member of the admissions committee, and *vice versa*.

Friends are also not appropriate authors for letters. Committees are tuned in to "listening" for letters that are overly familiar, suggesting that the letter writer may not be entirely objective. In contrast, professors are terrific sources for letters, as are employers and directors of volunteer programs. When seeking letters of recommendation, always ask if the person can write a "favorable" letter. Frequently, students assume that all letters of recommendation are, *by definition*, favorable, and this is unfortunately untrue. If letter writer can agree to produce a "favorable" letter, the student can be assured that the letter will be minimally appropriate for the committee.[58]

The worst letters read as follows: "Bob worked for me from 2007 to 2013." This is referred to as "damning with faint praise". In this context, the letter writer is likely avoiding a potential lawsuit by acknowledging only that the student was in his employ.[59-60] As our society becomes more knee-jerk litigious, facts-only letters are emerging as a mechanism for diffusing poor references...by not being references at all.[61]

When you apply for pharmacy school, you may be asked to waive your rights to read your recommendation letters. Waiving this right may increase the reliability of the letter because the author can speak/write more freely. Thus, do everything to assure that your letters are truly "of recommendation", and that they will secure your standing with the committee who receives them.

THE PERSONAL STATEMENT OR ESSAY

The essay component of the pharmacy school application is tricky. It is both a testament to character and a writing exam.[62] If you speak English as a second (or third, or fourth!) language, you could consider this essay a language test. Your writing style will either entertain the faculty or serve as a sedative-hypnotic for those poor souls, depending on what you write and how you deliver it. Have your essay stand out from the rest by starting with an unexpected sentence, a quote, or a single-word introduction. Tell a story. Take the reader where you want him to go.

Most essays have the same theme: "I have always wanted to be a pharmacist; it has always been my dream." This is likely not entirely true; chances are excellent that when you were small, you wanted to be a cowboy, a ballerina, or a long-haul truck driver. The committee knows this; they were once children as well. However, if you have a unique personal experience, share it. Tell the committee something that will make them laugh, cry, or think.

This sounds simple, but writing well takes more than a few minutes of poking a keyboard. Good writing that engages the reader takes thought and planning and editing, and then *more editing*. Watch for fluff that adds no additional meaning or offers no new information. Statements such as "I am beyond words at the idea of becoming a pharmacist" is hackneyed. Obviously you have words; you just used a few! Also, terms such as "very", "super", or "incredibly" are not terribly useful. Use the interview to add a personal touch to what was said in the essay.

Think of the personal statement a formal recommendation of yourself to the program. You want it to sound sophisticated and appear to be written by a well-educated writer. Thus, perfect grammar, syntax, and diction are necessary and expected at this phase of life. Odd or awkward language used only in an attempt to impress faculty will fall flat. Write the way you speak, and speak from the heart.

Watch for misguided attempts to share your personal gratitude for your education and experience. An essay from an applicant from a mid-tier undergraduate university, in an unheard of area of the US, that bangs on about how "proud" the student is to be so "fortunate" for his middle-class upbringing and "privileged" to attend the mediocre college appears sadly naïve and misguided. If you lack a full and cosmopolitan understanding of your roots and professional trajectory, leave it out of the essay and focus on what you can share with the admissions committee that gives concrete reasons why you are worth accepting.

Finer points about the personal statement include making reference to any aspect of your upbringing or education that allows you to stand out from the rest of the applicants. Some colleges refer to this as "diversity": meaning that you offer a perspective that cannot be found in most student bodies. Diversity means "non-white" to most casual readers, but this is not the definition of diversity to most admissions committees.

For instance, colleges of pharmacy are seeking applicants who have lived outside of the US (as children or adults) or who have international ties through family connections. Committees want to hear about fluency in other languages than English, also. If your parents were disadvantaged in that they did not attend college or another equally interesting circumstance, this, too, is valuable.

Applicants should not shy away from sharing stories of adversity or experiences that were teachable moments. For instance, if you worked in a senior care facility, hospice, or volunteered for a medical mission trip, this would be of interest in the name of diversity. However, when describing these experiences watch for inherently "clueless" and prejudiced language. An essay that depicts the "poor underprivileged community in Belize" is more likely to be insulting than illuminating.

An interviewer would be fully on-point to inquire exactly *how* these people were so pitiful to the student, which would establish an adversarial interaction—with the student on the defensive due to sloppy language. More appropriate and clinically relevant terms for describing helping societies such as these include "medically underserved", "rural", or "geographically challenged areas". Reading journals and more intellectual papers such as *The Wall Street Journal* or *The New York Times* will offer rich vocabulary options for the young writer.

Athletic or artistic accomplishments are also elements of diversity that are worthy of mention in the personal statement but again, here, use caution. The admissions committee may not appreciate basketball wins against a rival college or a gymnastics championship. Depict involvement but move on to develop more germane aspects of the essay such as your academic qualifications.

For example, perhaps you wish to explain a semester of poor performance when you experienced a personal setback or you may wish to write about a sudden change in your major, because you perhaps realized your desire to be a pharmacist just recently. All of these are real topics to write about and they reflect a real and dynamic life.

Another aspect of diversity is something that many students (if they are in this situation) are wary of offering for a committee to evaluate: whether they have a family and children. In this case, having a full life of responsibility and obligations does not make you a less attractive candidate for pharmacy school. Rather, the opposite is true.

Someone who has raised children, paid a mortgage, cared for an elderly or ill parent, or something similar is likely a prime candidate for pharmacy because they have a demonstrated commitment to maturity and caring for others. It is true that an interviewer cannot ask an application about marriage, age, and children, but students who want points on their application for diversity can increase their visibility by adding comments about these very normal aspects of life to their diversity statement or application.

When you finish your personal statement or essay, read it to yourself out loud to catch errors in logic, clarity, and flow of the information. Your ear will "hear" inconsistencies and your eye will catch spelling and grammatical errors. An impressive personal statement that is rife with mistakes or redundant phrases will be a disappointment for the reader who is looking for the best reasons to suggest acceptance for that applicant. Thus, take the minute or so required to find and eliminate faulty sentences, unclear references to your academic performance and life experiences, and worn out or clichéd expressions.

THE ACCEPTANCE PROCESS

Colleges of pharmacy are endlessly competing for the small pool of the best students who graduate from college or have the pharmacy prerequisites to attend a professional program. Admissions committees may continually revisit their approach to interviewing students by a certain timeline, such as accepting later PCAT scores, or waiting until all of the student's grades have been submitted. Committees from virtually all schools of pharmacy do this watching and waiting at the same time. Thus, these schools, for a brief period of time, are in fierce competition for similar or identical pools of human intellectual capital.

Schools which offer early acceptance letters directly compete with (and perhaps complicate the process of) slower or later admissions processes. Such temporal differences in acceptance timelines among schools forces a few colleges to issue acceptances early to exceptional students who are considering multiple offers. Students strongly interested in one program, but who have several offers in hand from other schools, can call the admissions director of their choice program and discuss options. No college of pharmacy wants a high-achieving applicant to slip through its fingers, so compromises can often be made to grab the best students.

Future pharmacists who are considering several schools but who do not have all of their data submitted may need to call each college and ask for the latest date a PCAT score or the most current GPA information will be accepted. They might also inquire about acceptance considerations that may be contingent on final grades at the end of the spring semester.

Offers made by colleges do get rescinded when students fail to fulfill the final requirements. However, the best students are frequently given slightly more latitude for admissions because the school directly benefits: they enroll a highly desirable student who will have a remarkable career and permanent positive ties to the college, a win-win situation for all.

Students who are not perfect applicants still have an opportunity for acceptance. Often schools offer admission letters in cycles, sending immediate responses to the top applicants early, then staggering additional offer letters as data are accumulated about who has committed to enrolling in the program. Thus, a student who is not accepted on the first round may be accepted in a later letter cycle.

Also, one or two students may be accepted to the college in a manner that could be considered "outside the normal channels", perhaps through the direct recommendation of a Dean or a university President. These university leaders often have the authority to request admissions for specific students who have exceptional promise but may not meet traditional academic standards. After all, GPA and PCAT scores are modest predictors of a measure of success in the first year, but studies are lacking with respect to predicting a student's overall success and future potential with these data.[44-45]

Now and then, these administratively driven specific student selections allow entry of what turns out to be poorly qualified students who require remediation and faculty intervention to stay in the program. This can generate ill will among the faculty who are saddled with offering these students extra help in their courses. Also, conflicts can arise when students fail, for example a 600 level class, and are then prevented from advancing to a 700 level course (of course, numbering systems vary).

When a student cannot advance to the next full year of the program, it creates a gap in the course load that often requires that faculty cobble together a "special project assignment" worth the credit hours lacking so the student can qualify as full-time both academically and financially. To many faculty, this is a form of academic rigging that only delays what they perceive as the inevitable—program failure and withdrawal. Thus, this pattern of rescue is not typical and should not be expected.

Finally, pharmacy programs will also have handfuls of students who accept the offer from the school and then later, for whatever reason, decline the invitation to admission. Thus, schools bargain against that certainty by leveraging wait-lists against the actual available number of seats in the program. Some schools may deliberately "over-accept" three or four students or bump students from the wait list to the accepted pool, estimating that this very number of accepted students will ultimately attend school elsewhere.

So, the admissions committee makes many outright decisions about students, while also "rolling the dice" for a few students in an attempt to predict their final decisions. Less qualified students who are not granted early or immediate acceptance to a school of pharmacy can take advantage of these buffers by calling the admissions staff at their program of choice, reminding them of their interest and offering to send additional data.

CHAPTER 3

MAKING IT THROUGH THE PROFESSIONAL PROGRAM

The transition from undergraduate school to a professional pharmacy program is often not a highly intuitive or obvious process in which students suddenly wake up one day, knowing every expected behavior and performance criteria for all professional students. Thus, most students enter pharmacy school with a sense of the program being a temporal extension of undergraduate school.

Students who have experienced a gap of time between college and the actual professional program also may be unaware of the professional expectations, even if they have been in the workforce for many years. Some pharmacy students have raised a family prior to enrolling in school, but they still have no idea what is expected of them in the professional school environment.

Thus, students will present on the first day of the program with a variety of beliefs, and perhaps mild confusion, about what lies ahead. To address the important aspects of the pharmacy school experience, the sections within this chapter depict some common expectations for professional programs and the rationale for these demands.

TEXTBOOKS

Required textbooks vary among pharmacy programs, and textbook publishers are forever enticing faculty to adopt their newest, or perhaps most expensive, version of a text. Usually, such textbooks are promoted to students and faculty without significant regard to the actual costs incurred by students, but increasingly, modern texts have CDs or other accompanying web-based supporting media for additional learning resources. Thus, the price of a new textbook may be worthwhile for students who enjoy using all of these extras.

Required class texts and other essential material should be listed in each course syllabus. However, frequently, these books go unused by the student, morphing into heavy paperweights or dust-collection platforms. Thus, non-required or "suggested texts", which may be faculty favorites or helpful review pieces, may also be listed in the syllabus or mentioned on the first day of class.

Also, on a few occasions, your professional faculty will have authored the recommended textbook. This could be a great "buy" and a memento of professional college. If you *do* purchase a faculty-authored book, get an autograph from the professor. This will be more meaningful later, even though it may sound silly at this time.

Aside from "real books", your institutional library may offer free, online textbooks for students. Depending upon the license purchased by the institution, one student at a time may be allowed to use the material, or the entire class may have the text available on demand. The librarian will know what the school has available for you and how you may access it.

To avoid any unnecessary spending for texts that you may not need or do not really want, ask current students what books were essential *to them*. You may get a variety of answers, depending on the study habits or techniques of each professional student, but the information is still valuable. Professional students are not usually penalized for choosing *not* to buy a text, and many times, the instructor simply recycles the "required text" part of the syllabus, neglecting to reflect on whether the book is truly needed anymore.

Laptops or tablets are increasingly being required for pharmacy school, and minimal technical requirements for such internet-ready devices are usually found (and updated) on the pharmacy program website. Laptops will be necessary for online testing when no computer laboratory is available for the students on-site. Also, many students find that reading and annotating course lecture notes in a paperless fashion on a computer or tablet is very efficient.

DOES WORKING "WORK"?

Often, students work during college to fund their education and to manage living expenses. Students must eat and have transportation, and working pays for these essentials. Thus, many students anticipate working during pharmacy school, especially during the first year. Indeed, students do manage to hold down part-time jobs, attend every class, and perform well in pharmacy school.[63]

Such juggling acts might be particularly difficult for students who have children or other family who need care and attention, but every year a significant proportion of students in this demanding multi-tasking situation graduate from a pharmacy program and find employment, and life then goes on. Even so, if you work around or avoid the need for a part-time job during pharmacy school, you may benefit from this freedom. Think about it: your coursework will be the most demanding effort you have put forth to date. Therefore, you will need to study many hours a day, every day, to keep up with the material.

So, having a job during pharmacy school may compromise your performance to the degree that you begin failing exams, a process that is difficult or impossible to reverse for some students. Even if you can maintain good grades and work at the same time, you can count on being exhausted. Sometimes students who work and attend pharmacy school actually fall asleep during class. They can be heard snoring in the back of the classroom, with their heads bent over their notebooks because they worked all evening, went home to shower, and then came to class.

Being stretched to the breaking point like this, for what probably amounts to just a few hundred dollars every month, does not necessarily build character, but it *can* make you crazy and miserable. In case you were wondering, sleeping during class may be "allowed" (but obviously not preferred) if it does not disrupt the class. Get used to it; you will see that people do strange things just to get by.

You may be able to avoid working by coordinating student loans to allow for some living expenses. Get a loan from your family if you need it (and pay it back; remember, you are entering a profession of honor). You may need to be frugal to live this way, but this will only last 4 years. You can surely exist modestly for that length of time for something so lasting and important. Then, you can splurge when you cash your first paycheck (or when you validate that the direct deposit successfully went through to your checking account).

Finally, students who work part-time jobs will not be given additional latitude in class. Professors rarely accept excuses about any work that causes students to be absent for important class information, arrive late for exams, miss exams entirely, or turn in assignments after they are due. Thus, complaining that an instructor is "holding it against you" because you work is childish and incorrect. Professors do not penalize students who work; they simply do not grant concessions for those who do. There is a difference. Face it, faculty "work", too, so either give up the job and attend school full-time, or leave the complaints at the door when you walk into class.

❝ Nothing is more annoying than offering timely pharmacy-centric articles and then having students whine, 'Are we supposed to read these?'
The answer to this?
'Of course not. You should only read these if you are interested in pharmacy.'❞

IN THE KNOW

Every pharmacy student is expected to be enthusiastic and informed about their course of study, ideally *before* they begin school. Along with this drive to pursue a pharmacy career, students should understand that by enrolling in a college of pharmacy, they have agreed to undertake a lifetime of learning that may extend beyond their pharmacy program in the form of continuing education.

A component of this drive for everlasting learning is knowledge of current events. Smart students read the paper, both the local "fish wrap" to know what is happening in the community, and a major newspaper with national and international news coverage. *The Wall Street Journal*, *The New York Times*, the *Los Angeles Times*, and the *Chicago Times* are perfect papers for keeping abreast of everything newsworthy.

Reading a daily newspaper should become a life-long habit that keeps you informed about your world in general and your profession, in particular. Interestingly, large papers such as those mentioned above usually contain an article or about pharmacy, pharmacists, or the pharmaceutical industry every day. Having access to this information will ensure that you are a competent, current, cosmopolitan pharmacist.

Keeping yourself "in the know" will benefit your patients, too. They will not only expect you to know more than they do about their health conditions, medications, and insurance plans but also they may ask you about new drugs and upcoming pharmaceutical trends which may change the face of healthcare and improve their quality of life.

COURSEWORK

Classes in pharmacy school are inherently difficult, and although students say that they expect this, they are often completely unprepared for the degree of work involved. The actual amount of work they will need to perform to be successful just cannot be imagined until they are well into it.* Students can browse the college's academic bulletin or program descriptions to estimate course expectations, but this will be surface knowledge. Pharmacy school is less flexible than undergraduate programs because the curriculum/course load timing is fairly fixed.

 ❝ When students choose not to attend class, ** **and then ask instructors questions that were answered in class, students are communicating the following message: 'my time is more important than yours.' Do you really want to communicate that to people who grade your exams?❞**

For example, all entering pharmacy students take the same classes, and withdrawing from a non-elective class is not an option unless there is a significant academic issue prompting it, such as a lengthy illness or a personal problem that requires a leave-of-absence to resolve it. Also, classes that you fail to complete as a first year student (P1) may compromise your

---

* *If you are interested in the minimum amount of information you will be required to know, glance at* **Appendix V** *for the list of the Top 200 Drugs for 2011, based on prescription sales. This is just a fraction of your expected knowledgebase.*
** *Obviously, illness-related absences do not apply.*

advancement to year two (P2 status). Summer courses for re-taking failed classes are not common and may not be program obligations. Thus, anyone who enters pharmacy school should have a mindset to finish the degree in the recommended time frame, as scheduled in the academic bulletin for that program.

Because professional school is a relentless torrent of classes, tests, and mandatory service that continues at least until gradation, the pharmacy curriculum usually cannot be modified for your preferences or habits. Students may be unable to take fewer hours; part-time students are rare.

Likewise, taking a semester/year off from school may only be accomplished through medical or personal leave, and there may be significant paperwork involved to allow the student to return. Generally, a verified/documented learning disability is one of the few mechanisms by which students can be granted small compromises in the curriculum. Such unique program adjustments are mentioned in more detail in **§Student Disabilities.**

Because the full-steam-forward approach is expected, an efficient mechanism of study should have been developed in undergraduate school. Even with an excellent preparation practice, you may need to vastly adapt your test readiness mechanisms. Gone are the days of frank memorization!

Interestingly, students who memorize discrete sets of information just for the test, only to forget it later are engaging in what researchers refer to as "bulimic learning". This refers to a veritable bingeing and purging of information with no real "learning" taking place.[64] This may serve a student well in undergraduate school when the courses are not as intensely packed with information, but this will be ineffective at this level.

Also, if the term "bulimic learning" was coined to refer to test-and-dump student strategies, then "pharmacorexia" may be the best way to explain the terrible phenomenon of opening a test booklet while simultaneously and completely blanking on every drug name and mechanism of action. Stress does strange things to students.

R͓X **" If you are physically well enough to come to class, you are expected to be present, prepared, and actively engaged in the learning process. Blowing off class is like throwing tuition money out of your car window while driving down the highway...silly and wasteful. "**

ATTENDANCE

Class attendance is considered by your faculty to be mandatory. Any day that you are physically well enough to come to class, you are expected to be present, prepared, and actively engaged in the learning process. When faculty see gaping holes in the classroom due to missing students, it is more than disconcerting to them; it can be insulting. After all, the instructor showed up and was willing to give his time, and he expects that students will do the same. Studies show that students who attend class perform better on tests than those who do not regularly attend.[65] In fact, specifics about absenteeism suggest that missing classes directly before or after an exam has a significant effect on student performance: frequently absent students perform more poorly on exams.[65-66]

Also, when students attend class, they benefit from real-time faculty-student interactions that offer important insight about professional conduct, speech, and appearance and faulty develop a sense of who the student is as a future pharmacist. This is required for letters of recommendation that may be requested later.

Finally, in smaller programs that enroll small student bodies (fewer than 100 students per class), the faculty can see faces and note patterns of absences for specific students. When students do not attend and then, later, request clarification for something they did not see the regularly scheduled class time, faculty are often reasonably less inclined to assist. They may think, "Everyone else was present for the information, so why wasn't this person?"

The most common *en masse* absences are before a major test in another class, such as biochemistry or medicinal/pharmaceutical chemistry, which are known for being very difficult courses. This is expected but not desired. Faculty prefer that students manage their time sufficiently to both be present and study well ahead of a test. Thus, missing one class to study for another is not necessarily accepted or acceptable but it is not openly criticized too often. In summary, attend class! Your faculty will sense that you are serious about school and they will be more inclined to help you when an absence is legitimate or necessary.

DURING LECTURE

As life-long learners, pharmacy students are expected to be well prepared for the lecture. Being "prepared" may mean reading a section of text prior to class, watching a pre-recorded video before class, or just having course materials ready for note taking. Such preparation should make class attendance more enjoyable. The student can follow along with ease as the lecturer reinforces information about which the student previously prepared.

Attendance and preparation is also important for clearing up misconceptions or misunderstandings about the material.

Some schools are re-investigating the use of the ancient Socratic Method for teaching professional students, which may be a future trend in colleges of pharmacy. With the Socratic technique, the students prepare in a special way for the lecture. Essentially, they teach themselves the material before class. Then, they use the actual scheduled class time to solve problems, clarify ideas, or address only certain topics as prescribed by the faculty. Thus, students who do not prepare appropriately cannot participate in class effectively. This model is not designed for re-hashing the prepared material, so students who believe that they can "catch up" during lecture often face disappointment with this model. It will not serve the lazy or ill-equipped student very well.

Whether the professor uses a traditional teaching method or Socratic lectures, neither will matter if the students do not commit to "seat time", as it is often called. Face-to-face student-faculty interactions—at a minimum—are necessary for faculty to learn enough about the students to write future letters of recommendation. Thus, students who are frequently absent will have no such relationship with the instructors. Next, talking to classmates helps to clarify material and foster friendships (and subsequent collegial relationships) that will be critical when seeking a job and participating in healthcare team collaborations.[67]

Finally, students should attend class because they paid for it. Although students too often trot out the tired (and not terribly clever) line of "I paid tuition, so I am entitled to do or have X, Y, and Z," this crude commercial viewpoint is true only to a degree. Furthermore, entirely exploiting the freedom of a professional program can give faculty a poor opinion of that student. Truthfully, tuition allows students access to course material, classroom lectures, and robust interactions with faculty to deepen their understanding of pharmacy so that they can earn a PharmD and (ideally) pass the NaPLEX. Tuition is not a payment rendered for a license to "go bananas".

Despite the strength of the evidence for attending class, a common tendency among some pharmacy students is to begin the year as attentive pre-professionals who are mentally and physically present. Then, after about two weeks into the program, they morph into tardy, unprepared, and disinterested people who intentionally skip class to sleep, socialize, or work part-time. Students would be wise to file that behavior under "No, Nyet, and Nein".

DISTANCE EDUCATION

Students may already be familiar with distance education or DE. If you have experienced a lecture online, over the internet, such as through the popular Khan Academy, you have experienced a form of DE. The Khan Academy hosts more than 3,000 videos and has more than two-million viewers monthly, a testament to its popularity and breadth of outreach.

Sal Khan, who once worked as a hedge fund investment researcher, created this DE opportunity after tutoring a young relative in math over an internet connection. He realized that learning material over the internet had broad appeal and could be delivered on-demand at almost zero cost. Khan's enormous success in this venture is instructive: DE—or the global university—is a trend that is here to stay.[68]

Therefore, many pharmacy programs are adopting DE techniques, expanding their reach and increasing student convenience. In the actual DE university setting, however, students do not watch videos exclusively, as they may in the Khan Academy. Rather, a lecture is delivered live and this lecture is streamed through communication software to other campus locations. Students can ask questions over DE using microphones or they can use an educational software interface to post questions and host discussions.

Thus, DE enables faculty to offer a lecture once to target not only the students in the class where the lecture originates, but also the tens to hundreds of students at multiple, remote sites that may simply be off-campus or in another area of the country.[69-72] A typical paradigm of the DE environment is a pharmacy school with a main large campus in addition to one or more college satellite campuses. Satellite campuses exist to offer educational access for people who cannot travel daily to a main campus or who are unable to re-locate to the main campus for the entire pharmacy school experience.

Questions have been raised about aspects of DE, particularly the apparent fragmentation of the lecture experience. Students have long suspected that students attending campuses at which the instructor is "live" enjoy better grades than remote-site students (where the teacher has no physical presence). However, the scientific literature at this time suggests that this is untrue. In fact, data show that students at both "live" and "remote" campuses of a DE experience have similar academic outcomes.[69, 71, 73] Thus, there appear to be no advantages conferred to "live" students as well as no *disadvantages* for "satellite" students.[71, 74]

Even so, to alleviate any perceptions of imbalance, faculty who teach in DE programs often travel to the distance campus to offer selected lectures in person. This establishes a faculty presence for all students in the course and offers better long-term engagement for students from remote sites. Also, faculty benefit from seeing new faces and making new connections. Even with these earnest attempts to reduce the friction inherent in a DE lecture, there remain problems, both real and perceived students who have experienced DE have these thoughts:

The downsides to attending a DE class is most often experienced on the remote campus, where students may not be able to see the face of the instructor and the instructor may only be able to see a broad view of the entire class with no distinct faces. This sense of "otherness" predisposes some students to talk amongst themselves during the lecture or even behave as if the classroom was an airport concourse where loud, simultaneous personal conversations are normal and justified. When the instructor on the other campus can hear the talking, it is annoying and disrespectful. Also, small groups of chatting students disrupt other students.

Thus, whether a class is live or conducted over DE, students should attend, take notes, and refrain from other activities not conducive to learning (texting, changing clothes, applying makeup, nosily digging through a book bag, etc.). Sleeping, eating, and shopping online are activities that students often assume are acceptable because they are quiet and "don't bother anyone" but faculty may be variously offended by either action, so caution is necessary. Some faculty do not mind student internet browsing and a rare professor will tolerate a sleeping student if overlooking the rudeness is more simple than interrupting the lecture to remove someone, but it is folly to believe that it is not noticed and remembered.

Finally, because there is often confusion about this topic, students should know that DE is *not* an online degree program. Online degree opportunities, such as the well-known Kaplan University or the University of Phoenix are likewise not a true use of DE. This distinction is important. Many employers stipulate that they will only hire people who possess a degree from an accredited, "brick and mortar", four-year university (read: no online degrees, please).[75-76] Currently, only Creighton University offers a formal online PharmD, but the rigor of admissions for (and student effort involved with) such online degree programs is uncertain at this time.[77]

LECTURE RECORDINGS

A byproduct of both DE and the modern classroom is that often lectures are recorded and archived as a college resource. Students may initially be confused, thinking that DE is the same as a lecture recording. It is not. With DE, the lecture is being broadcast to a remote *classroom*, not to individual students. However, if a regular or DE lecture is recorded, the students who attended either the live or remote lecture have access to these recordings after class, as individuals.

Thus, students cannot watch the lecture as it is being delivered in real time from off-campus sites such as the student's home. Because lecture recordings are so important to professional students, they should understand how lecture recordings are actually developed. This will give them infinitely more patience (and peace) for this process and, hopefully, an appreciation for the work involved in making these happen.

First, a lecture is delivered to the class using desktop software and it is captured with video and/or audio recording devices. Breeze, Tegrity, and Camtasia are common brands of lecture capture software that accomplish this. Then, while the lecture is being delivered in real time, an information technology expert (IT guy or gal) is sitting in a sound booth, monitoring lecture progress, correcting sound issues, and the like, as the lecture is delivered. This IT person is also on call for any lecture device malfunction such as a faulty desktop pen used to illustrate lecture concepts, or an issue with a slide projector or microphone.

Then, once the lecture is finished, the IT specialist will render hundreds of megabytes of lecture video and sound to a format that can be accommodated by multiple internet interfaces (if you enjoy a lecture on a tablet, a phone, and a laptop, thank your professional program's IT people; they are responsible for such cross-platform excellence).

Then, after rendering the lecture, the IT expert labels the file and places it in an electronic "home" on a campus server that can be accessed by enrolled students. Students often assume that the lecture should be available as soon as they leave the lecture hall, and they may even question the fairness of any delay in lecture uploading, asking, "Since I paid tuition, should that lecture not be immediately available to me when I demand it?"

First, students must appreciate that this rendering, labeling, and uploading takes time. Even if the lecture does get added to the server as quickly as possible, it still may not be immediately available to all students. Some schools deliberately restrict access to recorded lectures for a certain period. For example, they may permit access to them no earlier than 24 hours after the lecture has been given.[78] This allows errors to be caught and corrected and enables the IT professionals to deliver the best quality product to the students.

Podcasts are popular mechanisms for lecture recording as well. Although chiefly thought of as audio files, podcasts may also feature the slide presentation, depending on how the material is uploaded to the podcast resource location. ITunes University (ITunes U) is one such resource for this learning tool. Some podcasts may be audio-only clips, lacking images entirely, but again, schools must upload their sound files to the resource and this takes time. For example, ITunes U will "fetch" submitted podcasts perhaps once a day, so a delay should be expected between the lecture's end and the availability of a learning resource.

Students can also be impatient about recordings because they honestly may not know that IT specialists are assisting other instructors campus-wide, for the entire college (or more than one college) for all instructors, for all lectures every day. Thus, IT experts may be literally running from site to site to maintain a continuous stream of lecture recordings and postings for students. Sadly, many faculty and students ignore IT experts until something goes wrong. Having great relationships with college IT personnel is wise; they enable your college to function in the modern world, and they contribute enormously to the college mission.

It is important to know that lecture recordings were never meant to be primary methods of instruction. Some universities restrict recordings to remediation of students who are failing courses, and they are not released to all students at any time. Other schools respect the professor's authority and privacy and will not record their lectures out of supreme respect for the lecturer's standing and reputation (not all faculty wish to be recorded or find it acceptable). Unfortunately, students are oblivious to the tenuous nature of a lecture recording, whether they arise from traditional classes or DE courses, and they appear to use them in a manner that reinforces or reward student absences and promotes noncommittal and professional behavior.[79]

Although studies suggest that some students who only view lecture recordings (without attending class) may benefit from this habit, they only do so to a point. Specifically, student performance seems to decline when the student is overambitious, planning to watch more recordings than he can temporally accommodate.[80] So, watching lecture recordings does not seem to harm student performance, but it may not *improve* achievement.

Furthermore, a lecture may fail to be recorded or uploaded to the college server, or the recording can be incomplete or of such poor quality that it is not useful. Remember that humans are making and rendering the lecture videos, and those recordings can be deleted by anyone, as well, obliterating the entire lecture series. Finally, why students would pay *not* to attend class, and only choose to watch videos is baffling to faculty. Do the students have something more important to do?

HONOR

Honor is necessary in pharmacy. Pharmacists have access to potentially lethal drugs, addictive substances, and volumes of confidential patient information. A pharmacist without integrity is a future felon biding his time until arrest and lock-up. Thus, to ingrain early a mindset of honor and integrity in pharmacy students, colleges of pharmacy implement honor codes in multiple ways.

These codes may include general professional conduct and classroom behavior. They may also address specific issues of cheating, lying, and stealing. You may be asked to take an oath of honor at a White Coat Ceremony (see §**White Coat Ceremony**) and/or you may be asked to sign an honor pledge before or after every exam. Unfortunately, even with these codes and pledges, cheating is a problem in professional school.[81-83]

Cheating can be defined as deception (misleading others), coercion (blocking action others are entitled to make), and reneging (refusing to accept deserved but undesirable outcomes).[84] Academic cheating, which includes any acts by the student which are committed to dishonestly or unfairly gain an advantage over other students, is prevalent and may be increasing in healthcare disciplines.

Access to technology that can assist with cheating and the lasting importance of the education that is being sought are two distinct drivers of student cheating in professional school. Also, pharmacy school is expensive and time-consuming; every student wants the degree that reflects the enormous investment each student makes to the program. Strong signals such as these, along with a growing trend in a lack of personal accountability in students today, seem to propel such academic dishonesty.[85]

The predictability of cheating among professional students is reported to have "correlates" or predictable personal characteristics. Interestingly, studies suggest that GPAs and student race had less predictive power for cheating. Economic inequality did have some bearing on student trust, however, with respect to academic honesty.[86] The most influential correlates were the students' degree of idealism (especially that of females), relativism, and Machiavellian traits.[85]

Thus, students who had high personal values were less likely to cheat. Students who perceived morality as situation- and individual-based ("cheating is better than failing") were more likely to be dishonest, too. Finally, students who were more cynical and detached from their college experience were more likely to cheat.[85] When students cannot meet honor code stipulations, their future professional and business ethics may be in jeopardy.[87-88]

With the ubiquity of small electronic devices such as programmable scientific calculators with downloadable applications and equations, phones, iPods, and similar internet-ready devices such as apple watches, detecting cheating in a student population is like trying to hold a gallon of water in your hands. As technology advances, sophisticated methods of cheating tend to follow, and keeping up with these methods is next to impossible.[88] Sadly, students seem to regard these events rather casually, For example, in an eye-opening experiment, one pharmacy professor did the following:

In a class of almost 400 students who arrived to take a junior-level exam, students were explicitly warned on several occasions to leave cell phones outside the testing area. They were also told that if they did not follow these instructions, they would receive a failing test grade. Prior to the test, the professor *again* reminded the students that anyone possessing a cell phone would have one last opportunity to place it in a box at the front of the testing room.

Only eight students accepted this pre-test offer. Then, the professor showed the class a hand-held metal detector, explaining that he would randomly screen students as they handed in their test. Suddenly, 38 students "responded" by turning in cell phones they had retained in a direct violation of the course policy.[89]

From this study, it seems that some students selectively obey honor code rules that they find most compatible with their desires. This is unacceptable. Worse, when professional students are given an opportunity to uphold an honor code on their own, they often fail spectacularly. Worse, those who observe other students cheating rarely report such behavior, although this is often a mandatory component of an honor code.[90] If students struggle with honesty in school, when, exactly, will they choose to be honorable within their profession?

Students often bristle at the idea that faculty openly discuss blatantly offensive or dishonorable student conduct among their ranks. Only naïve students expect that severe or unprofessional transgressions will not be mentioned to others. A student who cheats, steals, or engages in illegal or unprofessional conduct has essentially waived his right to all forms of scholastic and personal privacy by being dishonest. In academic circles, notoriety is an effective mechanism for deterring dishonesty. No one wants to be shunned by colleagues; negative attention such as this can ruin careers.

PROFESSIONALISM

The term "professionalism"—and the lack of it, or "unprofessionalism"—is used frequently in pharmacy programs, but it is a very abstract concept, potentially meaning something different to each person.[91-95] For example, one person's "unprofessionalism" may be another person's "directness", "firmness", or "frank honesty".[96] Thus, to be safe, err on the conservative side of professionalism's definition. Also, always presume that every comment you make in public (and often in private) can be overheard by or passed on to someone important to your present and future, whether these be your professors or your patients.

Likewise, any behavior you engage in—while possibly permissible and legal in college—can be cause for an accusation of unprofessionalism in your pharmacy program. Professionalism committees in colleges of pharmacy exist to regulate these behaviors, and these groups may consist of faculty, staff, and some students.

The role of the Professionalism Committee, Board, or Council is to hear and adjudicate claims of unprofessional behavior about students within the college. Students should be aware that not all faculty who serve on these disciplinary boards are light-hearted and fair-minded. Ideally, there is a balance of personalities and philosophies on the committee to prevent uneven treatment of students (neither too lenient or too punitive).

Oddly, these committees are often evenly divided into temperaments based on the type of faculty serving. Basic scientists tend to be more nuanced and circumspect about professional student infractions, often more willing to ask investigative questions to interpret the "how" and the "why" of the infraction. In contrast, professional faculty are often more disciplinary, perhaps identifying with the professional student directly and feeling that the infraction represents a personal duty that they must correct swiftly. Professional faculty may sense that the student who committed the violation is somehow a poor representative of their profession, so they take these events much more seriously than the basic scientists present.

Also, if the professional violation is a drug-related issue, basic scientists who are pharmacologist (drug experts) may view the infraction as less serious. Often, these scientific types perceive drugs and alcohol not as personal vices but as chemical compounds with no inherent value; they are neither good nor bad. Thus, a pharmacologist's "take" on an illicit substance use allegation may be more relaxed, in sharp contrast to the PharmD on the committee who may be in favor of immediately recommending a 12-step program or program dismissal on the first offense.

When warranted, professionalism committees can charge students with unprofessional conduct and impose sanctions that range from probation, blockade from student government service, mandatory counseling, or program dismissal. The unprofessional charge also may be filed in the Dean's office and may appear on the student's transcript. Some examples of unprofessional conduct for a pharmacy student include (but may not be limited to):

- Cursing in a public venue
- Public drunkenness
- Illicit drug use/testing positive for illicit drug use
- Theft
- Assault/battery/domestic or child abuse
- "Sexting" either over the internet or a cellular device
- Sending inappropriate photos over the internet or a cellular device
- Making derogatory comments in public (or at the university) about other students or faculty
- Making verifiably false statements about faculty or other students
- Posting inflammatory rhetoric on social media (whether the page is "private" or a school-based page)
- Creating "secret" group pages that disenfranchise other students on social media meant for the entire class
- Haggling over grades with faculty in a persistent fashion
- Arguing about course or college policy
- Signing the name of another student on an attendance roster
- Being late for exams or laboratory sessions
- Wearing clothing deemed inappropriate for enrolled students (often, dress codes are implemented for pharmacy students)
- Refusing to accept final decisions about academic matters from faculty or administrative personnel
- Disrespecting staff
- Threatening students or faculty/staff
- Defacing school or private property
- Being arrested for any reason (guilt may not be considered; the arrest was sufficiently undesirable)
- Other behavior: if you are uncertain about its appropriateness, it probably is not.

Other aspects of professionalism seem to equate with student maturity. For example, a student may tell a professor that he is "unhappy" with a test grade or (ironically) a low score for professional behavior in class. This type of comment can be a mistake or an opportunity, depending upon how the

PHARMACY SCHOOL CONFIDENTIAL

message is delivered, how the professor accepts comments of this nature, and what the student does next after making the complaint.

Although this topic is fraught with controversy, it must be mentioned: faculty who harass (in any form) or demean students should be reported immediately to their Chair, and Chairs should be reported to their College Dean. Deans and other similarly titled administrators have indeed been found guilty of propositioning students, threatening students' grades or professional standing with dismissal or other punishments in exchange for sexual favors. They also have been documented bullying students (and faculty). Generally, students faced with these horrors fall into a normalcy bias, thinking that "this cannot be happening" when it certainly is. They shrug off the interaction as bizarre or anomalous and do not attend to the facts before them, a dangerous denial.

Students need to know (and never forget) that any faculty or administrator who inappropriately approaches them with such offers or conversation or who creates a situation in which the only extrication for the student is something illegal, immoral, or distasteful should be reported to the university President forthwith.

On that day.

Immediately.

This type of complaint should also bypass the Human Resources Department who most often serve to protect the university's interests only. A legitimate complaint of this nature must be followed up with an email or a formal letter again accounting the event, with times and dates, and it must be sent to several people above that offender's academic position. The more people who are aware of the illicit event or improper statement or action, the more protected the student will be. Students who are too timid to follow this course of action should contact a trusted faculty member who can guide this process confidentially and correctly. This also allows the student a mentor to share the tension and support him/her during such distress.

No faculty or administrator may retaliate against any person in the university, especially students, for valid, proven charges against them. For instance, they may not lower or withhold grades, deny assignments, or retain diplomas rightfully earned by students. They also may not tarnish the student's reputation with future employers for bringing about correct and justified accusations of malfeasance. These additional offenses are legally actionable and the student can sue the individual at fault as well as the university for implicitly condoning (by sheltering) such terrible behavior.

No faculty or Dean is protected in academia for such illegal or improper acts and, in fact, each of these people may be held to even higher standards than other community professionals due to the program's importance or prestige. After a student officially informs upper administration about the occasion, the student may also file a police report to support the academic paperwork in the event that it mysteriously "disappears". Students are adults with rights no different from any man or woman on the street. They should protect those rights by loudly and repeatedly calling out any person in the program who mistreats them and follow up on every complaint until it is satisfactorily and very publically resolved.

- **Professional Dress**

Professionalism extends beyond speech and attitude. When you become a pharmacist, your patients will expect to see clean, well-groomed, and professionally dressed experts when they seek medication counseling.[97-98] Pharmacy school prepares you early for this type of personal presentation by requiring professional dress as soon as the first year of classes. Some students may feel mild resentment about this requirement, perhaps wishing to continue the undergraduate style of casual: flip flops, shorts, or sweatshirts...or all three worn at once.

❝ You may have a class Facebook page. Keep it clean. Also, any special private group pages may be considered "school" pages because everyone involved has that common denominator: pharmacy school. Thus, what is posted on those private pages may be covered by university social media polices, too. ❞

Now and then pharmacy school allows a casual or dress-down day; otherwise, female students fulfill the dress code with a blouse, slacks or skirt, and shoes suitable for working in an office. Male students can choose a button-down shirt and slacks with a belt and clean leather shoes. Covering body art and or removing non-ear piercings may be wise for class and clinical appearances due to patient-care considerations. These restrictions may vary by region: a school on the west coast may be more permissive than a school of pharmacy in the south, for instance. Overall, a successful student will immediately begin emulating the habits and attire of a professional pharmacist. Dress for the job you want, not the student you are.

Similarly, faculty should model the very professionalism required of students. Studies show that when faculty are professionally attired, students have more confidence in the academic program.[97] Some people pooh-pooh the idea that a professional pharmacist's personal presentation matters, stressing that the pharmacist's communication skills are most important to patients. However, the majority of peer-reviewed reports confirm that patients regard a professionally dressed pharmacist as an authority in healthcare.[99-100]

THE INTERNET AND SOCIAL MEDIA

This section of the book could be short and sweet: do not friend professors on Facebook, and never post anything on the internet that degrades or criticizes faculty or your professional program. This is intuitive, but faculty and students still wrestle with social media, if the stories in the newspaper are any indication of reality. Thus, perhaps just letting the idea go at a simple directive might not be effective.

First, faculty understand that students are accustomed to social media and rely on it for their communication needs. Their utter comfort with it sometimes breeds a disrespect for the power it holds both immediately and in the future, when they are professionals with a public face.[101-103] Each student should approach the world-wide web as a permanent and un-alterable record of every image and keystroke sent over the wires.

In fact, anything posted on social media is considered to be "published". This includes any past internet postings from high school or undergraduate school. Studies show that most pharmacy school faculty will not extend connections to students over social media such as Facebook, and they likewise usually do not accept "friend" requests from students.[104-105]

❝ Students with entitlement issues should know that displaying these in front of faculty, other students, or patients creates resentment. Patients are especially offended because entitled people fail to communicate compassion and respect for others. Thus, cultivate personal behaviors that suggest that hard work and kindness matter. ❞

Pharmacy school admissions committees can, and often do, search for undesirable internet information about student applicants to "weed out" potentially unsuitable applicants. Some students also mistakenly believe that pharmacy faculty are not sufficiently savvy to locate information posted online by a student, and this could be a costly miscalculation; "older-than-you" does not mean "clueless".[104, 106] Aside from sullying your reputation in your professional program, consider the effect that bad internet information could have on your family, both the nuclear family (parents, siblings) you have now and the future family you may choose to have later.[103] Finally, consider anything posted online to be "forever".

Some social media or online postings may be *actionable*, too. This means that a lawyer could be in your future, specifically in the capacity of defending you from another lawyer who is spear-heading a lawsuit against you. In case you were cogitating on these concepts and require a refresher: slander is an oral defamation of an individual that is heard by another person that harms that person's character, and slander can include hand gestures. Libel, in contrast, is any written defamatory comment(s) that may injure the reputation or character of another individual.

Setting a personal goal of posting only true and positive information online (or not posting any information at all) is a simple rule that would well serve anyone.[101] Many unsuspecting pharmacy students have been unpleasantly surprised to overhear their instructors robustly and enthusiastically discussing a recent event posted online by a student, about another student, who exercised poor judgment. Also, it is a certainty that once discovered and discussed, these instructors are likely to remember this event for many years, especially during the time in which recommendation letters are needed for a residency program or a new job.

STUDENT ENTITLEMENT

What is entitlement? Does not the very word suggest that if someone is entitled to something, well then, they should have it? The answer to this is a qualified "yes" and "no". Two problems arise with the concept of entitlement. First, is the "entitlement" correctly interpreted, and next, is it feasible to fulfill the entitlement as it is described? Seemingly, with the recent shift in parenting styles, educational trends, and the cult of individuality, the singular rights and feelings of the young members of society are emphasized more than ever.

Thus, professional schools are dealing with fall-out from this shift in social norms in the form of entitlement issues.[107-111] To illustrate this idea, two different but real examples of entitlement events are depicted in the following section. One example pertains to society in general, and hopefully, it will be an obvious situation of entitlement. The example that is depicted next pertains to pharmacy school specifically, and it may be more ambiguous to students.

First, the obvious and non-pharmacy related illustration. Many students may recall this report of a tense situation on an Amtrak train that captured the interest of the US press and public. A woman on a 16-hour train ride from Oakland, California to Salem, Oregon was thrown off a train for speaking loudly and non-stop on her cell phone. Because she was knowingly in a designated "quiet car", she was violating the passenger policy for that train. Instead of choosing another car, she did exactly what she pleased, even when multiple passengers asked her to be quiet...during every one of those 16 (miserable) hours that she was on the phone.

This Chatty Cathy was eventually escorted from the train and charged with disorderly conduct for violating train policy, only to tell the authorities, and anyone else who would listen, that she had been "disrespected" *by being held accountable* for the rules and her over-the-top rude behavior.[112] As iterated previously, this one is obvious. Selfishly misbehaving for 16 hours is a significant *faux pas*, especially when many passengers requested that she simply observe the rules she implicitly agreed to follow when she chose to ride in the quiet car.

In contrast, more nebulous areas of entitlement are harder to ascertain.

A pharmacy-specific example might be summarized as follows: a common belief among pharmacy students that they are entitled to the professors notes/slides/study guides for every lecture because they paid tuition.[111] This is a common current theme among students. Some students may regard an entire educational experience as a commodity that can be purchased.[113-114] Indeed, this idea is raised by at least one student each year, and often by many students in one semester. Tuition, to these students, guarantees that lectures—and everything that the instructors create that goes into those courses—are the property of the student. Thus, as such, any faculty-generated course resources must be made available to all students on demand, they believe.

For example, students frequently demand that a professor "hand out/post a copy" of a specific slide that appears in a lecture but was not captured in the handouts. In effect, that student is actively refusing to take notes on the new piece of material, and instead, she is requesting that the information be *given* to her. This not only demonstrates entitlement but also suggests that the student is not serious about the class.

Why not write down the concept at the moment it is presented? Why wait for the professor to create a "personal memento" of the presentation in the form of an additional note? Sometimes, this selfish aspect of the request completely escapes well-meaning students. However, the meaning of these requests is not lost on the faculty who field these queries.

Another problem with this example is not about the intellectual property generated by the professor *per se*, such as the slide the student requested— or even the issues of copyright under which material belongs to the professor as well as the university (See **Chapter 4, §Course Packets, Lecture Recordings**). Rather, the real issue is that the student believes these notes are hers, *period.*[115] Other manifestations of student entitlement may be expectations of credit for simply showing up for class, unlimited faculty assistance with course material in the form of "study guides" or "practice questions", and a general simplification of course content to "be fair".

Rewarding such entitled expectations in the form of giving students every piece of information and rewarding them for lack of effort effectively devalues the pharmacy degree *in toto*. If the PharmD is available to anyone based on non-achievement outcomes, then what is the PharmD actually worth? The answer is this: the degree would be worthless. After all, handing out PharmDs to anyone, irrespective of effort means that undeserving individuals are being credentialed along with students who worked hard for the degree. Thus, protect the value and earning potential of your PharmD by asking more of yourself and your classmates. Shun entitlement at every opportunity.

❝ *It is very nice to be important, but it is more important to be nice. Remember this fact when you feel like the "entitlement monster" has you by the neck. Practice this thought continually throughout your professional experience!*❞

SELF-AWARENESS

How does a student know if she is behaving in an entitled fashion? Metrics to measure student entitlement exist in the scientific literature, a fact which may be of significant interest to students. Entitlement or an "exaggerated deservingness belief" often leads students to take actions in response to these beliefs. Thus, measuring the actual belief, as well as the self-reported likelihood of an action taken that was based on these beliefs, can be used to estimate student entitlement.

Academic Entitlement Scale[116]

Below is an entitlement instrument that is configured to a 7-point Likert scale. Likert scales are the typical survey choices of 1 = "strongly disagree" to 7 = "strongly agree". Two subscales of this entitlement instrument exist: entitlement beliefs and entitlement actions. Students should read each question and think about how strongly they agree or disagree with the concepts as follows:

Entitlement beliefs

- Instructors should bend the rules for me.
- An instructor should modify course requirements to help me.
- I should only be required to do a minimal amount of thinking to get an A in a class.
- I should get special treatment in my courses.
- I cannot tolerate it when an instructor does not accommodate my personal situation.

Entitlement actions

- I would confront an instructor to argue about my grade.***
- If I thought a test/assignment was unfair, I would tell the instructor.
- I would attempt to negotiate my grade with my instructor.
- I would argue with the instructor to get more points on a test.
- If I felt an instructor's grading was unfair, I would tell the instructor.

Studies show that answering "yes" to the belief questions correlates moderately with positive responses to entitlement behaviors. This means that students who believed these ideas often took action on these ideas. Of course, not all students with exaggerated academic entitlement beliefs will act on them, and some students will behave in ways that are not, in their mind, correlated to exaggerated entitlement beliefs. Naturally, there will always be statistical outliers.

Even so, students who answered the questions above with "yes" for most of the beliefs and/or actions may not think much of the assessment. Perhaps they will choose to think, "an older generation crafted this instrument, so of course, they are only doing what the generation before them did: criticize

---

***This is not the same as legitimately querying a bad test question, as addressed in Chapter 5, § "Testing" the Test.

younger people." Those students may be surprised to learn that *a PhD student* actually crafted the instrument, not some board of geriatric naysayers.

Promoting student discomfort with entitlement may be approached by indirectly appealing to the student's sense of mental health. Generalized entitlement beliefs are actually subcomponents of a narcissistic disorder. This personality trait can be scientifically measured and is defined by these characteristics, among others: expectations of performance to be recognized as superior without commensurate effort; a belief of being "special"; a sense of entitlement (unreasonable expectations of favorable treatment); and a willingness to take advantage of others.

Social scientists suggest that entitlement arises over time, through multiple and overlapping mechanisms that have been initiated before the student entered kindergarten. Perhaps the child was raised in a home in which parents over-praised every effort to the degree that accolades were expected for *any* effort.

Next, the community may have reinforced entitlement by supporting the idea that "all players are winners", a concept that is semantically null. Perhaps this was accomplished by giving every team a trophy at the end of a sports season, effectively rewarding each player and team in the same manner as the team who scored the most points.

Think about this for a moment. Would you enjoy being the most productive pharmacist in your store/department, adding innovation and convenience to your craft only to receive the same salary as the guy who arrives to work late, goofs off, and takes a two-hour lunch?

Probably not.

Clearly, you understand that not every attempt (or even a half-attempt) is a *winning* effort. Such warped concepts may begin in the home, but they are supported by communities and schools that inflate accolades for all students, suggesting that all work is terrific work. Statistically, not every student in a course can be an "A" student.

We all step up to the educational table with various skill sets and intellectual abilities. Schools that lack rigor and reward easy courses of study with high grades for all students perpetuate a grave disservice to those who go on to obtain more education. This is especially true if the next new experience is not a veritable organization of mutual admiration. This is explained in more detail below.

STUDENT ABILITIES

Students frequently discover, after a few weeks in professional school, that their coursework is much more difficult than they anticipated. You may be exposed to material you have never seen before; therefore, you may have absolutely no context for understanding it immediately. Perhaps pharmacy classes will seem like a new language for many students, and they will have no frame of reference to rely on for support. The reasons for this are multiple, and almost every student will feel overwhelmed at some point in a professional program.

Students need to know that an inconvenient truth exists. This truth is one that many colleges or pre-professional schools do not ever share with their students: their courses lack meticulousness. Reasons for this are numerous. For example, the undergraduate program could be out of touch with the realities of professional school demands and therefore is insufficiently challenging.[117-119]

A second reason for a lack of undergraduate course difficulty may be that the classes were taught only to the ability of the student, which may have been, on average, quite low.[119] Either way, the student (and perhaps the family of that student) mistakenly perceives that the classes are demanding and that real learning is taking place when nothing of the sort is occurring.

Another bad act among undergraduate schools is the trend of grade inflation, which was mentioned briefly before. This practice is not new. Literature dating back to the 1970s exists about this phenomenon.[120-123] The consequence of grade inflation is that students' scores and GPAs are higher than ever, but student abilities are not equally matched. Thus, the GPAs are not reflective of what the students know and what they can do.

Reasons for grade inflation vary from the incompetence of faculty in proper academic evaluation, a capitulation of schools to "gift" students with high scores, and the fault of accreditation bodies who abhor student attrition (See **Chapter 5, §Attrition**) pharmacy schools presently have a 10% average rate of attrition per class per year, which is a low value, in case you were wondering).[15] All three acts undermine true performance measurements, and an educated society, over time, will only suffer from this practice.[124-128]

Also, the name of a college class is no indicator of its true content or whether it can prepare students for more advanced study. When students have no other experience for comparison, they are truly are blind to any educational gap they have until they begin pharmacy school.[129] However, this statement is not meant to comment upon or address true student disabilities of learning, which are unique and covered in more detail below.

STUDENT DISABILITIES

Students do enter pharmacy school with learning disabilities. Section 504 of the Rehabilitation Act of 1973 prohibits discrimination or denial of benefits to (otherwise) qualified individuals on the basis of disability. This applies to any program conducted by federal agencies and any program that receives federal financial assistance, to name just two areas for which this law applies.

Criteria for classifying eligible students under the Rehabilitation Act are the same as those used under the Americans with Disabilities Act. Thus, students with learning disabilities present legal and ethical concerns to professional faculty as well as demand strategies that must be developed to address specific student learning issues.[130-131] Disabilities considered under Section 504 include psychiatric disabilities, specific learning disabilities such as attention deficit hyperactivity disorder and dyslexia, and frank handicaps such as blindness.[131]

Although different colleges have their own mechanisms for handling student learning disabilities or handicaps, special student circumstances usually must be documented by the student prior to entering the program or immediately after orientation, well before testing occurs in any course. Such accommodations made for students with legitimate educational barriers may include more testing time, a quiet and isolated exam environment, or different assessment tools.

Students with learning disabilities should not be discouraged from attempting pharmacy school. Almost every issue can be worked around with enough advance planning and creativity. If you are shying away from a pharmacy career that you truly desire because you believe a disability stands in your way, consider this unusual story about a most exceptional pharmacist:

In 1976, Anthony Burda was blinded at the age of 21 in his junior year of college due to an accidental poisoning. Burda was studying pharmacology with the hopes of being a pharmacist. However, his teachers at the University of Illinois strongly discouraged him from applying to pharmacy school. Undaunted, he applied for and was accepted into a pharmacy program, and he graduated in the top 10 of his class. After graduation, he was initially denied an application for a pharmacy license in Illinois. No stranger to challenges, Burda contacted the National Federation of the Blind. Then, with his persistence, the Federation's help, and two years of legal intervention, he obtained his license to practice pharmacy.[132]

Ironically, Burda works for the Poison Control Department of St. Lukes-Presbyterian Medical Center in Chicago. He uses Braille to "read" about toxicities and side effects (such as the blindness he experienced) so that he can communicate this information to his patients. Patients who call the Poison Control Center have no idea that he is blind. They are simply grateful for his assistance. As Burda puts it:

> "They all looked at me as some poor guy looking for a job who had a degree in pharmacology...I looked at myself as a very good pharmacist who just happened to be blind."[133]

Even if a student has no learning deficit and enjoys an absence of physical or mental issues that can complicate learning or testing, some students flounder in their studies and fail to ask for help. Their grades sink as they struggle to keep up and the insufficiencies accumulate. At the end of the semester, the student finds himself facing an academic committee who is tasked with deciding whether or not to keep the student in the program. Remember, "getting in" does not equal "getting out".

Of course, pharmacy students are not the only scholars who frequently face the dilemma of being inadequately prepared or failing to apply themselves with sufficient rigor to prepare for professional school. This is a common problem for many students of all disciplines. A wonderful story illustrates this concept quite well. Below is an opinion piece by *Miami Herald* columnist, Leonard Pitts. Although the entire article is worth reading, it is excerpted here and edited for brevity:

> "I scored 960 on my SAT. This was good enough for second best in my class and many congratulations and backslaps from teachers and administrators. Based on that, I thought I'd done pretty well.
>
> In my freshman year of college, I get to talking with my roommate, this guy named Reed, about our SAT scores. Reed sheepishly confessed that he scored "only" about 1200.
>
> That's when I realized I had not done pretty well. I had done pretty well for a student of John C. Fremont High, in the poverty, crime, and grime of South Los Angeles.
>
> As it happens, I started classes at the University of Southern California and came out four years later with my degree.

He then goes on to comment about such achievement gaps being "expected" for some ethnic/racial groups and some state's attempts to allow these gaps to persist through this "understanding" about student abilities and disabilities that are allegedly rooted in race.

> ...(T)hat two states—Florida and Virginia—have adopted new education standards under which they would set different goals for

students, based on race, ethnicity and disability (would create) separate and unequal performance standards for their black, white, Hispanic, Asian and disabled children.

These dissimilar standards reflect the achievement gap…(and) the best analogy I can give you is based in the fact that some coaches and athletic directors have noted a steep decline in the number of white kids going out for basketball. They feel as if they cannot compete with their black classmates. What if we addressed that by lowering the rim for white kids? What if we allowed them four points for each made basket?

How long would it be before they internalized the lie that there is something about being white that makes you inherently inferior when it comes to hoops?

It burns—I tell you this from experience—to realize people have judged you by a lower standard, especially when you had the ability to meet the higher one all along."[134]

This opinion piece is telling in two ways: the author acknowledges surprise that he was not as "educated" as he believed himself to be. However, he learned to accept this, and he worked harder to close this achievement gap. Next, the writer expresses the poignant and very true concept that no student should knowingly accept less than a rigorous program and the highest expectations, even if much work is required to reach those standards (and even if some students may fall short). Finally, abilities or disabilities aside, if your very best is still not good enough for pharmacy school, respect yourself enough to find something else to enjoy. The next 30 to 40 years of your life may depend upon it.

CHAPTER 4

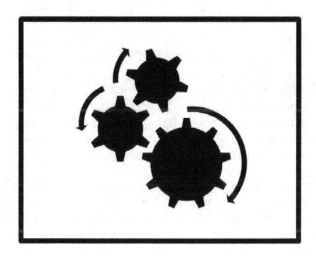

THE "INNER WORKINGS" OF THE PROFESSIONAL PHARMACY PROGRAM

THE PLAYERS: DEANS, CHAIRS, FACULTY, AND STAFF

Many students complete a PharmD with zero knowledge of who had leadership roles in their college and how those crucial individuals within the professional program were organized. This is unfortunate because professional students can use this information to their advantage when seeking resources or advice about procedures. All students should know the general hierarchy of and the relationships among "the players" in their college so that they always go to the right person with the right issue.

Much like the military's rank system for its officers, academia has a traditional and fairly predictable organizational scheme that allows smooth operation of the college and reduces duplication of effort among faculty.[135-136] Theoretically, if all members of an organization are certain of their responsibilities, then accountability can follow.[135-140] The academic "chain of command" offers just this type of organizational acknowledgment and accountability.

First, the head of the college will most likely be referred to as a Dean. The term may be strange to some people who do not spend significant time in academic circles; its Latin origin (*decanus*) refers to this authority figure being a "leader of ten." Historically, a decanus led cohorts of monks, who organized their education within monastic schools that were precursors to the modern university.

Thus, in colleges of pharmacy, the Dean is often the apparent college authority and this person may have a PharmD, a PhD, or both a PharmD and a PhD. Ideally, a Dean has held a Chairmanship or a similar authoritative leadership position for some time prior to acquiring a Deanship, but this is not always true. Infrequently, a Dean may be someone appointed for being non-threatening to upper administration and he/she may actually be an ineffective or destructive leader of a college.

Deans may also be hired from industry and such hires can offer innovation and new methods for accomplishing the college business. Because students cannot know intimate details of how and why a person was (or was not) selected for a Deanship, they will have no sense of this person's effectiveness or intelligence. In fact, the only "feeling" students may have about a college Dean is whether he/she is friendly or not; to them, this person is just a "face".

Even so, students should attempt to divine who has the real authority and who is the most relevant college representative (read: the "face" of their school to other faculty and administrators) campus-wide. This acumen can be obtained through conversations with faculty and plain observation of college happenings. Such academic-political savvy will be helpful for later job-seeking strategies and issues with employment.

Because pharmacy schools are historically and currently not as centrally prestigious to most universities as the college of medicine may be, leadership within the college of pharmacy may be lackluster or mediocre and cries to effect change in the college may go unheeded by university administration. The reason for this is simple: colleges of medicine are typically tied to patient care, which is university revenue. Thus, colleges of medicine often get the first choice of the best resources and pharmacy colleges are second or third in line for the leftovers. Understanding this as a student will put you miles ahead of many junior faculty!

The Dean of a pharmacy college may answer to the Provost, who answers to the university President, who reports to the Board of Trustees. The Board of Trustees may be comprised of citizens from the community, alumni, or other influential people. The Dean may also have an advisory board, who advises him about modifications to the curriculum, increases in tuition, or changes in college entry prerequisites. Boards may have different privileges at each college of pharmacy, but essentially, the advisory Board to the Dean provides balance and insight for his decisions.

Students may refer to their Dean as Dr. Smith or Dean Smith; both are appropriate titles of address. Additional Associate or Assistant Dean positions may exist throughout the college and these roles may have very specific tasks associated with the title. So, an Associate/Assistant Dean of Student Affairs may work directly with the pharmacy students, and the Associate/Assistant Dean of the Professional Curriculum may oversee course sequences and content. Also, an Associate or Assistant Dean may assist the executive Dean with college functions.

Next, Chairmen (or -women) usually lead departments within the college, and they may hold a PharmD, PhD, or both. Chairs report to the college Dean. Departments "own" curricular instruments such as certain courses and resources that are used to educate students, and Chairs preside over the faculty who administer these courses. The Chair can hire new faculty and advise faculty and staff about various matters within the college.

If a college has divisions instead of departments, then Division Directors may lead these areas instead of Chairs. Divisions may also be used to subdivide large departments. Usually, Chairs lead departments which have unique scholarly foci. For instance, some colleges find convenience in having a research department and a clinical department.

Staff are *non-faculty* individuals who support the functions of the college in various capacities. For example, Deans and Chairs may have executive assistants to help them with tasks of daily administration. Staff are also critical for college information technology, educational support, student resources, and other activities essential to the function and success of the college. Staff often report to the Chair of the department in which their position is based. Some may report to specific faculty, if they work directly for them as assistants.

Faculty are organized within the abovementioned departments or divisions, according to a traditional academic hierarchy. For example, most colleges refer to entry-level faculty as Assistant Professors, and the promotion order usually follows in this manner: Assistant Professor, Associate Professor, and Professor (also unnecessarily referred to as "full" professor). Clinical faculty may have other modifiers in their title such as "Clinical Associate Professor".

Faculty who are adjunct may have modified titles, too. Adjunct faculty are often part-time employees, and these two terms (adjunct/part-time) may be used interchangeably now and then. Also, a student/resident preceptor with specialized training and skills, who trains professional students may be permitted an adjunct role within the college. This adjunct status would be based on an application for this appointment and a departmental review and approval.

Research Assistant Professor, Research Associate Professor, and other research-labeled positions are additional titles that are meant to distinguish among faculty duties and roles within the college. Faculty report to department Chairs or Division Directors, and they may participate in committees which may report to a Dean. Because students chiefly interact with faculty as instructors and mentors, this component of the college is described in greater, student-specific detail below.

Sometimes, an inexperienced pharmacy student asks why his teachers are not all "real" pharmacists."[141] The answer is simple: rarely will a pharmacist in practice have sufficient expertise to cover every area of pharmacy at the level of detail needed for students. Practicing pharmacists may be more generalists than specialists. Thus, to address the didactic needs of the college, teaching faculty have various backgrounds that may be generalized into two areas along the lines of the departmental foci: that is, scientific and clinical areas.

66 *If the speech (in a lecture) is not malicious, vulgar, profane, racist, or deliberately unprofessional, universities usually support the faculty's right to teach as they wish. As long as speech is free, everyone has an equal and unassailable right to be heard. This freedom, however, does not necessarily include a "right" to never be offended.* **99**

So, faculty may be clinical pharmacists who teach and work in a clinic or hospital affiliated with the college to fulfill their role as faculty in the college. Clinical college faculty may also be adjunct professors who operate private pharmacies and teach now and then, bringing a community pharmacy perspective. For example, adjunct faculty with the college may be preceptors for student rotations.

Other college faculty may be scientists who have research and teaching duties in their areas of expertise. Such experts may have PhDs in pharmaceutical sciences, pharmacology, toxicology, pharmacokinetics, physiology, pathology, immunology, and related fields. More information about this is presented in **§Class Structure**. The goal of having clinical and basic science faculty in a college of pharmacy is to cover every aspect of pharmacy education in the most efficient manner possible for the ultimate benefit of the students within the program.

- *General Faculty Characteristics*

Even if students understand that their instructors have the necessary scientific or clinical expertise to be teaching, they may be surprised to learn that university faculty, in general, are rather liberal from a philosophical point of view. In fact, a large proportion of basic science faculty do not ascribe to any religion.[142] This statement in no way suggests that all faculty are atheists, unreligious, or lacking spirituality.

This fact is just that—a fact: note that university faculty, as a cohort, do not represent the general population in myriad ways, and this is just one specific (and consistent) example of how they are unique. Science faculty in general, and scientists in particular, such as those who deliver much of the first- and second-year pharmacy school curriculum, are reported to have political viewpoints that are skewed away from typical public perspectives. You may have observed this trend in college, one of the first places students step outside of their comfort zones into the zany and creative world of higher education.

Professional (and graduate school) science faculty may especially fit this unusual professional mold. For example, fewer than 10% of academic scientists self-identified as "conservative" (approximately 6% held Republican political values); almost 70% of the science faculty considered themselves to be "liberal" or "very liberal." In contrast, less that 25% of the lay-public self-identifies as "liberal/very liberal."[143]

In contrast, pharmacists who teach are not visibly categorized in the scientific literature with respect to political or philosophical leanings, so one may assume that the profession is more heterogeneous. This diversity may be one of the wonderful aspects of working as a pharmacist. Pharmacy seems to warmly welcome all types of people with varied worldviews.

Students from deeply religious homes or those who come from areas where conservative viewpoints are the norm can initially feel uncomfortable in professional programs when mingling with the abovementioned faculty.[144] Faculty may say and do things that are completely unexpected and perhaps unfathomable to these students. These students can find some resolution for this cognitive dissonance by remembering that academia is the last safe home of unfettered thought and free speech. In fact, the granting of faculty tenure was originally intended to protect intellectual thought and speech in the university, permitting the instructor to use satire, sarcasm, horror, or pointedly provocative words to convey ideas.[145-147]

Students who lack this understanding about science faculty often engage in behavior that demonstrates their ignorance. For example, students have audio- and video-taped lectures or seminars in which faculty were espousing comments which were "disagreeable" to the student for the purpose of deliberately exposing or exploiting the professor and the university.[148-149] If the students who participated in the attempted "outing" better understood faculty dispositions and leanings, such classroom experiences would have been less surprising or perhaps less "offensive."

Of course, if the professor removes his clothes and behaves bizarrely, this type of "lecturing" may justifiably raise eyebrows. Such an event occurred at Columbia University in New York in 2013. The school responded to this wild act of professorial disrobing with the statement:

> "(We) are committed to maintaining a climate of academic freedom...faculty members are given the widest possible latitude in their teaching and scholarship...(but this carries) corresponding responsibilities."[150]

Thus, the school still operated under the tenet of freedom of academic speech and thought (and apparently, actions). Furthermore, universities can bring a lawsuit against any student who makes such recordings, because they can violate university copyright or policies regarding course ownership.[148]

COMMUNICATION WITH FACULTY

A student applying to pharmacy school at this time may not recall a world without the internet, instant messaging, Skype, FaceTime, texting phones, PowerPoint slides, and e-mail. However, the faculty who teach your courses have indeed witnessed the advent of these wonderful educational tools, and they well remember life before such paraphernalia were universal features in our lives. Because of the ubiquity of such powerful and useful gadgets, students may relax about the etiquette surrounding their use. Thus, all students should remember that any communication to faculty through electronic media (e-mailing, texting, etc.) must be done with extreme care and consideration for every message, every time.

To stay below the Dean's (and the Professionalism Committee's) radar, regard every written communication between you and faculty as sacrosanct. Thus, each electronic or paper message you send to a professor should be respectful and brief. Anything that can be forwarded or saved is an especially sensitive submission, and the importance of civility in these matters can never be understated.[151] Appropriate e-mails from students to faculty include notices of upcoming class absences due to scheduled appointments, unanticipated or sudden illnesses, or other legitimate reasons. Proper inquiries also include questions about the timing of make-up exams.

Additional suitable queries might be course-clarification questions about material covered by that professor. An inquiry of this nature naturally requires that the student attended class when the material was presented, and that he attempted to understand the information *prior to* asking for more details. Some faculty prefer to use web-based discussion boards such as those found in Blackboard or Moodle (or other learning platforms) to handle questions. With this technology, all students enrolled in the course can view the question and the answer at their leisure. Questions can be made anonymous, too.

E-mails about actual tests and quizzes, other than the timing of them, may be problematic. Some schools of pharmacy forbid re-iteration of test material in any format, including e-mail (See **§Honor, §Testing and Student Evaluation**). Thus, appointments to talk to faculty may be required to discuss test results and request question/answer clarifications. Faculty usually cannot share grades with students over e-mail, either.

E-mail is inherently insecure, and an incorrectly typed e-mail address can misdirect confidential student data. Therefore, inappropriate texts and e-mail messages include asking about grades (there will be a formal posting method listed in the syllabus), challenging faculty on test questions in a hostile or demanding manner, and sending e-mails that can be interpreted as outright solicitations for better grades.

Before you e-mail an instructor, consider that faculty usually arrive at work each morning to find an accumulation of 50 to 80 e-mails that arrived overnight. Thus, your e-mail may take 4th or 15th position after e-mails from a Dean, President, or other faculty.[152] E-mailing a faculty member twice within one day with the same question is unnecessary. In effect, you are "prompting" this professor to respond to you, something a student should not attempt. Any student e-mail that does not represent a true emergency will be handled by the professor as he deems appropriate.

Students should remember, too, that some research may be required by the instructor to fully and accurately answer an inquiry. Therefore, e-mailing a professor, and then walking into her office an hour later to "discuss the e-mail" is extremely presumptuous.[153] Just because *you* only see the faculty member in your morning class does not mean that she is not teaching elsewhere, completing manuscripts, writing lectures, attending meetings, or performing research outside of that morning period (See **§Faculty Duties**).

A point often overlooked by new students is that pharmacy school faculty talk to one another daily, perhaps hourly. Faculty are consummate and prolific communicators who live and breathe "information". Of course, faculty conversations and data sharing exist in every program or college, but this proclivity of your instructors may carry more weight in professional school. At this level of the game, student behavior—both good and bad—is rapidly circulated, and may rise to the office of the college Dean if it is egregious enough to warrant the attention. The general rule for professional school is that the Dean should not know your name unless is it associated with virtue and hard work.

An increasingly frequent form of communication between faculty and students is frank criticism of an instructor's policies or offerings during the course. For instance, if an instructor is generous enough to see that a bonus opportunity can be created and that students would benefit from it, she may offer a few extra points for some lower-level work in or out of class.

When students email to criticize the points offered (too low), or that the points were not added to the final course average (instead of a test or quiz), or that the bonus was not available for a month so that they could get around to it, the instructor can rightly assume that the audience is not responsive to the bonus and deny the privilege in the future. Indeed, some students feel very comfortable critiquing seasoned, terminal-degree holding faculty about everything from their dress to their course packet. This is unwise behavior every time.

Unless a student also has teaching experience at the professional program level, holds a similar degree, and has experienced the chore of creating, deploying, and grading lessons and exams, a knee-jerk negative appraisal of the class and a full cataloguing of every perceived personal injustice committed by the instructor will be more than unwelcome. In contrast, a heart-felt, two-line email expressing enthusiasm for a topic, gratitude for the instructor's time or energy, or a quick note to share appreciation is always welcome and can go a long way to building good will with faculty.

> **℞** *" (Faculty should) admit when they are wrong. If a test is incorrectly scored, faculty should amend this. A student graciously pointing out an exam error might be the only way a professor learns that something is wrong. "*

FACULTY DUTIES

For success in your professional program, knowing what you need to do in pharmacy school is half of the equation. The other half is comprised of information to describe what faculty within your college do for you in the scope of their employment. The most important obligation faculty have to students and the college is to teach courses as described in the college catalog or academic bulletin, to be present and punctual for every lecture, and to test students accurately and fairly on the information they have learned. Professors are not required to entertain or amuse students. Often the lecture you enjoy (or don't) is part instructor personality, part subject material. Therefore, making every topic interesting for your class may be impossible.

Also, some instructors simply have no interest in being humorous, provocative, or more than mildly appealing. Remember, academia is a warehouse of diverse personalities and belief systems. If you are fortunate, you will have a handful of stand-out faculty who will increase the scope of your education by adding current events or thought-provoking topics to the class. Being funny is also a wonderful lecture delivery tool, and this certainly will keep students coming back to class. Unfortunately, because some of your faculty are probably the quirkier members of an enlightened society, you may find their brand of comedy eccentric, strange, incomprehensible, or even objectionable.

Although briefly mentioned above, regarding faculty activities outside of the classroom, students must understand that when faculty leave the classroom, they are not "off" work. Students are usually clear about equating a lecturing professor with a "working" professor. However, they may be less certain about that instructor's role when she is not in front of class. Instructors frequently log more than 50 hours of work a week (there is no overtime pay for faculty) just to keep up with departmental and college expectations and obligations beyond the classroom.[154]

In fact, faculty have contracts with the college, and detailed descriptions of their duties are described within these documents as well as the percent efforts they must devote to certain tasks. For example, a professor who teaches and conducts research may have a 25% teaching/75% research appointment, so his time must be generally divided in that manner as much as possible each day/week.

Professors may choose to adhere rigidly to their contract and perform tasks within their job description, immediately returning to their personal lives. This is perfectly acceptable. Naturally, some teachers view their occupation as a *quid pro quo* arrangement of "I teach and perform research, and the university pays me." Other faculty may willingly take on additional and uncompensated roles, such as class advising, helping with student fundraisers, or being highly visible after class and accessible for student interaction. Just as no reward is offered for going beyond the call of professorial duty, no penalty is imposed on an instructor who simply does her job.

Thus, due to the diverse and numerous duties and responsibilities of faculty, students should not be too disappointed if an instructor cannot be available each time *they* are free to chat. Never equate an office presence with freedom to hobnob with students; although, this is obviously a delightful and rewarding activity for many faculty who genuinely love their students and want to know about their lives. Pay attention to posted office hours in the syllabus and respect them as much as possible.

The sad mathematical fact is that every hour that a professor spends with a student, whether she is socializing, advising, or just listening...is an hour not given to that instructor's professional obligations, or worse, taken from her family due to her artificially extended work day. Most faculty tend to be very patient and non-confrontational, so they may never reveal that those two hours spent, for example, consoling a student over the loss of a pet meant that they had to finish a manuscript at 2 AM, collapsing into fitful, brief sleep before rising at 5 AM and returning to work the next morning.

Other than lecturing, advising, and testing, an important obligation faculty have to students *and their colleagues* is to admit when they are wrong. For example, if a test is incorrectly scored, the faculty should amend this. A student graciously pointing out an exam error might be the only way a professor learns that something is wrong.

Thus, students should speak up early and often, albeit politely, about confusing test data. Also, in class, instructors are obligated to say, "I don't know", to student questions beyond the scope of their expertise. Students should not expect any professor to know *everything*. Questions are welcome and can add to the class discussion, but students should realize that "I don't know" is a terrific and truthful answer.

RESOLVING PROBLEMS

Now and then, students will encounter problems in their professional program. These issues may be frustrations with classmates, unhappiness with grades or tests, confusion about class material, or general inquiries about procedures and processes in pharmacy school. When students do not understand the inherent chain of command in academia, they can approach the wrong people with inappropriate questions and receive incomplete answers. Thus, all students need to know some basics of the art of complaining.

First, any course issue must be taken up with the immediate course faculty. This is only fair. Giving faculty a chance to explain or correct a problem may be the fastest and most pleasantly surprising solution. Often, mistakes are simply unnoticed until a student mentions them. Incorrect test grades, malfunctioning class equipment, or cheating classmates can always be brought to the instructor of the course. Also, a student can speak to a class representative, who may serve as the voice of the class body. This representative can collect student observations, investigate complaints, and inform faculty on behalf of many students at once.

Then, if the student is unsatisfied with the course instructor's advice or decision, the next step might be (and usually is) to contact the course coordinator or curriculum director for the department. Directors may be appointed to handle professional education and oversee general course coordination, and specific course coordinators bring together the team who teaches the entire course over the semester or year. Both are suitable people to approach, with the order of command being the specific course coordinator and then the curriculum coordinator.

Next, directors or supervisors of overall pharmacy professional education may advise course and curriculum coordinators and resolve disputes or decisions arising within courses when the desired outcome cannot be achieved for the student. Next, the Chair of the department is usually the subsequent line of contact when the immediate professor, course/curricular coordinator, or director of professional education cannot answer the question. Taking an inquiry to a department Chair is entering the upper administration of the college, so students need to be certain that the question is well researched and meaningful.

If a Chair cannot reach a resolution for a student, the Dean may be the last step, but this should be undertaken only after approaching each of the previously mentioned people and meeting with failure. Students who refuse to engage the chain of academic command in this manner and circumvent the process immediately lose any authority they had over their problem. They can be perceived as "going around" the appropriate faculty or attempting to game the system.

> ❝ *Knowing who to approach with a problem in pharmacy school may be as important as knowing who __not__ to approach. Students who are familiar with the college protocol for posing questions about the pharmacy program or its faculty may find that they receive answers to their questions faster and that the answers are more satisfying.* ❞

Students are often shocked to be accused of going around the chain of command. They often state that they were not aware that a protocol was in place; so, obviously, how could they have followed it?

Welcome to adulthood, where you can be held responsible for things you *do not know*, as well as for the concepts of which you are aware. A wise student will inquire about any necessary or preferred procedure for asking questions/filing complaints/registering dissatisfaction. In the end, the student may have to accept that her way is not going to be *the* way.

Not everything that a student wants to have changed really needs changing. Furthermore, students who post grievances on Facebook or other social media as the problem is being resolved lose any standing in the argument. Keep the problem about yourself to yourself and follow the protocol for the best possible outcome.

Also, the pharmacy program is not a democracy, and faculty exist not to make students happy but to educate them. Students cannot "vote" to change the way a course, or the college, is managed. Rarely, a student will threaten to take a complaint to the university administration or, more foolishly, to the local newspaper or television. Such over-the-top behavior is viewed as a hostile gesture, and could result in charges of unprofessional behavior or dismissal from the program.

Likewise, heckling faculty with the same question over and over because you do not like the *first* answer is also unprofessional. The answer to the question will probably not change, no matter how many times you repeat the question. Furthermore, trying to "wear down" faculty in this manner may come back to haunt you. Thus, any student seeking answers through the hierarchy should be a model of propriety and restraint. In the end, students must adapt to the current administration of the program or find another school.

CLASS STRUCTURE

Classes in pharmacy school are usually team-taught. In undergraduate school, you may have had one professor for biology, cell biology, and genetics. One instructor might have taught every chemistry class, too. In large universities which cover multiple and diverse areas or topics, having many professors teach different elements—or team teaching—is the norm. Students say that the best part of team teaching is having a new face every few weeks and a new teaching and testing style. Oddly, these are the very reasons offered by students to explain why team teaching is also quite terrible.

In a team-teaching paradigm, faculty with expertise in specific course content will instruct students on that material only. For example, a successful researcher in renal injury may teach an entire kidney unit in physiology, or she may teach a unit on diuretics. Likewise, a specialist in cardiovascular pharmacology may handle the hypertension drugs for your pharmacology class. Some faculty members are professional educators, so they may teach multiple courses across various topics.

- *Teaching Excellence*

Because science is the basis of pharmacy, and because basic science is a global profession, you may have professors within the course teaching team who were born and trained outside of the US (recall that 98% or so of the world lives *outside* the US). So, English may not be the first, *or even the third*, language of the instructor. Thus, depending upon the linguistic ability of the professor, you may be unable to understand the lecture at all.

This is unfortunate while also being quite common, and often virtually unchangeable, depending on the degree of frustration of the student and the level of engagement of the department and college administrators. Students who graduated from large, metropolitan universities are often the most accustomed to the issue of faculty's lack of language fluency and they tend to either tolerate linguistic difficulties or to overcome these obstacles faster than students who came from smaller, more homogenously populated colleges.

When language barriers present insurmountable challenges for students, they either stop attending class or complain to course coordinators about the problem. The usual actions at the level of the college are to tell the students to read the notes and review the recordings. Also, students are asked to make an appointment with the instructor who has difficulty with English to resolve issues, but typically, when these uncomfortable situations arise, the professor who is causing the problem for the students may be the only person left out of the conversation. Thus, the "solution" to the problem is often no real solution at all.

" Faculty may not speak English as a first language, or may have a heavy accent. Expecting international faculty in a professional program is prudent. Students unfamiliar with such (or who resist this truth by asking other faculty to "fix" it) are less likely to understand course material well under these conditions. "

During circumstances such as these, the fact that no changes are made in the lecture roster to remove the unintelligible professor may come down to hidden specifics. For example, often the instructor is contractually obligated to teach a specific number of hours per semester or year, and this cannot be changed easily or without imperiling the instructor's livelihood (see contract details in the previous paragraphs). Even if no compromise can be reached about a professor's language inadequacies or her poor communication skills, students should refrain from abjectly demeaning any professor who has language difficulties.

Even though this is a popular refrain among less savvy students, objecting to unintelligible speech is not racist or elitist and engaging in poor behavior because of a poor speaker is simply rude. In reality that instructor may speak more languages than the students who are giving her a hard time. So, mocking faculty dialects, accents, or pronunciations is also taboo. Chances are excellent that somewhere on the planet, your accent, dialect, or pronunciation is amusing to others, also.

No person has the market cornered on speech and enunciation (*although National Public Radio has some really excellent broadcasters who are worthy of emulation if you have the time*). Even so, because this is a recognized issue in higher education, the English Fluency among Lecturers in State Institutions of Higher Education Act which was passed in 1990 allows individual State Boards of Education to certify English fluency and impose penalties when these matters are not addressed satisfactorily to the enrolled students.

The Act was promulgated to ensure that students were adequately educated and to provide students with excellence in education with the highest standards of instruction. The framers of the Act understood that instruction and conversation are elemental for imparting knowledge and that if students cannot understand faculty, then the instruction failed.

Finally, the Act acknowledges that "to address questions to an instructor and to receive understandable answers to those questions represents a consumer right, a civil right, and an educational imperative."* Students who must listen to professors who cannot be understood may rightfully interpret the lecture as unimportant because no one is concerned that it be delivered intelligibly. Thus, the Act suggests that English fluency is not negotiable, and students can take satisfaction in knowing that their needs are seriously considered at all phases of secondary education, especially in schools of pharmacy.

- **Faculty Evaluations**

Teaching excellence involves much more than language, however. As covered later in **§Faculty Duties**, your instructors should arrive to class fully prepared and early or on time. They should be obviously pleased to be there and offer an instruction that is the best you have received to date. This is the hallmark of a superior professional program: engaged, dedicated, enthusiastic faculty who keep you motivated to attend class and wanting to know more about the topic.

The department that pays these faculty to teach their courses and the college in which the department resides are all interested in student feedback about lecture quality and content. Thus, students are frequently encouraged to offer anonymous evaluation in the form of a score and comments for every professor who teaches their courses. Usually these evaluations are offered after an exam, and students may wish to punish an excellent teacher for difficult exam questions (this is obvious to administrators, by the way). Better students with greater maturity can see past the rigor and actually be glad for

---

The English Fluency Among Lectures in State Institutions of Higher Education Act can be accessed online using a search engine, and it will be tied to each state's Board of Education listings

it, properly evaluating faculty for their passion and persistence in encouraging learning (not memorizing).

Students need to know that addition to their critiques of faculty, professors are also evaluated by their peers (other faculty) and these data are combined to give the department and college a fuller picture of their effectiveness (not their "hotness", trendiness, political views, or popularity). This helps to balance and distinguish student evaluations that are based on "sucking up" to students, "teaching to the test" and simply "being entertaining".

In contrast, some (and thankfully rare) evaluations are no more than a verbal assault on a person in his/her place of work. These arise when students do not appreciate that they will pass through that program in only four short years. Faculty, in contrast, can work in that environment for decades and their workplace (and the critiques within it) matters to them.

Smartly crafted and deployed evaluations identify problem faculty who need assistance or frankly, should find another line of work. Most or all of your faulty have never been taught to teach you (it is not a formal portion of PhD programs, and it is not a common PharmD component). Rather, they are asked to teach, perhaps as an extension of other obligations to the college such as clinical service or research, and this extension is contractually renewed annually with the allotted time for teaching assigned as needed.

When you become a pharmacist, your work goals will mirror theirs: that you do the job to the best of your ability, with the greatest authority based on the latest information, and that you deliver it effectively. Unfortunately, the idea of "effective" is difficult to define. Thus, here is a limited list of elements of minimally effective teaching:

- Course objectives are clearly stated, achievable, and measurable (that means testing).
- The instructor is organized, offers transitions during the lecture to facilitate learning and summarizes main points at the end.
- The lecture includes relevant background and facts, current and evidenced-base data, examples, and offers alternative explanations to facilitate understanding.
- The instructor is audible, clear, and enunciates with the appropriate diction and vocabulary for a terminally educated professional.**
- The instructor begins and ends the lecture ON TIME, with appropriate prescribed breaks.
- The instructor senses when students do not understand/are having difficulty and amends the lecture to remedy this.

These criteria define consummately effective (the best) and hopefully enjoyable teaching styles (the instructor meets the previous criteria as well as these)....

- The instructor offers cosmopolitan, sophisticated lectures, expanding the content beyond "course facts", including relevant details to "round out" the educational experience.
- The instructor uses engaging support (video, audio) and is responsive to shifts in classroom behaviors (varies lecture pace accordingly)
- The instructor is well prepared but flexible enough to shift pace, direction, or discussion spontaneously as the lecture evolves and students interact.
- The instructor's enthusiasm for the students and the topic is obvious.
- The instructor stimulates questions and involvement, solicits feedback, and clearly answers questions.
- The instructor encourages diverse points of view and allows relevant student discussion.
- The instructor is comfortable with "I don't know" as an answer to a student question.
- Testing is rigorous and covers course content with the purpose of supporting mastery.

Students should evaluate faculty fairly: if the scale presented is 0 to 5, then surely only a handful of faculty would deserve a 5 as this is the best score possible. Better teachers may earn 4s, and mediocre teachers can be awarded 2s and 3s, with the faculty making the most effort (although with less effectiveness) being given more 3s. The worst teachers should be honestly scored, too. Scores of 1 or 0, if it is used, can help faculty improve teaching which benefits everyone in the end. Sadly, students tend to cram most faculty into the 3 to 4 categories, reserving 5s for their favorites and 2s and 1s for the toughest teachers, irrespective of excellence. This is not the purpose of the scale and it does not facilitate program improvement.

Finally, no student can cause a single professor to be terminated over a solitary bad evaluation although gossip often suggests that this can occur. The truth is that no student has that much individual power, but many students have a strong voice over legitimate instructional concerns. Honestly, only temporary or adjunct faculty (which are rare) are actually at the mercy of bad evaluations to the degree that they may be eventually unemployed. Thus, students should offer prudent and constructive criticism to help faculty teach better and criticisms should be levied with the face of the faculty in mind: picture the person you are reviewing, and you will likely strike the right balance of helpful and wise feedback.

COURSE MATERIALS

- *Course Syllabi*

Course materials available to pharmacy students vary by school, but typically, all students will receive a course syllabus for every pharmacy class. Depending on how the courses are structured, syllabi may also differ for each class. For example, attendance may be mandatory for one class but not as critical for another course. Some classes tie grades to attendance, so read the details and assume nothing. Also, read every syllabus offered for each class to determine differences in expectations or grading and testing policies across the curriculum.

Even though the syllabus is the first course material you will receive, and you will be at your highest level of enthusiasm for your professional program when you receive it, *every semester* without fail, students ask faculty questions that are answered in the syllabus.

They do this simply because they did not perform the due diligence on their end. This lack of task commitment frustrates faculty who are peppered with queries from such lazy students. *Yes, these students are lazy*: instructors gave hours of their time to prepare and distribute the syllabus and some students did not bother to read it.

Also in the syllabus, exam deployment will be described, and this may be somewhat standardized at the department or college level. Therefore, testing across classes may be similar, but faculty can add pop-quizzes, graded out-of-class assignments, presentations, projects, and readings. Also, with more course material being available online, some instructors may require pre-class viewing of brief videos. Some students estimate that two to three hours of preparation for each hour of class is appropriate or necessary.[172] This is all explained in the syllabus, so read it thoroughly and consider the syllabus to be a personal, if informal, agreement between you and the professor.

- *Course Objectives*

Another surprise that awaits students in professional school is the independence that faculty are granted to host their courses as they wish, as initially suggested above. Thus, a biochemistry professor may host daily pop-quizzes at unannounced times, and a pharmaceutics instructor may require short multiple choice tests to be taken on audience response devices (also known as "clickers"; more on this in **§Audience Response Devices or**

"Clickers"). One professor's technique for course delivery may be different from that of another professor, and this is perfectly acceptable; although, students may think that these differences are somehow "unfair."

Therefore, students may complain, "Well, Dr. Smith allows us to...."; "Well Dr. Jones never makes us....". Unfortunately, such statements are ineffective strategies for eliciting change; students do not set course formats or content. Moreover, students should not ask faculty to comment on or attempt to manipulate faculty who direct or teach within other courses. If intervention is needed, this would occur at the level of a department Chairman (or a professional curriculum advisor), and even then, the instructor may still impose her course preferences. Thus, the general rule for pharmacy classes is that an instructor's rights to a specific course ends where the other instructor's course begins, so to speak.

- *Course Packets*

Even though a thorough explanation of the syllabus has been provided previously, students often confuse the course syllabus with a *course packet*. Course packets or course notes may be given (or sold) to students, and these bulk print jobs consisting of several hundred pages may contain the slides or presentations that the faculty have created for a particular class.[155-156]

Course packets are valuable to students because the sheer volume of information cannot be easily transcribed during lectures. This does not mean that course lecture information *cannot* be written down, only that such transcription is difficult.[157] Note-taking is intended to be combined with listening and remembering.

Because course packets are not meant to substitute for attending class and taking notes, faculty who issue "incomplete" packets (in the opinion of the student) are not obligated to supply extra slides or material to the students at any time. Submitting a list of course objectives or a simple course outline is fair game for course packet submissions. Thus, taking notes is the answer to having a complete course packet, and students are expected to anticipate the need for extensive writing and annotating of their packets.

Often, minimal course packet offerings may mean that more substantial notes are made available immediately prior to class, uploaded to campus educational software. Thus, before class, students can print notes they wish to have from this software interface or download these new notes to laptops or tablets. Course packets may also be revised mid-course if an aspect of science has changed.

Pharmacogenomics is one such course that covers an exploding and ever-evolving discipline. Thus, as discoveries are made, course material may be updated to reflect such innovation. Such amendments are characteristics of responsible teaching, and students should expect to have a few fresh class notes posted to provide the most current information. The downside to immediate and frequent lecture material postings is that students must engage in ongoing printing to keep abreast of continually emerging information.

- *Lecture Recordings*

Class or lecture recordings that are delivered over the college intranet or portal and stored online provide secondary study tools to enhance learning.[158] See more details of this in **§Distance Education**. Lecture recordings are meant to be secondary devices for learning and some universities restrict their use to remediating students only. When recordings are available without restrictions, some students will watch or listen to recordings as soon as they are available, reinforcing that day's material.

Other students wait until a few days before an exam, and attempt to launch a marathon lecture-viewing session. Students may even convert these presentations to an audio file for listening without the aid of slides. Students should be sure that downloading and sharing lecture recordings are not prohibited. After all, lectures are meant for enrolled and tuition-paying students only. Thus, students who download lectures instead of watching them from the host website or software may be violating university copyright, and they could face sanctions for this activity.

Students want to keep in mind that academic aids such as those described in this chapter (course packets, lecture recordings, etc.) were not common resources for the very faculty who teach you today.[159] In fact, your current professional faculty, when they were graduate or professional students, were probably armed for lectures with a mighty pencil and reams of paper (or a fancy pen, if they were more affluent).

In those days—and your faculty will remember this vividly—they literally wrote their fingers numb for every class. Also, your faculty accepted that not everything said in lecture was written down. They relied on memory for filling in the gaps, and they may have the same expectations for you, too. Indeed, the present time offers educational advantages incomparable to any era preceding it, and these advancements will only improve over time.

Thus, students may not be aware that frequently, faculty are the sole decision makers about whether a lecture will be recorded, and this stems from the inherent freedoms conferred by an academic environment. The instructor s material, voice, and any images that bear a likeness to him is the property of that instructor. The course materials are specifically intellectual property and the rest are forms of personal property.

So, a professor who refuses to record a lecture due to poor attendance may have every freedom to do so. Likewise, an instructor may record a lecture and then stop the recording to take questions or review upcoming test material. Recordings are "perks", not rights, so students should hold an "attitude of gratitude" for these technological marvels and the generous faculty who allow them.

CHAPTER 5

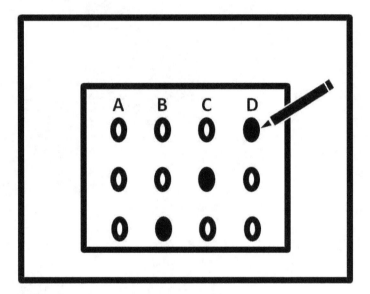

EXAMS AND STUDENT EVALUATION TOOLS

Quizzes, exams, and similar testing instruments are common ways to evaluate student performance and mastery of program content. Quizzes and tests may be online, paper-based, or administered via "clickers" (explained in §**Audience Response Devices or "Clickers"**). Each testing mechanism is unique with respect to the time and effort required to prepare and administer it, and each testing method has significant pros and cons.

Paper exams, which offer test questions in a test "booklet", usually include a Scantron (answer) sheet for "bubbling" in answers. Paper tests are a fairly common means of standardized testing, and the time given to complete the exam is usually set for the class based on the number of questions contained in the test. Thus, the instructor estimates the time needed for all students to complete the work.

Because paper exams tend to be administered in crowded classrooms, a minimum of two test versions may be made. These tests (Test A and Test B) contain the same questions, but the order of the questions varies. Exams are handed out in an alternating fashion, so that no Test A student is sitting next to a Test B student. This technique is used to decrease potential cheating: the answers on the Scantron for Test A will not match answers for Test B. If cheating is a *significant* risk, more than two test versions may be used. However, this represents an enormous effort for faculty to create, randomize, and key (provide answers for) each version.

Also, during exams—both paper and online—students may be forbidden to ask the instructor anything directly pertaining to the test. Exceptions to this rule may include alerting the faculty to typographical errors or gross omissions that could change test outcomes or confuse students and waste valuable test time.

Students are also often not permitted to leave the test area, even to use the restroom. Bathroom breaks should occur before the exam starts. When students are permitted personal breaks, the student may be asked to turn in the test, be escorted to the restroom, and receive the test for completion once re-seated. Such supervised procedures have evolved over time in response to unique attempts by students to cheat on exams.

After testing is complete, irrespective of the method used for testing, the material covered on the test is not discussed, written, or recorded in any manner. This rule is often written into the honor codes by which all entering pharmacy students pledge to abide. Also, each student may be required to sign a short form of the honor code on each exam, vowing not to share information during the exam or discuss test questions after the exam.

ONLINE TESTING

Students may know that paper exams are being phased out and replaced with online, computer-based testing.[160-161] Thus, first year students may be expected to have a laptop or tablet as mentioned before (or an internet-ready device that is approved) for these tests, when they become available (if they are not available already).

Students who cannot acquire the use of a laptop or tablet for the test may be offered one by the instructor or may be offered a paper test version instead. Also, pharmacy schools may have sophisticated computer testing centers, in which individual desktop computers are separated by privacy screens. These testing centers may be separate rooms from the lecture hall, used by all colleges in the university.

Students and faculty can immediately appreciate the *environmental* benefit online testing offers to Mother Earth. Consider that a first-year exam may consist of 20 pages of paper. Then, these 20 pages are probably printed for more than 100 students. This represents *at least* 2,000 sheets of paper for each test administered, plus any additional print jobs due to corrections or printer errors.

Another advantage of online testing for the student is the immediacy of grading. The test score may be directly uploaded into an educational software program such as Moodle or Blackboard. Then, students can view the grade and receive instant feedback about their progress at the end of the test. Also, electronic testing immediately allows faculty to remove poorly written questions from hundreds of tests in one keystroke, automatically re-calculating each grade in a matter of seconds.

R̲x̲ **" *Students who are not accustomed to online or computer testing may balk at the idea of testing on computers because they cannot "show their work." These students should know that the NaPLEX (discussed in greater detail later), which they will take after graduation, is entirely computerized.* "**

Even with technological advances in computing, online test integrity and security are ongoing concerns. To assure test security, online testing software is often coupled with proprietary computer browser-lockdown software. The student is required to download this locking software to their tablet/laptop prior to the exam, and the exam can only be accessed through this browser add-on.

Once in the test, the computer screen is locked at "maximize", and students cannot open another window, browser, or application during the exam. Furthermore, testing software may have built in timers to close the test at an appointed time, prevent backtracking, or prohibit printing exam material.

Additionally, lockdown software can be programmed to accept online testing from only specific IP addresses, such as those from within specific zones of the campus, to prevent any off-campus test taking. To accomplish this, the acceptable campus IP address is entered into the browser software by the instructor, and students access the test with a password. Even if an IP restriction is not in place, testing software can show the IP address from which a student takes an exam, confirming test security.

Other security measures include logging every student keystroke during the exam using by-the-second timing of every student entry. These data can be used to compare students across the class to ascertain if cheating is occurring with other techniques.

When students complete the online exam and submit the test for electronic grading, the test interface closes, preventing students from changing answers. Another feature of computer testing is automatic question and answer randomization. Not only are the questions in unique orders for every student, but also, the correct answers will be located in different places. Thus, question 12 for one student may be correctly answered with "A", and this same question is number 30 on another test, with a correct answer of "C". Such re-ordering of test data makes cheating too difficult to attempt.

Students who are not accustomed to online or computer testing may balk at the idea of testing on computers because they cannot "show their work." These students should know that the NaPLEX (discussed in greater detail later), which they will take after graduation, is entirely computerized. White-boards (dry erase-like boards) are offered for working NaPLEX calculations; no paper is needed. Thus, students who are already comfortable with online testing may have an advantage when taking the pharmacy board exams. The ACT, which you may have taken for entry into college, will be laptop/tablet-based as of 2015.

AUDIENCE RESPONSE DEVICES OR "CLICKERS"

Another testing mechanism that is common among schools of pharmacy is testing via an audience response system or "clicker" method. Many schools of pharmacy require these for students in addition to the laptops/tablets. Clickers are hand-held remote devices about the size of a cell phone. They have a small window to view alpha-numeric data and a keypad. Batteries supply power for these devices, and they must be registered for the class in which they are used, typically on a website students access once they purchase the clicker. Some clickers require multiple separate registrations to function in every class.

Clickers offer real-time data that are entered by students, and they can be used for taking attendance (students "click in"), quizzes, or rapid-response student self-checks for understanding the course material. The latter use is similar to a game show in which the audience votes and the results appear on a screen—this is the same technology. When used for quizzes, clickers are typically used for short exams, perhaps with fewer than 10 questions. Thus, the student may be given a paper quiz containing questions, and the student can initially work out his answers on this paper (to show work, calculate problems, etc.).

Then, the final quiz responses can be entered into the clicker for grading. The paper is retained by the instructor for record-keeping and future reconciliation with clicker data, if necessary. Then, the clicker device uploads the quiz data into educational software that the student can access after class to view his score. Students may not immediately appreciate the initial expense of a required clicker (about $30), but they do appreciate such devices later because they get hooked on the instant exam feedback.

Sometimes, clicker devices can be used in parallel with longer paper exams, allowing students to input responses on a Scantron test answer sheet while entering the data semi-discontinuously into the clicker. Thus, the student can enter his answers all at once, at the end of the exam, or he can enter one response or a few answers at a time, as he goes through the exam. When this type of mechanism is employed to test students, the clicker data are normally unofficial, and the Scantron represents the official test score. The clicker data give the student an estimate of how well he performed in real time.

Students often forget that clickers cannot tell them much about bad exam questions that are eventually thrown out. Clicker software may not be integrated with the test-reporting software, and faculty may not bother to change clicker test key information to account for these adjustments. Another major drawback of clicker usage for *official* test scores is that often several versions of a test are deployed (as described previously) so students must enter their test version first before entering clicker data to assure that their responses are keyed correctly.

66 *Life is inherently unfair, so you will find that some classmates can pass all exams without attending class or seeming to study at all. Others will attend class and every review session only to make middling grades (or worse). Constantly assess your study strategy to seek improvements and increase efficiencies. Be willing to drastically alter the way you prepare for tests.* 99

When students enter incorrect test versions into the clicker, their responses are graded against the wrong key. Furthermore, some clickers prevent a student from correcting the initial test-version entry. Often students are completely unaware that they have mis-keyed their test version at all (clickers may not show which version of the test was entered); although, the devices may show the answers chosen and allow students to review and modify these selections until the test closes. Once a test closes, clicker data cannot be changed. Also, each "click" made by every student is recorded, time stamped, and held in a database, just like entries made in computer testing environments.

If clickers are used for official scores, the faculty hosting the exam may not allow students who mis-key their test version to be re-scored with the *correct* key. Faculty may impose the entire responsibility of test-data entry on the student, and many times the only evidence of a mis-keyed test is a devastatingly low grade after the exam is over.

Of course, students have argued that since a paper version did exist (remember the paper used to work out initial answers?), then the instructor can simply use the paper quiz to re-grade the answers, ignoring the mis-typed clicker information. Usually, faculty will not do this, even if the paper quiz had completely correct answers, and this situation can be instructive for students. Such potentially heavily penalties for carelessness directly translate to pharmacy: a mis-calculated drug dosage can cause a patient's death. Thus, one can never be too careful too early.

As technology improves, these types of devices will be replaced with phones, laptops, and tablet devices to engage students and provide feedback. Then, the student will shoulder the entire burden of maintaining device integrity and functionality to fully participate in class.

TESTING PREPAREDNESS

Professional students tend to be highly focused on grades, and such hypervigilance about scores can rise to the level of a distraction from the fundamental mission of pharmacy school: to acquire knowledge that fulfills the requirements of a PharmD (and master sufficient information to pass the NaPLEX, See §NaPLEX). Ideally, these students will then move on to a successful career armed with the best and most current information in their discipline. Such a far-away goal often gets overlooked in exchange for the more immediate feedback of grades.

Because this attitude is not likely to change in the future, students should, at the very least, know what goes into a test and how tests are evaluated to assess if they are fair and true instruments of competency measurement. Of course "knowing what goes into a test" does not mean "knowing what is on a test."

Even today, some students believe that it is appropriate to ask a professor, "What do we need to memorize for the test?" Students who inquire about test content in this manner may be viewed as rude and immature by the faculty (and other students who know better than to inquire). Asking what is on the test is improper, period.

Doing so is much like asking the judge of a footrace to move the finish line back a few feet for one runner only, so he can complete the race with less effort. Even restating test-content inquiries as follows: "What should we focus on for the test?" or "What do you believe is important for us to know?" does not fool anyone. These questions are conceptually identical to simply asking what will appear on the test.

Some students try an oblique approach, asking, "How should I study for the exam?" This is disingenuous, too. Experienced faculty may respond honestly, telling the student, "How would I know?" After all, each person may need a unique study approach, so how one professor would prepare for an exam may have no relevance to how a student would study. This, again, is merely an end-run around the actual question of "what is on the test", an inquiry that students should not make if they want to be taken seriously as professionals who can handle a rigorous program.

If students spent the same time studying that they give to attempting to pry loose test questions from faculty, they would have nothing to worry about. To this end, great ideas for studying are everywhere and there is likely a method that will appeal to almost every learning style. For example, Quizlet, a free online resource (quizlet.com) allows students to make and share "flash cards" for studying.

Also, students may choose to read into an audio recording app and listen to the recording while running, lifting weights, or leaning against a tree outside. Also, audio files can be burned to CDs for listening to while driving to class. Facebook pages are also wonderful formats for ping-ponging study tips and getting clarification about concepts from classmates. Before a test, Facebook class pages for pharmacy students are overloaded with querying and answering by students. The atmosphere on these pages is usually respectful, polite, and helpful.

Finally, as always, all of the studying in the world will not matter if you do not show for the exam. Thus, if a test window is posted, be present at the posted time. Often, professional school exams are given over one and one-half to two hours due to the length and complexity of the material. All students are expected to arrive at the indicated test start time.

Students who enter the test site after test deployment may be denied a testing opportunity, and the college may impose sanctions of unprofessional conduct on students who do not consider a test start time to be an important event. Entering a test late disturbs students and distracts test proctors who are present to ensure test integrity. Sleeping late, studying "just a little more", or the belief that you do not need the entire exam period for the test are poor excuses.

Now and then a student will miss an exam. This can happen to the most prepared and punctual student. Cars break down, trains stop traffic, and illnesses circulate among students (and their families). So, missing a test once in a while is nothing critical. Most pharmacy schools have test-absence policies such that any illness that causes a missed exam must be documented by a physician in the form of a letter or a note every time this occurs.

Each note for the absence will go on file in an office such as that of the Associate/Assistant Dean for Student Affairs or someone with authority over student absences. Usually, this person only can authorize an absence from an exam and permit a make-up test to be offered. If this is the case, then the course coordinator must work through this administrative office to obtain information about absences and potential excused make-up tests. Also, the make-up exam may have to be completed by a certain time due to upcoming test reviews. Only students who have taken the exam may attend a test review for that exam. Moreover, each day that a student delays a make-up test is another day to fall behind.

Some students who cannot bear the pressure of testing will find themselves "ill" frequently, missing a series of tests so that they can have a later make-up test, likely taken in isolation, and at a time more agreeable to them. This behavior is a form of cheating, and it is detected fairly quickly. Notes for excused absences begin to pile up in the student's file, and the authority presiding over student absences may send an e-mail to the faculty to "warn" them of this problem.

Also, faculty often "compare notes" about students, and they can catch on to purposeful test delaying tactics as well. Students, too, notice this activity, and they talk to each other as well as to faculty. Students who make a habit of delaying tests with mock illnesses or random excuses can be brought before an Honor or Professionalism Board or Council and sanctions can be imposed on the student. For example, the student may receive a zero on the next missed exam, irrespective of the excuse for the absence.

TEST REVIEW

After an exam, faculty may choose to host a test review at the next class meeting time. During test reviews, the class period may not be recorded as it might be during a traditional lecture. Students may not be allowed to take notes, either. During these special reviews, which are entirely at the discretion of the instructor, selected questions that most of the class missed may be reviewed and explained. At this time, students can ask additional questions and discuss test material to clarify concepts.

Such testing and review confidentiality serves multiple purposes. First, it decreases faculty work of re-creating new tests every year. Next, it protects test security in that no test file or old test material is in circulation. Although students may have enjoyed having test files or folders of old exams in undergraduate school, this is considered to be unprofessional behavior at this level. Such "test preparation" amounts to no more than memorizing old questions instead of focusing on learning course content.

"TESTING" THE TEST

Multiple-choice and true-false tests take significant time and talent to write. Also, longer tests (more items to answer), tend to be more reliable indicators of student competence.[162] So, to measure the knowledge of a large group (such as a class of pharmacy students), lengthy multiple choice exams are typical of the pharmacy school experience.

It may be surprising to many students, but the best test, according to many faculty, is one which allows the better performing students to make higher scores (As), with the mid-performing students comprising the bulk of the Bs and Cs, and the more poorly performing students receiving lower scores (Ds, but hopefully not less than that). A test that produces this very score pattern is considered to be thorough enough to separate the best students from the rest of the pack.

Not all students enroll in pharmacy school with the same abilities, and further differences in performance will arise from study habits and effort. Furthermore, an exam for which all students receive As and Bs is thought to be less rigorous and a less accurate measurement of actual learning. Faculty have been known to criticize colleagues who have "all As" for a test, because they understand and agree with this concept. However, this idea is usually not popular with students, but it should be understood, nevertheless.

The best test should specifically measure student competency with respect to what is being taught. For example, a test in pharmacokinetics is narrowly designed to measure student competency in just that: pharmacokinetics. If it includes math problems, as it certainly will, it may challenge students less proficient at math. Thus, the test would not only measure knowledge of pharmacokinetics but also another subject or ability—for at least a few students. The test would better measure true competency in pharmacokinetics for students who have no mathematical liabilities. Therefore, in this example, the test is not really a pure pharmacokinetics test for each student.

Tests can also fail to measure course content mastery because the student has a weak vocabulary. The student may not be aware of this deficit until attempting to decipher strange words (to the student) within a question or answer. This basic inadequacy would present an additional stratification among students taking the exam. Therefore, students who are more "widely read" (translation: better and more holistically educated), or who have more experience in pharmacy and the vernacular of the field, may breeze through nomenclature that is foreign to other students.

Because these differences in ability exist and faculty cannot control for each discrepancy in student preparedness in this regard, special statistics are used to gauge the reliability and validity of exams to ensure that they measure what they are created to quantify. Such statistics arise from student score data, and faculty can use these numbers to find "bad" questions after a test has been deployed. Many times, the flawed questions are eliminated from the test and points are restored to each student so that students are not be penalized for "incorrectly" answering a bad question.

Two common statistical points used to measure test reliability and validity are the point-bi-serial correlation and the p-value. Each test question for which statistics are performed should have one of each. Briefly, the point-bi-serial correlation tells faculty whether the students with the higher test scores are answering that particular question correctly (they should). Simultaneously, the statistics tell faculty whether the more poorly performing students missed that question (this is more likely). Point bi-serials range from 0.1 to 1.0, and higher values (0.8, 0.9) reflect "better" questions.[163]

The p-value for each question indicates how many students (as a percent) answered the question correctly when this value is multiplied by 100. High p-values are "easier" test questions because more students answered them correctly, and low p-values indicate more "difficult" questions for the opposite reason.[163] In fact, test questions with four multiple choice responses and p-values approximating 0.6 to 0.8 are considered appropriately rigorous questions for most tests. Test question p-values that are either very low or very high may suggest problems with the question or an issue with the entire class's comprehension of the material. For example, a question with a very low p-value may have been addressed material that was not covered in class or perhaps it was presented, but the concept was completely confusing for most students.

Because students may have never seen actual test statistics until now, and this information might be useful or interesting, an actual test statistical report for a real pharmacy school exam is depicted in **Figure 1** (previous page). First, note that 39 students are shown to have taken the exam (under the **Graded** column in the Figure).

This represents the number of students who had this test version only (Test A, for example); other students had a different test version (Test B, perhaps). Test A and B student data are analyzed separately, but they can be compared. In the Figure, to the right of the Question number, under the "Reliability" column, each bi-serial and p-value for every test question is listed. Three unique questions are "boxed in" within the figure (Questions #2, #5, and #13). These three questions will be compared below to analyze student performance assess the quality of the test question.

Question			Reliability	
Question	Points	Graded	Point Biserial	P-Value
Question1	1.00	39	0.43	0.85
Question2	1.00	39	0.15	0.59
Question3	1.00	39	0.22	0.64
Question4	1.00	39	-0.01	0.74
Question5	1.00	39	0.59	0.77
Question6	1.00	39	-	1.00
Question7	1.00	39	0.19	0.87
Question8	1.00	39	0.34	0.82
Question9	1.00	39	0.56	0.77
Question10	1.00	39	0.27	0.87
Question11	1.00	39	0.32	0.97
Question12	1.00	39	-	1.00
Question13	1.00	39	-0.14	0.97
Question14	1.00	39	-	1.00
Question15	1.00	39	0.07	0.95
Question16	1.00	39	0.48	0.77
Question17	1.00	39	-	1.00
Question18	1.00	39	0.16	0.97
Question19	1.00	39	0.61	0.90
Question20	1.00	39	0.33	0.87
Question21	1.00	39	0.53	0.97
Question22	1.00	39	0.04	0.95
Question23	1.00	39	0.38	0.72
Question24	1.00	39	0.15	0.90
Question25	1.00	39	-	1.00
Question26	1.00	39	-	1.00
Question27	1.00	39	-0.03	0.64
Question28	1.00	39	0.42	0.79

Figure 1. Test statistics for a first year pharmacy exam.

First, for Question #2, test statistics reveal a bi-serial of 0.15 and a p-value of 0.59. These data are found under the **Reliability** column, specifically under the **Point Bi-serial** and **P-value** headings, respectively. We can convert the p-value to "the number of students who answered the question correctly" by multiplying this value by 100. Thus, slightly less than 60% of the class answered the question correctly. This p-value suggests that the question is appropriately difficult, given the standards mentioned above. However, the bi-serial value was very low, and both statistics must be considered together.

Thus, the students who normally perform well on the test did not answer this question correctly. Therefore, the question did not separate poor performers from strong performers. Such divergence in statistics may reflect a question anomaly: the question may have been mis-keyed or ambiguous, or the information in the question may not have been covered in class at all. Therefore, the question may need to be tossed out and all scores may be adjusted to remove the penalty of "missing" this bad question. So, the question had apparently appropriate "rigor" but inappropriate discrimination ability.

Question #5 has p-value of 0.77; therefore, many students in the class answered the question correctly. The question also has a bi-serial value of 0.59. This indicates that students who normally do well on the exam were among those who answered the question correctly. This is desirable; the question likely discriminated the stronger students from the weaker students. Collectively, the statistics suggest that this question was rigorous and a good discriminator.

Question #13 has a p-value of 0.97 and a bi-serial value of -0.14. Thus, most of the class answered the question correctly, and because almost 100% of the students were correct, this inherently means that weaker students were included in the statistics, lowering the bi-serial. Taking both statistics together, this question was a poor discriminator of strong *vs.* weak students.

The question may have been too easy, and it may be revised or deleted for next year's exam or substituted for a more rigorous question. Now and then, an "easy" question is given as a "gift" to students. This is rare, and when it occurs, students who complain about the gift discourage faculty from future generosity (yes, crazy as it seems, students do complain about a question that is too easy).

As previously mentioned, test statistics can help faculty catch inadvertent errors in the test production process. Because tests may pass through many hands before reaching the student, questions can become mistyped or improperly worded, and test keys can have errors. This would show up immediately in a point-bi-serial analysis.

The faculty member would see a value below 0.1 for that question, a circumstance that warrants investigation.[163] Also, test statistics that depict excellent questions one year may reflect poor questions in another year, even though the question did not change. Every year new students bring new talents (and deficits) to the testing environment. So, test statistics are a continually moving target for faculty to address.

Finally, the test statistics presented here are only two of several types of analyses used to measure test reliability and validity; faculty may also use more discriminating tools to gauge test excellence. With such data available to faculty for every test, most students will be ill-prepared to challenge faculty over test questions. Rarely do students understand test statistics—if they know they exist at all. Without bi-serial and p-value data, the student who challenges a test question is basing his argument on his opinion, which may lack research or experience. There is a chasm of difference between opinion and scholarship.

Furthermore, outright challenging test feedback is perceived by faculty as inflammatory and is likely a dead-ended pursuit.[110] Allowing students to influence course and exam content defeats the purpose of the educational experience. Faculty are trained and mandated to deliver an accredited program with a specific body of knowledge to pharmacy students.

Student interference at this level undermines the purpose of a professional program.[164] Asking questions about tests is expected, but the language of inquiry is important. The more mature students will approach faculty with a tone more reflective of "I am uncertain about this question that I missed, and I would like to learn from my mistake. Can you help?"

MAKING THE GRADE

Most grading scales are set by the university, and this scale is virtually immutable. Thus, the scale will appear in each class syllabus along with the course description and requirements. Some college grading scales are deliberately long on significant figures to prevent issues of rounding.

For example an A may fall within the range of 90.00 to 100.00, so an 89.96 would be a "B." Therefore, asking the instructor, "Can you round up my grade?" is tantamount to requesting that the instructor violate the college grading policy, an action that can be construed as academic fraud or grade tampering.

Students who tell faculty, "I will do anything to raise my grade." or "Can I do something for extra credit?" are in dangerous territory. Not only are these comments useless but also they may be offensive. Exactly what does the student propose that was not previously available (but simply not utilized) in the form of extra help, faculty office hours, and tutoring?

Any assistance offered to the student by the actual course instructor, if available, must follow a timeline convenient for the faculty, not the student. Also, waiting until the semester is almost over before expressing concern over grades is considered a poor approach to getting help. After a certain time has passed, nothing can be done to improve the study habits or the student's understanding of the material for that course.

GRADE MODIFICATIONS

- *Curves*

Another aspect of grading that many students take for granted is the "curve." This mathematical application and manipulation of student scores allegedly began in the 1960s when faculty began scoring male students higher to protect them from being drafted to serve in Vietnam.[165] Keeping the men in college likely saved many lives, but these grading trends remained long after the risk of being drafted had passed.[166] Interestingly, and perhaps unknown to students, is that many faculty are vehemently opposed to the concept of curving course averages, although some acknowledge that curving grades has a positive influence on their teacher evaluations.[124, 165-169]

Furthermore, some students see curving as a "right." An example of this type of thinking can be inferred from the story about students at Johns Hopkins University who boycotted a final exam to share their "feelings" about grade curving.[170] Exercises like this are unfortunate because faculty may feel compelled to curve grades.

Thus, they may curve scores to prevent artificially negative teaching evaluations that bear no relationship to their teaching ability or effectiveness. Such events then reduce teaching evaluations to a series of "Like" buttons such as those on Facebook: meaningless tick boxes. So entrenched is the curve mentality that a few professors have even claimed that they were fired for not curving test scores.[171]

Faculty expect grades that arise from well-written and properly deployed exams to fall into a special pattern (as mentioned previously) referred to as a normal distribution or a bell-shaped curve, which is *not the same* curve as the additional point curve adjustment introduced above. Thus, faculty expect that the strongest students (who are statistically a minority) will perform best; most of the students in the class will distribute in the upper to middle area of the curve (the "bell"); some will fall below the middle of the curve; and a few (another statistical minority, but at the other end of the spectrum) will fall below the curve, in the lower grade ranges.

Curves that are point adjustments to increase the scores of the entire class are applied after all of the grades are submitted to the course coordinator at the end of the semester. This way, the faculty can analyze the data from every student in the course. This concept is important.

All scores must be known by the instructor *prior* to curving scores. If annoying a course coordinator is the goal of the student, this can be accomplished most rapidly by showing ignorance of this concept and its application early in the semester, by asking after the first exam if scores will be curved. After the first test, obviously, the semester is not over and not all scores are known; thus, this question is silly and irritating.

Even if students understand that curves, if used, are applied at the end of the course, not every student will grasp the concept that a curve may not help students terribly much. Thus, an explanation of how curves function in a real class is provided below. Appreciating how curves work (*and how they do not*) will decrease unnecessary worry and questioning on the part of the student, and it will decrease the annoyance and time spent by faculty answering uninformed questions by students.

First, curves are mathematical contrivance to adjust grades to account for differences in instruction among the teaching team (different lecturing styles can affect learning), inherent and unavoidable errors in test question creation, and other variables that affect learning objectives. Notice that this list does not address increasing student satisfaction or raising low scores that make students unhappy.

Interestingly, students who question tests that they perceive to be "unfair" often stop asking about that test when their scores are modified upward after a curve, when they get the score they believe they "deserve" or prefer. Oddly, that "unfair" test seems to be just fine and the righteous indignation and deep concern for the rest of the class mysteriously disappears. Faculty see this each semester and are not fooled by any of these faux altruistic inquiries about exams.

Table 1 (next page) offers an example of grades for a class that just ended; thus, all of the test scores have been averaged. You can see the final grades for these 25 students under the ***Average*** column. Using these averages and a grading scale as depicted in **Table 2** (next page—the letter grade distribution for these 25 students would be as depicted in **Table 3** under the *Before* heading.

Table 1 Student Grade Samples		
Studen	Average	Curved Score
1	98	100
2	90	92
3	88	90
4	86	88
5	86	88
6	80	82
7	78	80
8	78	80
9	76	78
10	76	78
11	76	78
12	76	78
13	74	76
14	70	71
15	70	71
16	70	71
17	70	71
18	68	69
19	66	67
20	64	65
21	62	63
22	60	61
23	60	61
24	50	51
25	40	41

Table 2 Grading Scale	
Grade	Range
A	90–100
B	80–89
C	70–79
D	60–69
F	59 and below

Table 3 Letter Grades (N)		
	Curve	
Grade	Before	After
A	2	3
B	4	5
C	11	9
D	6	6
F	2	2

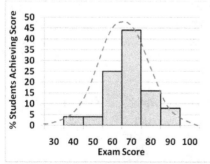

Figure 2. Grades before Curve Applied

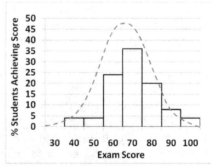

Figure 3. Grades after Curve Applied

Once commonly used approach is often applied to final scores, setting the highest average as a "100%", or a perfect score, because it was the best grade. This two-point addition would be made to *all scores for all students*, raising them modestly. Note that there were not many more A's after the curve. Specifically, one C was improved to a B, and one B was improved to an A. These adjusted outcomes are also depicted in **Table 1** under the heading *Curved Score*.

To view the distribution of non-adjusted grades in another format, see **Figure 2.** In this Figure, the grades shown are slightly skewed to the right when compared to a "normal" grade distribution. The dashed line overlaying each chart represents the Bell Curve or a typical normal distribution. This rightward skewing of the data indicates that more scores were in the lower grade range.

Figure 3 depicts the curved performance. This distribution is more "normal" but not perfectly "normal". The purpose of the curve was not to fully normalize the grades, but it was to make them *comparatively more normal*. Still, the curve imparted a reasonable adjustment for student performance, and the curve left the stronger students with the highest scores, while lifting the weaker students a small amount. This small adjustment is also apparent in the class average which increased from 72.5 to a 74 (a mid-range "C").

Thus, students should appreciate from this example that curves may not offer a significant difference for the class overall (or individual) performance. In fact, the more controllable variable would be personal performance. Other curving methods can be used, such as adding points to all scores without creating a perfect top performed (as we did above). Faculty vary in their enthusiasm for curving and with respect to curving technique.

If a curve is not applied to scores, on some occasions extra credit may be offered. Extra credit is not a required course provision, and any extra point opportunity is a generous gift to be graciously received by all students. Extra points may be granted by way of allowing one quiz in a series to be bonus-points instead of a grade, offering extra assignments to complete outside of class, or offering additional test questions for bonus points immediately for that test score (See **§Pure Performance**).[172]

Faculty attitudes about grades and extra credit, which can seem negative to students, are buttressed by the technological advantages conferred to students in the present age. Chances are excellent that most of your instructors did not have course packets, lecture recordings, or the internet for learning tools.

Thus, their perception may be that the students of today already have a marked advantage over those of the past. This impression may predispose many instructors to be less lenient about student laziness and entitlement-rooted extras in the form of curves and extra points. In the end, if grade-enhancing opportunities are offered, they must be offered to *every student* at the same time, under the same conditions to be perfectly fair.

- *Pure Performance*

When curving or extra credit is offered, students may forget that the grade they receive is reflective of an accumulation of bonus points which might have raised a score an entire letter grade, in the best of circumstances. This "bump" may mislead the student to perceive that the enhanced grade is his true performance in the course. It is not. At this point, ideally, the instructor will show the student his actual, non-enhanced grades to reveal his true abilities and actual standing in the class.[165]

Thus, each student should objectively evaluate his grades without enhancements or extra points to ascertain his true mastery of the course material and not his embellished outcomes.[166] Finally, telling a professor that a test grade *must be wrong* because, "I am only an A student" will get you nowhere, really fast. Clearly, this type of statement is not true (at least not for that course or exam), so such whining sounds more like a challenge than a self-reflective or introspective and meaningful comment about grades.

FAILING

Occasionally, students do not pass pharmacy courses. Many reasons for this exist. First, the student may have not studied effectively, and grades may reflect poor time management and study skills. Also, students are invariably accepted into pharmacy programs who have no business being there. They may have qualified for the program "on paper" but could not do the work once enrolled.

This happens at every pharmacy school each year and sometimes it is because a few unqualified applicants were admitted by way of "knowing someone important." These students frequently have no real desire to be in the program, and they may be "going to school for" a parent or other family member either out of perceived obligation or due to strong influences pushing the student to pursue the career. Other students are admitted that had such poor previous training that they simply cannot do the work at hand and no amount of remediation is sufficient to address their deficits.

Ideally, students are adults who can choose their own course of study and profession, so forced professional education should be rare. Sometimes, students who perform poorly in professional school were simply bad choices made by the admissions committee. Perhaps these weaker students were chosen from lower ranking areas of the wait-list because slots were vacant after the top choices were made. Also, students can change their mind about being a pharmacist in the first semester and stop trying to make good grades.

Most schools of pharmacy require a "C" or better in program classes to earn a passing grade. Grades below a "C" ("D+", "D", "D-") may cause the student to be placed on academic probation for a period of time. During probation, if the student earns another non-passing (below "C") grade, she may be dismissed from the program. Academic probation is a time of serious introspection and self-improvement; therefore, the student may be required to step down from any class offices or clubs to ensure that her time is exclusively spent on academics.

Many schools require a student with a deficiency (one who earned an "D" in a class) to repeat the course, often in the summer. These classes may be one month long, effectively cramming 14 weeks of school into 4 weeks. Summer classes enable students to make up deficits without compromising the program schedule and having conflicting courses that might occur at the same time. Often an "F" or failing grade may not qualify for a summer remediation and may be a required "retake" the next semester, putting the student behind one year.

Once the summer class is passed, then student can proceed through the program on time. The grade of the re-taken course may replace the failing grade. If the student fails to earn a "C" or better in the re-taken class, she may be barred from continuing in the program until the deficit is rectified, which may mean repeating (and paying again for) the entire previous year or, depending on the circumstances of that student, a failed summer offering or remediation may mean program dismissal. No student who is accepted and enrolled is guaranteed to stay. In fact, students can be, and have been dismissed in the last month of their fourth year of the program! Frequently, too, students will drop out of the pharmacy program if they are unable to make a passing grade in a repeated summer course. Apparently, this is evidence that the course work is too difficult or not sufficiently interesting to keep up this level of effort.

LEAVE OF ABSENCE

Students who have academic or personal issues (read: medical, mental health, family, etc.) may opt to take a leave of absence from pharmacy school. This leave is structured and documented at the level of the Dean of the College. Typically, reasons for leave must be obtained in writing and a plan is implemented to allow the student to return to the program within one year of departure. A readmission process may apply for the return to pharmacy school, and other requirements may also apply.

For instance, a scholastic committee may want to evaluate the student's performance after returning to assure that the student is healthy and able to complete a course of study. Although extended leave beyond one year can be granted to students on an individual basis, students who do not return within one year may have to reapply to pharmacy school and complete with other new applicants with no particular privileges for having been in the program previously.

ATTRITION

Students may believe that anyone who enters pharmacy school must graduate. This is not true. A process of student loss over the course of a pharmacy program, or student attrition, does occur. Attrition is a natural sorting of the professional school population much like the aptitude-based sieving that occurs between high school and college—and then again between college and professional school.

A few people who find that the field is not as appealing as they had hoped will self-select for leaving it. Still, even with the abovementioned factors at play among individuals in professional schools, actual attrition rates across the nation for pharmacy colleges are alarmingly low. Logical minds would assume that a rigorous program would have a high drop-out rate, but this is not true for most professional programs.

An explanation for low attrition might be found with accreditation committees, who seem send disapproving glances toward programs that fail significant numbers of students. In fact, colleges of pharmacy can be scrutinized for high drop-out rates, so colleges will actively strive to assist students in multiple ways. In fact, so many resources are often available for student academic help that failing the professional program is *actually difficult*. Of course, this never means that a professional program must go beyond the scope of routine assistance to bail out a student who is lazy, uninterested, or simply unsuited for pharmacy.

CHAPTER 6

THE FIRST YEAR

The first year of pharmacy school may the toughest year of all because of the seemingly insurmountable "unknowns" that will confront you. Much like beginning a new job, the first year in a professional program may be a strange brew of finding classes, printing course material, joining professional clubs, and then realizing that this adventure is the equivalent of a full-time job (See **Chapter 3, §Does Working Work**?). In addition, you will be faced with entirely new course material, more work volume than ever before, and a greater speed of material delivery.

Faculty will not slow down to accommodate students at this level. They expect all students to find a way to manage note-taking and retention of information. Faculty are also not obligated to repeat material that students did not hear because they were talking, inattentive, or absent. As mentioned before, if something appears on a slide, and it is not in your handouts, write it down. Pharmacy faculty are not responsible for providing every detail to you.

Because the actual content of pharmacy school classes is of great interest to most incoming pharmacy students, this is described in within this chapter to explain what is generally offered across programs and to explain why the curriculum is organized as it is. Some representative course titles and descriptions are given in this chapter, too. Naturally, these classes will vary somewhat from program to program; thus, the list is not meant to cover every potential class or course combination offered in every professional pharmacy program.

❝ The first year is often confusing and demoralizing for some students. The difficulty of the coursework may have been underestimated. Sometimes, students are disappointed to learn that the study of pharmacy is not what they anticipated. More information about the field prior to enrollment might have prevented such disillusionment. ❞

COURSE DESCRIPTIONS

General titles (which function more like categories because of the diversity of offerings) of potential classes in the first year are listed below, along with brief descriptions of what these might contain.

Table 1 Potential Courses for the First Year	
Course Title	*General Course Description*
Introduction to Drug Delivery; Drug Dosage Forms; Pharmaceutics, Pharmaceutical Sciences, Principles of Drug Action, etc.	Teaches students about the various dosage form classifications (capsule, tablet, solution, etc.) and how they are created. May introduce basic physical laws that apply to dosage formulations, from liquids to solids. Routes of drug delivery and basic drug chemical kinetics are introduced along with fundamentals of structure-activity relationships.
Biochemistry	Focuses on energy (sugars, carbohydrates, proteins, fats), chemical equilibria, major metabolic pathways and relevant biologically based information such as nucleic and amino acids, cell membranes, and

Table 1 Potential Courses for the First Year	
Course Title	*General Course Description*
	enzymatic reactions.
Physiology, Pathology, Pathophysiology, Immunology, Microbiology, etc.	May be offered in different formats, depending on the pharmacy program. May allow students to advance their current knowledge in each scientific area pertaining to medicine and human health, or they may represent the student's first exposure to such material. Covers topics needed to understand the purpose of medications used to treat or cure human disease.
Medicinal Chemistry	Consists of, literally, the chemistry of drugs presented later in the curriculum. Drug structure, solubility, activity, combinatorial chemistry, computer-aided dug design, and natural drug sources. Also introduces receptor and membrane interactions with drugs, initiating a foundation for pharmacokinetics.
Pharmaceutical Care	Introduces data gathering about patients and medication management strategies to reduce morbidity and mortality. Teaches students about drug therapy problems such as unnecessary therapy, adverse drug reactions, and patient compliance issues.
Community Pharmacy, Introduction to the Pharmacy Profession	Focuses on pharmacy in the context of other health professions and discusses job opportunities. Identifies the roles of the pharmacist in US healthcare, specifically describing multiple specialty professions.
Pharmacy Calculations	Teaches students about measurements of volume, weight, length, specific gravity, density, etc., as well as how to use pharmacy laboratory instruments. Offers instruction on interpreting prescriptions and medication orders. Offers lessons in producing different dosage forms as well as buffers, infusions, and parenteral admixtures.
Pharmaceutical Sciences, Pharmacokinetic Applications, Pharmacokinetics	Describes drug absorption, distribution, metabolism, and excretion and emphasizes related mathematics to describe pharmacokinetic parameters such as therapeutic window, steady-state/constant-rate drug regimens, and individual patient characteristics that affect dosing.
Pharmacy Systems, US Health Care, Understanding the Healthcare System	Describes various components of healthcare costs, patient access, distribution of drugs, and healthcare organizations. May focus on legal and regulatory issues of controlled substance management using pharmacy technology and inventory control.

Table 1 Potential Courses for the First Year	
Course Title	*General Course Description*
Introduction to Pharmacy, The History of Pharmacy	Explores the profession of pharmacy and evolution of pharmacy focusing on the role of pharmacy and patient care. May offer details about the pharmacist's role in state and federal health care issues. Pharmacy professionalism may be discussed and students may participate in different activities in the clinical setting with other health professionals.
Nonprescription Drugs, OTC Therapeutics, Patient Self-Care	Describes non-prescription drugs with an emphasis on how patients care for themselves using these products. Students are taught how to assess self-treatable conditions and how to instruct patients to use multiple OTC medications.
Biotechnology	Describes basic elements of biotechnology, such as recombinant DNA and monoclonal antibody technology and may include applications of biotechnology in the diagnosis and treatment of disease and discussions of how biotechnology products will affect pharmacy in the future.
Clinical Applications	Discusses patient cases to integrate overall course material.
Patient Communications	Teaches communication skills such as how to interview or counsel a patient. If a separate course in cultural awareness/diversity is not offered, cultural/religious/traditional influences in patient care may be discussed here.
Medical Terminology	Teaches medical terminology relevant to the pharmacy practice environment.
Compounding	Instructs in the art, science, and technology of pharmacy compounding, typically in a laboratory environment. Products made in the laboratory may be kept for personal use by the students.
Lab Information	Teaches the basic principles of access and utilization of drug information resources both paper-based on online.
Transforming Healthcare, Interprofessional Opportunities, Healthcare Teams	Offers details about the health care system and how interprofessional collaborations are needed to manage patient care.

Because each school of pharmacy has its own mechanisms for orienting students to the field, some first-year classes may be significantly unique in content and timing. For example, some colleges of pharmacy offer courses such as gross anatomy or personal finance. You may also have classes in histology, clinical physical chemistry, or you may be asked to research drug information in scientifically acceptable databases.

Laboratories may be included for these experiences, or the courses may be exclusively in lecture format. Some schools of pharmacy even offer biostatistics to orient students to reading clinical data. An introduction to pharmacy practice class may offer information about the history of pharmacy as well as instruction on patient counseling. Other courses or laboratories may teach students how to write and interpret a prescription. See **Chapters 7, 8**, and **9** for more information.

Due to these programmatic differences, on the rare occasion that a pharmacy student transfers to another school, a summer course may be required to make up a deficit in course content that differed between programs. For instance, a student who completed one year of Program A may transfer to Program B, and Program B offered pharmacokinetics in the first year.

Program A did not. Thus, the student who is transferring will take this course over the summer to get up to speed with his classmates in Program B for next fall. Otherwise, in general, most colleges of pharmacy manage to impart the same information to students over the course of the entire program so that all US pharmacy graduates possess a similar body of knowledge for practicing their profession.

R̫ **" Another potentially intimidating aspect of starting a pharmacy program is the number of new faces you will encounter. Some students do not realize that these "future colleagues" will have a significant influence on their professional school experience. "**

Electives are not common options for students in the first year because core courses are necessary to build a foundation of pharmacy knowledge. In fact, the massive volume of information needed for a student to simply advance to the second year of the program diminishes the time (and the energy) available for an elective option. Often, students compare the first year of pharmacy school to "drinking water from a fire hose". The comparison is apt: trying to quench thirst from a water source capable of moving at more than

100 gallons per minute* is painful and may require enormous task commitment and resiliency for success.

EXPECTATIONS

Along with onerous coursework, student expectations about testing in the first year are often fearful or anxiety-producing thoughts. This need not be the case. Many students may be in a program that offers professional school exams at predictable intervals, such as every 6 to 8 lectures. Also, tests may be given in blocks, a method that is popular with students and faculty, alike.

With block testing, students have exams during strategically spaced testing weeks in which no classes are held. Studying and taking exams are the chief foci during this time, and many students appreciate the decreased distraction of attending lectures. In contrast, some students may dislike block testing because more than one test may be given in one day. Peruse the syllabus of your classes to determine if your program offers block testing, because this may profoundly affect a work schedule for students who are employed while in pharmacy school.

As mentioned previously, some faculty estimate two hours of study are needed for every hour that a student is in class.[173] Take this to heart. If you honestly prepare well for each lecture, then, in class, you are merely reviewing material that you have seen, decreasing the attention you must pay to minute details. Such strong preparation is encouraged, as is being prepared for all tests well before each test. Students spend enormous energy worrying about test questions (See **Chapter 5, §Testing Preparedness**), attempting to nail down every detail in the notes which they believe to be a potential test question. This is too much work and wasted time. The students would do better to be more creative than this.

For example, to guess what information will be testable, think like the instructor. Does the professor repeat certain information in class? If so, this could represent a test question. Does the teacher ask questions of the students? If a question is asked, and it goes unanswered, this can prompt an instructor to use this question on an exam. If the professor writes information for students to view, this may be important to the faculty in the context of testing. Also, if quizzes or reviews are given, these questions may re-appear in modified format for tests.

Aside from preparing for class and predicting exam questions, another potentially intimidating aspect of starting a pharmacy program is the number of new faces you will encounter. Some students do not realize that these

---

Yes, different hoses have different diameters and thus different flow rates. Don't overthink it.

"future colleagues" will have a significant influence on their professional school experience. Treating others inappropriately, selfishly, or rudely will have lasting negative consequences for the student who misbehaved. A smart student will immediately recognize the importance of his classmates' opinions and will be approachable and professional. After all, you will very likely be working with (or for) a classmate or upper classman in the future, so getting off on the right foot is essential.

Because each student has his own expectations of the first year, perhaps reading actual comments of P1s would be informative, or at least, entertaining. Thus, some thoughts of students in the first year of pharmacy school are depicted below:

> "One of the things that your school will not tell you, nor *(sic)* your friends, is how emotionally and mentally taxing pharmacy school is. If not for the material, than *(sic)* for the expectations of the school or the manner in which courses are taught. You find yourself sitting next to a dual PhD *(sic)* on one side and on the other sits the wiz *(sic)* kid who powered into pharmacy school riding a 4.0 after two years of undergrad. Suddenly you are no longer a big fish in a small pond... and you come to the realization that there are individuals, perhaps several, in your class who could mentally wipe the floor with you."[174]

> "I have finished a whole month of Pharmacy School! Pharmacy School is a great deal different from Undergraduate studies! I go to class for 6 hours a day, come home, and study for another 2-4 hours!."[175]

> "...Pharmacogenetics and biopharmaceutics have been not quite as interesting as I expected. (deleted text) guides us relatively slowly through a review of basic genetics and is just now skimming the surface of population genetics. The terms (recessive, dominant, allele, genotype, etc.) that we must learn are dryly linked in lecture to obscure genetic diseases like sickle cell anemia or G6DP deficiency."[176]

> "...In our biotech lab...basically we were going to be "diabetics" for two days....Easy, right? Well, first off, I have no diabetics in my immediate family, and I have never been a big one to inflict unnecessary pain on myself. With this assignment, I was going to be sticking myself with a needle four times in order to get a droplet of blood to check my glucose levels."[177]

> "Fascination grew while learning terms like "Stool Softner" *(sic)* and the fact there were medications that made you pee. In fact, the "pee pills", HCTZ and Furosemide, were the very first drugs I learned. By the end of the summer I found myself enjoying what I was doing, but still had no idea that it would transform into my life-long profession."[174]

"...The second semester of pharm care involves a lot of case-studying, where we are required to develop a care plan using soap* notes. There have been a couple times where a patient came to our class and us *(sic)* students had the opportunity to ask the patient questions as a group, and come up with the most appropriate care plan for the patients' condition. I find this class very useful since a lot of pharmaceutical practices are using the soap-note system."[178]

"One day, I got an e-mail saying that a community pharmacy is hiring first-year students. As much as I told myself that I should wait, I applied right away. The inner me just couldn't stand not having a job...plus the extra cash is always nice! So here I am, been working since September and I'd say having a job during first year is actually quite manageable. I work one weeknight per week and every other weekend."[179]

"Even those who put on the most stoic of faces, are internally crumbling. Many are too proud to admit their struggles or to admit their frustrations. After years of being used to academic success, it is a bitter realization that one may be forced to struggle to earn merely average grades."[174]

"This is my second quarter of my first year of pharmacy school. Last quarter was tough, but I would say that I expected worse. I was prepared for the workload and I was used to the workload, as my two years of pre-pharmacy courses were a challenge too."[180]

"After approximately the third lecture of the school year, everyone in my class decides where his or her seat is. Not just for the day or week, but every day for the next two semesters. If we didn't change classrooms every year, I'm sure our seats would be the same for the entire six academic semesters. We just DO NOT move. Why is this?"[181]

ACTIVITIES

The first year of pharmacy school includes the option of running for a class office and joining clubs or interest groups. If holding a class representative position is interesting to you, honestly assess whether you have the time and energy to devote to this extra obligation. Chairing a fundraising committee, leading your class to national recognition in service, or speaking to faculty on behalf of your classmates is rewarding. Some people enjoy an outlet for their extroversion, leadership skills, or teambuilding talents.

Such extracurricular activities can increase the breadth of your school experience and showcase your time-management abilities.[182-183] Also, some

---

Soap Notes: An acronym for subjective, objective, assessment, and plan. This is a technique for documenting patient encounters.

student organizations may have national offices, and you may choose to participate in these higher-tier groups when you graduate, extending your association with the organization for your entire career. An interesting statistic reported in the scientific literature is that students heavily engaged in social and professional clubs or organizations were found to be more likely to enter residencies after graduation.[184] Serving your future profession in this manner is worthwhile and may be exciting. However, keep in mind that—to some potential employers—such roles may have rather limited value: any offices or obligations you undertake in school are likely to matter little (or not at all) to a future employer.

Thus, run for office, serve on a committee, or participate in class functions because you truly want to do it. Never forget your actual purpose for enrolling in school: to obtain a PharmD. Resist succumbing to distractions from this most important mission. If your grades slide due to excessive "participation", hand off your job to someone else and concentrate on your studies. Nothing else is really more important than your scholastic performance. For those interested, popular pharmacy organizations are alphabetically listed in **Appendix III**, along with descriptions of each organization and relevant websites.

Additional aspects of the first year involve many opportunities to "trip up" for students. There will be laboratories in various forms that can consist of real wet-lab work for compounding to labs, to labs or "practicals" for making pharmaceutical equipment such as IVs and syringes, and some may be sit-downs for talking and learning about patient cases. They all may be referred to as "labs" and this can be confusing. What should not be confusing is that all students, for all of these opportunities, should show up and be professionally dressed as dictated in your student handbook.

Often, students assume that these more casual "labs" do not require their presence or proper dress and either show up in flip-flops and shorts or do not show up at all. This can cause a faculty member to file a professionalism complaint against the student that can be time-consuming to deal with a harmful to the student's reputation and standing. Yes, it sounds terribly petty, but pharmacy school should be treated like a real "job", complete with attendance, proper time given to the task, and the required dress and decorum.

BETWEEN YEARS

The summers between the first and second year (and again between the second and third year) are usually devoted to an Introductory Pharmacy Practice Experience (IPPE) or an "IPPE rotation". The first-year IPPE is typically hospital pharmacy, and the second IPPE summer may focus on community pharmacy. Academic credit for IPPEs may be 4 or more credit hours, but schools may vary with respect to the duration of the IPPE, which can range from 4 to 6 weeks.

Because these IPPEs stress similar skills, they will both be presented in this section. Students are lead through the IPPE by preceptors, or special instructors who mentor and teach students pharmacy practice skills in real-world pharmacy settings. Such training is necessary for students to transition from learning about pharmacy to practicing the craft. Important to this transition is the requirement of a white coat and visible name badge to be work at all times as well as the respect of patient confidentiality.

During an IPPE, whether for community or hospital pharmacy, students will be evaluated on basic competencies. For example, the student should be familiar with the layout and arrangement of the pharmacy, including how each employee supports the mission of patient care. Also, the student should have mastered the prescription processing procedure in the form of choosing, counting, labeling, and packaging drugs for patients. Often, one prescription per day, as a minimum, must be processed to "count" toward mastery of the IPPE rotation. The student should be able to give medication instructions to patients, too, and often one documented patient counseling session is required.

Some minor compounding techniques may be learned in addition to skills for maintaining a drug inventory (stocking, pricing, recording supplies, etc.). How to process medication ordering and subsequent secure storage of those drugs may be taught to students, too. During IPPE rotations, students may be exposed to, perhaps for the first time, the economics of medication use and how insurance does or does not assist with drug payments.

Students should be able to access and interpret drug information as well as understand scheduled drug information and related paperwork. During every IPPE, students are expected to be professional and ethical, displaying compassion for the patients who seek care at the pharmacy. This professionalism should also extend to other members of the healthcare team. Again, attendance is mandatory and these sessions can be graded for competency, independence, and any requirements of the rotation or experience.

A difficult concept to grasp for a minority of students is that summers will no longer be free (if they ever were). Remember, you signed up for four years of training, not four consecutive nine-month periods of education. Thus, the last summer you enjoyed before professional school may truly be the last time you will ever have three entire months of liberation.

If you cringe at the thought of giving up summers forever, think of your college faculty: they work year-round, too (and frequently 7 days a week). Welcome to the adult universe. After your first IPPE between year one and year two, you *may* have two months after the IPPE to enjoy family time or to investigate other options that help you acquire experience. However, this will probably be the last time you have such generous time off.

Another first year consideration that all students should think about early and often is internship hours, which are required prior to applying for a pharmacy license. Each state has a different requirement for mandatory internship hours and IPPE rotations can count toward this total. Students may submit proof of these hours to their state boards of pharmacy when they apply to take the board exam. An affidavit of intern service may be required as proof that the hours were completed, and this is a legal document signed by the pharmacist(s) who supervised the internship. Finally, the internship period can be fulfilled in more than one pharmacy setting.

Some states may also grant "credit" for hours of experience substantially related to the practice of pharmacy, but this is given at the discretion of the state board, and it should not be expected. Sometimes, first year students hear about the hours needed to apply for professional pharmacy licensure and they immediately think, "That it is impossible!" For example, the most common requirement across the US is 1,500 hours (a few states ask for 2,000 or more hours), and some states require a minimum of several hundred hours in a pharmacy experience *outside* of professional school. Also, age requirements for licensure application may depend on the state where the license is obtained. Think about this during your first year of school to ensure you have all that you need (and perhaps more than required) to sail directly into licensure and employment.

THE SIGNIFICANCE OF THE WHITE COAT

Most colleges of pharmacy across the nation participate in a special ceremony to christen the initiation of their professional pharmacy education programs. These are typically referred to as "White Coat Ceremonies".[185-187] Such ceremonies may be held before classes begin, usually in the evening, and students' families and friends may participate in the ceremony.

The purpose of the ceremony, led by college faculty is to ask each new student to reflect on the symbolism of the white coat of the pharmacist. The ceremony emphasizes that the health and welfare of our society depends on the skill and morals of healthcare professionals such as pharmacists. Thus, the white coat represents pharmacy as a discipline for the public good, as pharmacists provide services according to values that benefit everyone.

Just as the white coat will literally wrap around your physical form, the coat also symbolizes how the pharmacy profession will literally envelope every aspect of the pharmacist's life. Once a student has graduated and entered the workforce, he becomes a minor public figure of a sort, something that a few students will not anticipate or prefer.

Thus, behaviors that upset the morals or laws of the pharmacists' community become events by which to judge him. For example, a pharmacist charged with "driving under the influence/driving while intoxicated" may lose his job, and his patients will certainly have an opinion of the matter after reading about it in the newspaper. Thus, the white coat symbolizes such public visibility.

CHAPTER 7

THE SECOND YEAR

Students who make it through the first year of pharmacy school are well on their way to earning a PharmD, whether this feeling registers with them or not. Finishing the first year of a professional program entrenches a student into the culture and mode of learning that will be needed for the rest of the journey. Students who can get this far usually make it to the end. As they say, "Well begun is half done." Therefore, by the beginning of the second year, students have adapted to the study schedule and the responsibilities that go along with a difficult program.

Attitudes of P2s, compared to P1s, are obvious. Their speech reflects their thought processes, which have been shaped by approximately 10 months of higher education. They no longer complain about "unfair" test questions, and instead they strategize with the faculty about how to better prepare for exams. They are less excited about bad grades and more grounded with respect to what they must do to recover from low scores. Also, they plan for multiple tests in one day instead of spending energy trying to petition the faculty to move one of the exams. Thus, the maturity and ease of the student body is increasing, and P2s begin to exude a calm acceptance of what they have signed up to do.

This is a good thing.

> R **" Think of electives as complementary training, enabling you to possess unique skills when you graduate. Students with a residency in mind may want to focus exclusively on electives that fulfill requirements toward that residency.. "**

COURSE DESCRIPTIONS

The second year of pharmacy school is a little less frantic than the first year, so surprises should be few. You will be well aware of the system used by the college and you will have basic information about courses and most college instructors. You may even have a few professors you truly enjoy (and a few you take pains to avoid). By your second year, you are also a budding (but not fully bloomed) repository of facts and opinions for new, incoming students. Remember that you represent an entire profession in their eyes, so focus on being helpful and using your special qualifications to enhance the education and experience of other students.

Possible courses for your second year in pharmacy school include separate courses in medical topics and second waves of first year pharmacy courses, building on the knowledge you obtained previously. Some representative courses for second year students are depicted in the table below.

Table 1 Potential Courses for the Second Year	
Course Title	*General Course Description*
Drug Delivery Systems, Dosage Forms, Pharmaceutics, Pharmaceutical Applications	Presents various drug dosage forms and administration techniques.
Pharmacotherapy, Therapeutics, Drug Therapy, Disease-based Therapeutics, Organ-systems-based Therapeutics	Describes appropriate use of medications and may include lab data interpretation, medical management of diseases, and drug side effect monitoring.

Table 1 Potential Courses for the Second Year	
Course Title	*General Course Description*
Drug Literature, Drug Information, Scientific Analysis and Interpretation, Medical Literature, Applied Drug Information	Offers methodology for peer-reviewed literature retrieval, data and study design analysis, and drug information dissemination.
Pharmacokinetics	If not introduced in the first year, may offer insight about drug metabolism and specific human kinetic analysis. Drug excretion or accumulation calculations may be offered, and strong mathematical skills may be required.
Medicinal or Pharmaceutical Chemistry	May build on first year offering and delve more deeply into structure and function of drugs and receptors, emphasizing second messenger systems and signal transduction pathways.
Professional Development	Can include courses in etiquette, writing curriculum vitae, interviewing skills, patient counseling training, or learning new languages to reach a broader patient base.
Ethics, Professional Integrity	May offer case studies to illustrate ethical problems and resolution. May include studies of the law and how boards of pharmacy sanction professionals who behave in a dishonorable manner or perform illegal actions.
Pharmacology	Informs the student about drug mechanisms of action at the receptor level, and may be subdivided into organ-system pharmacology or disease-state pharmacology
Microbiology, Immunology	Provides foundational information for treating disease states, subject-specific and intense learning about focal topics to understand how therapeutics mitigate illness.

Note that different schools may use the same name for rather different courses, or some colleges may structure the order of early coursework in a unique way, as mentioned in the previous chapter. For example, one school may require statistics in the first year, whereas another program might hold statistics in the second year or not at all.

Thus, these listings are, again, representative, and they are general descriptions for courses that are broadly offered in most programs. Also, remember that subject material may be more fluid in certain programs:

physiology may be incorporated into pathology: creating a pathophysiology unit, or typically combined courses may be separate classes (such as therapeutics and pharmacology). Material that seems to fall under one category such as pharmacokinetics may be studied in an introductory pharmaceutics class, too.

You may be allowed an elective at this time. Choose this wisely. Most students try to guess which elective is the easiest "A" and take that class, whether they have a genuine interest or not in the topic. This is a waste of your tuition, and it insults the instructor who assumed your enthusiasm about the subject. Work a little and immerse yourself in a choice elective; never discard an opportunity to increase your experience.

Think of electives as complementary training, enabling you to possess unique skills when you graduate. Students with a residency in mind may want to exclusively focus on electives that fulfill requirements toward that residency. Not all electives can be applied to residency prerequisites, so ask before choosing a course.

You may interact with patients at this phase, too. Something to consider when assisting patients, whether they are in a teaching hospital, clinic, or neighborhood pharmacy is that any patient may refuse to allow you to interact with or treat them. Some patients do not want students "guessing" about their care, and they may not want their privacy invaded. These are legitimate feelings and they must be honored every time.

Do not assume that any patient wants or needs your help, and never mislead a patient about your student status. Some schools provide ID badges for students with color coding and large typeface letters that spell out "STUDENT" under the individual's name. In some states, impersonating a professional healthcare provider is a misdemeanor.

Many teaching hospitals have policies that protect patients from unwanted care and allow them to call an attending physician at any point in their care. In this situation, the physician who oversees the patient has the final word. At the end of the day, *students should remember that each patient's right to care and privacy always trump the student's educational and training privilege, without exception.*[188]

EXPECTATIONS

Students in the second year are important resources for incoming first-year students. Class officers from the second year may be called on to orient newly elected officers, assisting them to set up their student government. Also, second years may have study materials they can sell to or share with new students. Second year students in colleges of pharmacy are ideal students. They are not so experienced that they are not interested in anything and everything related to pharmacy, and they are not so new to the system that they cannot participate fully in the social and intellectual activities of the college. Also, a second year student is, by now, disabused of many of the entitlement beliefs frequently held by some first year students. In the second year, career aspirations are still creative and lofty, and the excitement of the PharmD is entirely enticing.

In this year, and in the third year, your program may invite you to participate in a pre-residency experience to identify students who are interested in future residencies. In this experience, you will be paired with a preceptor or college faculty who will mentor you through the residency application process. They assist the student with ensuring the correct electives have been completed and that the student's CV is properly written and inclusive of details important to for residency interviews.

For pre-residency activities, students may participate in seminars and meet with current residents to discuss details about the experience. A pre-residency mentorship can help students choose a program that best fits their goals and shepherd them through the process of writing a letter of intent to the residency program they hope to enter. Pre-residency skills for students at this time may include the creation of a research project for eventual publication in a scholarly journal or for presentation as a poster at a national meeting.

To give you an idea of how the second year may differ from the first year, some student comments are provided below:

> "In starting pharmacy school it seems as if the world is yours for the taking...(a)nd then a funny thing happens. That hopefulness, that strong desire for learning is slowly chipped away like waves crashing against a cliff. Eventually you become a shell of yourself, merely moving through the motions and responding to questions when asked."[174]

> "Lately, we have had a few guest lecturers come in and talk about pharmaco-economics and infectious disease. They relate these topics back to genetics, and I have found both the lectures to be really interesting. I switch back and forth between taking notes on computer and hand-written notes in this class because sometimes my hand can't write as fast as the professor teaches the class."[177]

> "I have already begun to learn about the different fields of pharmacy during rotations. Doing rotations during the semester may seem like a lot, but it is worth it. We are able to see what we are learning in class

be applied to the real world of pharmacy. I can go to Measuring Therapeutic Parameters or Pharmacokinetics one day and then the next I am in the hospital seeing what we just learned put in action. It all works together so well."[189]

"Part of the reason is that you cover topics in multiple courses. Med chem will talk about SSRIs, SNRIs, and TCAs, and then pharmacology will discuss those and then we'll have a lecture on the same classes in therapy. You are, in effect, exposed to the material in three, or more, separate courses, often with a slightly different perspective. In a way, you are being tested on the material three different times and, eventually, you realize that you have actually learned said material."[174]

ACTIVITIES

Similar to the summer after the first year, IPPE rotations will be offered in the summer after the *second* year. As previously mentioned, unlike first year IPPEs, these IPPEs may emphasize community pharmacy instead of hospital pharmacy. See the previous chapter for information about this experience.

Such IPPEs extend the student's capabilities, focusing on the hospital setting as students develop specific skills related to the responsibilities of practitioners working in these settings. Also similar to the first IPPE, these are usually 4-week experiences with preceptors, who evaluate the student's competencies. These IPPES will differ from later experiential practice opportunities, which will be more clinically focused and more reliant on what the student already knows and can apply. Learn what you can in these IPPEs; you will use this information later.

CHAPTER 8

THE THIRD YEAR

The third year of pharmacy school represents a gigantic shift in program format and student and faculty expectations. After four consecutive semesters in a professional program, third year students more resemble the professionals they will become. Thus, P3s, as they are known, are highly enthusiastic but not necessarily idealistic or easy to impress.

The reality of the task of completing a PharmD is apparent to them, and these students are seriously engaged in learning at this stage. Although P3 students spend less time socializing (exactly when would this occur?) than second year students, they have amassed rich experiences which they willingly and generously share with upcoming and incoming students.

Therefore, the gift of having third year students participate in new student recruitment and interviews is wise and fortunate for everyone involved. P3s have an ease and confidence that inspires their underclassmen and enthralls potential incoming students. Third year students also reinforce to faculty what is important about a pharmacy education and remind them of time well-spent in the classroom. P3 students offer a wealth of worthwhile pharmacy information and experience, so they are highly valuable pre-professionals *right then,* and their worth to society will only increase over time. Oddly, and perhaps sadly, third year students do not so much as move into their fourth year as they seem "dissolve" from public view over time as the second year class moves in to assume the P3 responsibilities in a seamless transition.

> ℞ **" The third year of pharmacy school represents a gigantic shift in program format and student and faculty expectations. After four consecutive semesters in a professional program, third year students more resemble the professionals they will become. "**

COURSE DESCRIPTIONS

Coursework decreases in the third year with respect to the volume of lectures that you attend. However, your new duties and electives will keep you more than busy. In the third year of pharmacy school, coursework is more specific. For example, electives offered in the third year complement the student's potential major area of clinical concentration or preference.

So, you may take classes that prepare you for specific patient interactions. For instance, you may be taught how to assist psychiatric patients or manage patients with difficult-to-meet or complex needs such as diabetic patients. Thus, third year classes exist to transition the student from a more didactic program to a clinical experience. Also rotations are offered that may have a clinical or academic focus. These are depicted below.

Some representative courses for the third year are described below. As always, some of these experiences may be offered sooner at other colleges, or they may not be offered at all. If these topics interest you, be sure to scrutinize closely your program's catalogue of courses to ensure you are on the best path to suit your talents and interests.

Table 1 Potential Courses for the Third Year	
Course Title	*General Course Description*
Pharmaco-economics, Applied Pharmaco-economics, Economics of Pharmacy,	Instructs students in best practices for managing drug therapy in a cost-effective manner. Students learn basic management

Table 1 Potential Courses for the Third Year	
Course Title	**General Course Description**
Pharmacy Finance	skills and decision documentation.
Specific Medical Subjects: Neurology, Psychiatry, Oncology, Endocrinology, etc.	Prepares students for patient encounters and they emphasize clinically relevant aspects of these subjects.
Contemporary Topics, Current Events	Provides information about recent advances in pharmacology and pharmaceutics, focusing on pharmaceutical chemistry, pharmacology and pharmacogenomics.
Therapeutics, Pharmacotherapeutics, Pharmacotherapy	Offers principles of pharmacology and therapeutics related to clinical practice. May be subdivided based on therapeutic category such as immunotherapy, chemotherapy, etc.
Human Diseases, Pathophysiology, Disease Diagnosis, Human Pathology	Discusses etiology and mechanisms of common diseases, integrating pathology, physiology, and drug therapy.
Pharmacy Administration	May discuss pharmacy management, leadership, marketing, and financial aspects of the profession. Communicating effectively, negotiating conflict, and strategic planning may be included.
Specific Basic Science Topics: Microbiology, Cell Biology, Genetics, Biotechnology, etc.	Provides the scientific foundation for the study of disease and therapeutic management.
Nonprescription Medications	Guides the student into over the counter preparations and distinguishes these from prescription products.
Pharmacist Communication, Conversations in Pharmacy, Pharmacy Education, etc.	Emphasizes professional interactions with healthcare providers and guides patient counseling.
Pharmacogenomics	Illuminates emerging topics in genomics and correlates individual genetics and therapeutic efficacy and toxicity.
Pharmacology	Emphasizes the mechanism of action of drugs at the level of the receptor.
Medication Safety, Drug Side Effects, Medication Quality	Offers insight into proper usage of medication with an emphasis on patient safety and recognition of common side effects.

Rotations, both academic and clinical, are usually one-month experiences, and 11 months of rotations may be required. Rotations that are academically based may involve teaching and limited test question preparation, among other activities. For instance, a P3 with an academic rotation alongside a basic science faculty member may include preparing a seminar for a journal club meeting, researching a new topic for presentation within a specific elective, participation in faculty meetings, and providing student instruction and evaluation, working with underclassmen, and assisting faculty with various duties. Also, P3 academic rotation may involve creating pharmacy educational outreach materials and hosting forums to educate patients and the public about timely topics in pharmacy.

These roles within an academic rotation will be necessarily limited of course. Some aspects of grading other students can be problematic or they can represent conflicts of interest (after all, P3 students are not faculty with the attendant rights, privileges, and measures of recourse for their decisions). Now and then, faculty may unfairly take advantage of academic rotation students by having them run errands, grade tests (likely inappropriate), and create exam questions. The idea of an academic rotation is not to have the P3 student shoulder the job description of faculty.

An academic rotation should be a genuine learning opportunity. Attentive faculty will create an education environment that buttresses the ability of the student and expands the scope of their skills by allowing the student to present lectures to gain teaching experience (and additional resume points) or to facilitate (but not be entirely responsible for) class discussions. Typically, a month-long academic rotation will be comprised of 160 hours (40 per week), so this rotation has the appearance of an academic position, perhaps complete with office hours and scheduled assignments.

Clinical rotations may offer experiences at pharmacy sites and clinics and P3 students may be expected to prepare a research project to present at a pharmacy meeting. In a clinical rotation, P3 students may be asked to participate in journal club and prepare lecture material. They may have additional duties in the form of being present at night or on weekends to deliver supervised pharmacy services in hospitals or clinics.

Rarely, but worth mentioning, a retail pharmacy experience during this year may involve performing questionable duties. For instance, popular but unregulated and often illegal herbal preparations, diet aids, or homeopathy products are sold in retail pharmacies that advertise holistic health care services. Such products are sold entirely for the profit they bring; none offers meaningful outcomes for patients. Unsuspecting students have been asked to provide scientifically inaccurate information to patients for a fee (that the pharmacist collects) and many times, these students return to their program with feelings of guilt, shame, or anger over the anti-science nature of their rotation.

Likely "going along to get along" is the best strategy because the rotation is approximately one month and it may offer a grade or a specific type of feedback that is part of the student record. The student really has no power here and unfortunately no "voice". So, doing what is asked, irrespective of the perceived reprehensible nature of the duty is probably the safest course for the rotating student. After the month is over, the experience is over and they have a terrific if unusual story to share.

EXPECTATIONS

In the third year, students are expected to blend professionalism with what they learned in the first two years of pharmacy school. Also, in this year, students begin to develop and follow their own interests in their profession. The third year is the time to begin pre-contemplating residencies, as well, and examining their grades to ascertain if they are competitive for this type of additional training. Because P3 students often express extraordinary enthusiasm and insight about this year of college and their observations are often amusing and thoughtful, some commentary from P3s is presented below:

> "I am at the end of my third year of pharmacy school which means that over the past week I have had a lot of "lasts": my last final exam, my last didactic lecture, my last time sitting in *my lecture hall seat*. Many of my classmates were, appropriately, excited about these lasts, but I have found that what I am truly excited about are the "firsts" towards which we are all quickly moving."[190]

> "My third and recently completed year completed the pharmacology and therapeutics of the remaining organ systems including oncology, infectious disease, and psychiatric pharmacotherapy. We also completed an immunization course as well as sterile product and chemotherapy preparation.

> This was our final year of classroom work and felt like the homestretch! My first IPPE was direct inpatient at (deleted text) where I participated in rounds with physicians and residents, interviewed patients and collaborated with the pharmacist on patient's medication regimen.

> During the following semester I was at (deleted text), which is an inpatient psychiatric hospital. There I had the opportunity to spend the day at each unit such as adolescent, geriatric, and intensive adult.

I even observed mental health court where both the patient and hospital are represented and sit in front of a judge regarding whether or not a patient can safely be discharged. Our third year closed with a week long course on pharmacy law and our assignments for the next year's advanced pharmacy practice experience (APPE)."[191]

ACTIVITIES

As the comment above suggests, P3 students will use what they learned in the IPPEs that occurred between the first and second year and the second and third year to begin performing more clinical tasks in the context of actually providing quality pharmacy care in the form of advanced pharmacy practice experiences (APPEs). At this time, students should be thinking about past preceptor experiences and weigh these thoughts as they make decisions about future experiential opportunities such as residencies.

At this stage of advanced training, a preceptor may matter more to the student because the interaction may be less about what the preceptor can teach the student about the science and the practice of pharmacy (because the student is well-versed in this discipline by now) and instead may hinge more on the overall student-preceptor relationship. This interaction should be optimal because the preceptor will be grading the student on what might be perceived as minor aspects of the APPE such as appearing at any scheduled meetings, completing all work, following through with all requests, and adhering to practice site standards and regulations.

An ideal preceptor will promote personal and professional growth in student pharmacists. Because preceptors may volunteer to take students at their worksite, they may not be paid for their instruction and mentorship. Instead, some colleges will offer adjunct faculty positions in trade for the preceptor's willingness to train students. Colleges of pharmacy always need excellent preceptors for the hundreds of students who need clinical training.[192-195]

For third year students, a great preceptor is not a "given".[196] So, some schools of pharmacy offer preceptor-training courses to improve the teaching skills of these student mentors. However these skills training sessions may not be able to improve bad attitudes or poor business practices. For example, some preceptors do not want student input or opinion, preferring to tell the student what to do and when to do it and this can undermine or prevent the development of independent problem solving.

These types of preceptors may also not encourage independent student research to answer questions, and the preceptor may lack sufficient skills to motivate students.[197] Some preceptors are just not engaging teachers and may use grades or scores to obtain student compliance. Be forgiving if possible: perhaps the method the preceptor uses to train her students is simply all she knows about teaching.

Good preceptors assist the P3 to blend with the current staff and students and offer instruction along with independent learning opportunities. The best preceptors will support the student without denigrating his weaknesses. Instead, the student's deficits can be turned into learning experiences. Whether you have a wonderful or severely challenged preceptor, wring out every piece of information possible. Maximize your time and super-size your experience with your own motivation.

During these APPE's all students will be evaluated regarding their ability to communicates relevant, concise, comprehensive, and timely information in oral and written forms that is clear and uses the correct terminology for a future pharmacist. The students are also monitored for their ability to listen to patients and obtain the needed information to fulfill a request. They are also, at this stage, graded on their ability to prevent problems with patient interactions in addition to solving any problems using science- or evidence-based data. Indeed, this APPE is modeling all of the relevant tasks of a future pharmacist!

CHAPTER 9

THE FINAL YEAR

By May of the third year, students will be starting activities related to the fourth and final year of school. In the P4 year, pharmacy school is entirely different from the preceding years which have prepared you for advanced pharmacy practice experiences (APPEs) that occur between the third and fourth year. With more than 100 hours of pharmacy experience under your belt from your first three years in pharmacy school (via previous IPPEs), as a P4, you will learn about actual patient care in multiple settings such as acute, ambulatory, and long-term care, and community environments. You are nearing the end of your preliminary educational journey, and maybe you will have some time to reflect on the choice you made more than three years ago. Here is one opinion:

> "As I approach my fourth and final year of pharmacy school, I finally have a moment to breathe and reflect. Born and raised on the west

coast, I decided to venture out east to experience a change in culture. Before I knew it, I found myself in (deleted text) at (deleted text) University School of Pharmacy. I quickly found myself immersed in a completely foreign culture only to be amplified by the most challenging years of my life. I had no idea what I was in for three years ago when I began the next chapter in my life but could not be happier that I chose this career path."[191]

Hopefully, in your final year, you too will be happy with the choice you made as you work your way through the actual application of prior formal classroom training. In the fourth year, students may be assigned to clinical rotations in a major teaching medical center affiliated with their program, or they may have experiences in unique practice sites such as the pharmaceutical industry, biotechnology companies, or government. APPEs, also referred to as clerkships, will require many hours for fulfillment of the P4 skills set. Virtually all academic health centers in the US offer such clerkships to fourth-year students.[198]

COURSE DESCRIPTIONS

Because there are no typical courses during this final period, your last year may be entirely experiential. APPEs are typically 4–6-week rotations that span the academic year, and students may be required to be present at community, hospital, clinical practice, industry, or ambulatory care sites. Thus, you may need to travel to other regions of the state to acquire your hours. A smart student will contact the preceptor at the rotation site to inquire about necessary travel and accommodation arrangements well before the information is needed. Some schools require the students to take electives that are pertinent to their APPE work. Of course, these classes will be taken in addition to seminars, journal clubs, or required project work with other students.

EXPECTATIONS

Students participating in APPEs will be working 40 or more hours a week, so holding a second job is probably not feasible. Work hours will certainly conflict with rotation schedules, which are not democratic. The rotation is the student's first priority. Some rotations, depending on the site, may require drug screening or proof of immunization against specific pathogens such as hepatitis. Attendance is required at every APPE rotation meeting, whether the experience is scheduled for an evening or a weekend/holiday. Also, rotations may include work for the student that exceeds the traditional work day of "9 to 5", and students must prepare for this. Any student who believes that he will not work long past "closing time" is delusional.

During APPE rotations, every assignment given must be completed for the student to receive credit for hours that count toward licensure requirements. Students will be evaluated on their professionalism, as well. Although rotations are not structured like the previous didactic lectures for which testing occurred and grades were awarded to students, preceptors will "grade" the student on his ability to perform assigned tasks. This evaluation *is* the grade, and a passing grade is not guaranteed. For some institutions, the student may also evaluate the preceptor.

APPE rotations may also allow the student to more narrowly focus on subspecialties of pharmacy by offering training in a specific topic such as cardiology or psychiatry. Rotation choices will vary by institution. To see what rotations are potential offerings among schools of pharmacy, see the list to the right:

To view the rotation through the eyes of the P4s, see the comments by students from US schools of pharmacy below. Names of individuals or institutions have been redacted for privacy.

Potential Rotations

- Academic Pharmacy
- Acute Care Pharmacy
- Ambulatory Care Pharmacy
- Community Pharmacy
- Community Management
- Community Outreach
- Compounding
- Critical Care Pharmacy
- Drug Information
- Hospital Pharmacy
- Infectious Disease
- Long-Term Care
- Managed Care
- Nuclear Pharmacy
- Oncology Pharmacy
- Pediatrics
- Psychiatry
- Public Health
- Regulatory Pharmacy
- Retail Pharmacy
- Rural Community Pharmacy
- Trauma

"This Acute Care rotation focuses on cardiac care as you are rounding with the Heart & Vascular care team. I rounded on a daily basis with the interdisciplinary team (nurses, social worker, dietician, PT/OT), but also had the opportunity to round with the Cardiology team (MD, fellow, resident) and spent a few days rounding on other floors with a hospitalist. (text deleted) gives you plenty of practice writing notes and orders in charts.

You develop SOAP skills as you need to follow basic information on every patient on the floor in addition to choosing two patients to follow closely via daily SOAP notes. (text deleted) will assign articles to discuss based on topics you suggest—we discussed current treatment guidelines for AFib, HF, and anticoagulation. (text deleted) will also arrange things so you can watch a cardiac surgery if interested."[199]

"I rounded with trauma and critical care doctors, giving my input occasionally (*sic*). I presented patient cases and information on new drugs and therapies. I attended committee meetings like antibiotic stewardship. All of these activities helped me to solidify the information I'd learned in class."[199]

"Request denied—was the response I got when I submitted a request to do an HIV clinic rotation at the county hospital...I was told it was because my preceptor would be on vacation for a week at the beginning of my rotation."[199]

"(I gained) in depth knowledge of toxicology and mechanisms of drug overdoses."[199]

"(I) familiarized myself with many uncommon specialty injections and oncology medications. I also gained a better understanding of the insurance process."[199]

"(I learned) about how hospital pharmacy works, (to) follow all areas of the pharmacy, learn(ed) how to make intravenous fluids, fill inpatient medication orders, learn(ed) about Pyxis, review(ed) all topics related to cardiovascular and also review(ed) antibiotics, attend(ed) weekly pharmacology conference with medical residents."[199]

"(I) became proficient in the treatment of "common" toxicology situations."[199]

APPEs may also include actual patient interviews and medication counseling to address multiple patient problems. Then, after you interview ("work up") a patient, you will present this patient data to your supervisor. Prior to meeting your patient, you may have little or no information to prepare for the interview other than laboratory data or some other written chart information. This aspect of the rotation will enable you to understand the spontaneous nature of health care and diverse patient concerns that can significantly influence the advice you give.

Both you (or you within a team) and your preceptor may discuss potential medication management strategies, and after a plan is agreed upon, you may prepare a patient therapy recommendation for the patient. You may even be asked to send this to the patient and the patient's physician, perhaps calling at a later date to confirm that all is going well. Thus, in this experience, you will have initiated patient care and performed a follow-up with the healthcare team. While these assignments are being completed, you may be asked to write a paper such as a drug review, or you may be asked to document the effects of a specific drug category on a certain patient population in the form of a manuscript.

Your APPE may include opportunities to learn the basics of drug information research and how to locate, scrutinize, and use correct sources for data regarding pharmaceutics. Every statement a pharmacist makes with respect to patient mediation management must be supported by the appropriate scientific literature. Otherwise, the advice is just an opinion and not a professional recommendation. Like a journalist, who usually requires three sources for his facts, strive for a couple of peer-reviewed citations to support your medication management treatment plans.

The advantage of unique patient interactions on these rotations is that you will witness diseases that you might have never seen otherwise, and more importantly, you will observe how multiple diseases or conditions affect the patient on a personal level. You will also meet tragically ill people with enormous scientific literacy and self-awareness about their predicament.

Then, you will interact with people who are continually in need of medication because of their lifestyles, and who are completely out of touch with the impact of their own habits. You may meet the smallest patients you have ever seen, who are only hours old and require your creativity to find drug formulations that meet their needs. In contrast, you will speak with people who are two to four times your age, allowing you to appreciate how a lifetime of choices or circumstances will contribute to health, or the lack of it, in later life. In short, the fourth year is the time for really practicing your profession and helping patients in your community.

ACTIVITIES

- *The North American Pharmacist Licensure Examination: The NaPLEX*

The North American Pharmacist Licensure Examination (NaPLEX) is one of the immediate hurdles for every PharmD who wishes to practice pharmacy. This exam is taken with permission after the student has fulfilled the required education as set forth by their state's board of pharmacy. Around May, at the end of the fourth year, students can prepare for this exam by taking practice tests. Upon graduation, each college of pharmacy issues to each student a Certificate of Education proving he has the necessary training to be a pharmacist. This Certificate then allows each student to obtain an Authorization to Test (ATT) with the North American Board of Pharmacy. An ATT is necessary to register for an appointment to take the NaPLEX.

> R̞ *** Students who have completed their degree and are ready to take the NaPLEX should be aware that, of the 185 questions on the exam, only 150 are actually used to calculate the score for the test...No indication will be given on the exam to reveal which questions count and which do not. ***

The NaPLEX assesses the graduate's overall knowledge of pharmacy practice to demonstrate professional competence. Exam passage does not license the PharmD, but it is a step in the process that leads to licensure. The four and one-quarter hour test is approximately $500. The 185 questions on the computer-based NaPLEX fall into three general categories.

First, slightly more than half of the test covers the assessment of pharmacotherapy to assure safe and effective therapeutic outcomes. In this area, you must interpret patient data and demonstrate proficiency with dosage forms and regimens. In this section, direct recall of drug mechanisms of actions will be required. Roughly one-third of the test measures knowledge in the safe and accurate preparation and dispensing of medications.[200]

Being able to properly dispense medications requires recall of multiple types of pharmaceutical calculations that you mastered in previous years, as well as recall of brand and generic drug names. Some of this information may be used again in the NaPLEX section that covers pharmaceutical compounding. Within the final section of the test (roughly 10% of the exam), the test candidate will provide proof that he can assess, recommend, and provide healthcare information that promotes public health. To do this, he must be able to locate and understand different types of drug and health information and use this data to educate patients.[200] Here are some sample questions for those who are curious about this exam (answers are supplied in **Appendix IV**):

> Question 1: Magnesium stearate is commonly used as which of the following type of pharmaceutical ingredient in tablet preparation?
>
> A   Tablet disintegrant
> B   Tablet glidant
> C   Tablet opaquant
> D   Tablet lubricant
> E   Tablet polishing agent
>
> Question 2: Which of the following dosage forms by definition contains alcohol?
>
> A   Emulsion
> B   Elixir
> C   Solution
> D   Suspension
> E   Syrup

Question 3: Which of the following is useful for relief of symptoms or as a preventive therapy in patients with xerostomia?

A   Non-alcoholic mouthwash
B   Alcoholic mouthwash
C   Sugarcoated chewing gun
D   Stronger mouthwash
E   Sugarcoated mint

Question 4: Passage of drugs across the placenta to the fetus occurs due to which of the following?

A   The drug has a high positive charge
B   The drug has a high molecular weight
C   The drug has a low molecular weight
D   The drug has a negative charge
E   The drug is very hydrophilic

Question 5: Which of the following processes will increase the water solubility of drug?

A   Absorption
B   Distribution
C   Elimination
D   Hydroxylation
E   Excretion

Question 6: Which of the following acts as a surfactant?

A   Psyllium
B   Senna
C   Milk of magnesium
D   Docusate
E   Bisacodyl

Question 7: Another name for Cardura is:

A   Amlodipine
B   Diltiazem
C   Doxazosin
D   Nifedipine
E   Terazosin

Question 8: Ultram is also known as:

A   Codeine
B   Hydrocodone

C	Oxycodone
D	Propoxyphene
E	Tramadol

If you could not answer any of these questions at this time, you have powerful knowledge about what you need to do to perform well on the NaPLEX. If you could answer most of the questions, and you are not enrolled in a pharmacy program, you are probably ahead of the curve with respect to general knowledge, and this should serve you well in a professional program. Students who have completed their degree and are ready to take the NaPLEX should be aware that, of the 185 questions on the exam, only 150 are actually used to calculate the score for the test. The questions not counted in the score are "test" test questions to assess the test's validity and the appropriateness of the questions. Of course, no indication will be given during the exam to reveal which questions count and which do not. This is the mystique of the NaPLEX!

- ### *Multistate Pharmacy Jurisprudence Examination: The MPJE*

Part of applying for licensure includes another test, the Multistate Pharmacy Jurisprudence Examination or the MPJE. This exam tests your knowledge of both state and federal laws that apply to the profession of pharmacy. You will need to know the basics of pharmacy such as general rules for dispensing medication to patients.

Like the NaPLEX, this exam is conducted at specific testing sites and it is laid out in a two-hour computerized, 90-question format. Not all states require this $200 test for licensure. Instead, some states have specific jurisprudence competency instruments. Thus, pharmacists seeking licensure in Arkansas, California, and Virginia will have unique licensure obligations. The majority of the testable information on the MPJE consists of knowledge of laws pertaining to pharmacy practice.

Specifically, can you recognize the duties, responsibilities, and privileges of the pharmacist, compared to other pharmacy staff? You will also be asked about laws governing how you order and dispense drugs, especially controlled substances. Students should know how to keep records of such acquisitions, too.

On the MPJE, PharmD graduates will be expected to know the difference between prescription and non-prescription medications, and who can prescribe such drugs. Concerning the written prescription, the student will verify that she knows what constitutes a valid and legal prescription and what is needed for computerized or electronic prescriptions. Competency regarding prescription limitations will also be queried. The student should be able to demonstrate that he knows how to fill a prescription, dispense a properly labeled medication with the correct patient information, and document procedures as needed.

A minor component of the MPJE includes competency assessment in federal and state regulations pertaining to the manufacturing and distribution of both prescription and non-prescription drugs as dictated by the Food, Drug, and Cosmetic Act and related legislation. Knowledge of controlled substance handling is queried, too.

- *And Beyond*

The fourth year is the also the time for applying for residencies. When students are well into the P4 year, major decisions about residencies may be too late to make. Thus, having early and accurate information about this process is essential. For example, smart students will be investigating potential post-graduate programs by talking to preceptors, current residents, or a residency director, if the school has one.

In the fourth year, too, students will be putting finishing touches on their curriculum vita (CV) so that this document can be shared with possible preceptors and anyone else who might help place you into your residency choice. You may want faculty or a previous employer to review your CV for omissions or inaccuracies. The CV should be correct, professional, and brief. Students may wish to tailor their CV and letters to best fit the residency they most desire, so these two sites may offer more specific assistance in this regard:[201-202]

- American Society of Hospital Pharmacists Residency Directory: *http://www.ashp.org/menu/Accreditation/ResidencyDirectory.aspx*
- American College of Clinical Pharmacy Residency and Fellowship Directory: *www.accp.com/resandfel/*

Students in their final year will also want to identify early possibilities for letters of recommendation. Letters should come from past or current employers, any faculty or pharmacy school advisor, and any previous or current preceptor who can not only address aspects of your knowledge and abilities but also identify any weaknesses that can be improved.

Unlike applying to pharmacy school, you may choose to ask for a copy of these letters so that you can anticipate any questions in the residency interview. At this stage of your life, letters are almost always shared and, in fact, at the professional level, sometimes the recipient of the letter actually drafts a first edition. Then, the letter's author will tidy it up, add a personal touch, and sign it. This sounds bizarre, but it is an accepted practice in academia.

Faculty cannot recall every important detail about every student (or colleague) for whom they are asked to write letters. Thus, students should smile and "roll with it" if the person who is asked to write the letter requests a preliminary draft. Once complete and printed, these letters are typically sent with an application for the residency that can be due at the end of the semester (December) or by January of the following year.

Speaking of materials and timing, your school transcript may be requested, so this may need to be addressed early to avoid being late. Schools do not often respond immediately to transcript requests, and they do lose the request now and then. Be pro-active and request your transcript information well before it is needed and then double check that your materials reached their intended destination.

Students who are not interested in a residency at the end of their four years may use the information above to prepare for a job, too. A residency is not a given for all students, so if you are not interested in/competitive for a residency, increase your chances of landing the job you want by keeping an updated and tidy CV and inquiring about whether letters of recommendation are desired by a prospective employer.

CHAPTER 10

POST-GRADUATION

After you graduate from pharmacy school, you will be a PharmD. You have worked diligently four years to earn the title of "Dr." so you should know how to use this honorific accurately. For example, you are now (depending on your gender) Dr. Bill Smith (Dr. Jill Smith). You can also choose to go by the following: Bill Smith, PharmD (Jill Smith, PharmD). However, you will never sign your name Dr. Bill Smith, PharmD (Dr. Jill Smith, PharmD).

To use both titles is redundant and uninformed. Any additional degrees can be listed after your PharmD in the order of ascension, if you have them. For example, you may be Bill Smith, MBA, PharmD, PhD. Or you may be Jill Smith, MSN, PharmD. Never list Bachelor's degrees anywhere in your title. At this level of the game, it is assumed that everyone has this minimal level of education.

Also, any certificates you have earned may be listed after your PharmD designation. For instance, you may receive board certification as a pharmacotherapy specialist, so your title would be amended to include this: Jill Smith, PharmD, BCPS. Additional certification titles and their definitions are described later in this chapter.

Although graduation is thrilling and joyful, you may truly be so tired of school (and paying tuition), that going any farther with your degree induces feelings of nausea. Paradoxically, some students are ready to jump into the postgraduate activities described in this chapter, but they may wonder if they qualify for these experiences. Students may be interested to know that anyone with a GPA higher than 3.5 is very likely to be competitive. Finally, students who worked *prior* to pharmacy school are more likely to select (and be chosen for) residencies after graduation, a fact that often surprises students.[184]

Residencies are often offered by the institution from which the PharmD graduated and they can be found across the country in diverse patient care settings. Leaving a home institution for new expertise is worth contemplating for the new PharmD because such experiences are often rich with opportunity. Going far afield allows the PharmD to learn new methods, approaches, and ways of thinking while making new professional contacts.

R**x** *" A residency provides the student with much more than additional clinical or community skills, a residency can give the PharmD an advantage in the search for employment...and provide a network of professional contacts for the graduate as he determines whether the specialty he is studying is worth a life-long commitment. "*

Residencies, which emerged in the 1930s for pharmacy graduates, are optional at this time. However, these programs of study may be mandatory by the year 2020,[203] an idea that is unpopular with some current pharmacists. These professionals argue against mandatory residencies, suggesting that the PharmD alone well prepares any pharmacy graduate with the necessary skills to treat patients.

Arguments against compulsory training also indicate that forcing post-graduate experiences on all PharmDs may eventually degrade actual pharmacy training. Colleges of pharmacy, they predict, would eventually rely on residencies to fill any educational gaps. Theoretically, this might de-motivate faculty in pharmacy colleges to stay current and maintain programmatic rigor. Thus, a population of pharmacy professionals seems to view potentially mandatory residencies as a form of graduate remediation; residencies, in their opinion, should remain elective.[204]

Residencies are also often referred to as post-graduate years one and two (PGY1 and PGY2). Each PG1/2 program is typically at least one year in length, and some pharmacy colleges provide nine-month residencies.[205] Residencies can be community-pharmacy- or health-system-based post-graduate experiences.

Graduates may want to know that most (85%) of the US community pharmacy residency programs are associated with a college or school of pharmacy, and several residency practice sites may be available as post-graduate options.[206-208] Community pharmacy post-graduate tracks can teach the new graduate how to operate an independent pharmacy, and health-system residencies enable the new graduate to master clinical skills in a concentrated fashion.[209-210]

Students are often surprised to learn that residency slots, at this time, are not as abundant as the number of graduates seeking those residencies. Many reasons include needing appropriate residency directors and lacking funds to pay for training as well as the resident's stipend and benefits.[211-213] Federal money in the form of "pass through funds" can be obtained from the Centers for Medicare and Medicaid Services for health-system (hospital-based) residency slots, but community pharmacy residencies do not have access to these funds.[203, 208]

For those unfamiliar with governmental budgeting strategies, pass-through dollars are funds collected by organizations that can be pooled to offer grants or awards to other institutions. In 2010, this discrepancy in residency opportunities prompted the National Association of Chain Drugs Stores to offer $1,500,000 in grants to nonprofit colleges and schools of pharmacy who collaborate with independent or chain community pharmacies to foster PGY1 community pharmacy residencies.[214]

WHY TO DO IT?

A residency provides the student with not only additional clinical or community skills, but also the residency can give the PharmD a distinct advantage in the search for employment.[209] Residencies provide a network of professional contacts for the graduate as he determines whether the specialty he is studying is worth a life-long commitment.[215-217] In contrast to the more traditional pharmacy residency, fellowships are postgraduate training programs to offer *research skills* to PharmDs.[218-219] Fellowships may be one or two years and they foster professional growth of the PharmD such that she can perform independent research funded through grants. So, scientific and proposal writing along with statistics may be included in the research training.

HOW TO DO IT?

To apply for a residency, a student may use the Pharmacy Online Residency Centralized Application Service (PhORCAS). Not all residency programs use PhORCAS, but for those that do, this is the sole mechanism by which students can apply for those slots. PhORCAS can be investigated further by viewing this site: _https://portal.phorcas.org/_. Before applying through PhORCAS, a student will have been registered by the National Matching Service's Matching Program.

This Matching Service will provide the student with a five-digit code for identification within the system. Also in the online Matching Service, you will rank your preferred programs in the order of interest. In fact, if you want to co-locate with a significant other, you can each register for Matching and then identify yourself as part of a couple when ranking your programs.

Students should understand that the Matching Program and PhORCAS are _separate_ online services. PhORCAS disseminates the application information and the Matching Program makes the final residence assignment. Thus, no application materials are sent to the Matching Service. If your residency program does not participate in PhORCAS, you will still need to register with the Matching Service, and then submit your materials to your residency site separately, in the manner they request.

Students who want to browse the residency Matching site to learn what fees and activities are required for registration should visit this webpage: _www.natmatch.com/ashprmp_. Students often ask about applicants who do not get "matched" to their program of choice. Students who do not get accepted into their desired pharmacy residency can be taken into their second choice programs through what is called a "scramble" to fill unfilled residence slots.[220-221]

When students are inquiring about residency programs, they should ask basic questions pertaining to the _overall_ program. First, you need to know how many positions are open. Also, you want to know what types of PGY2 experiences can be had after this first year (PGY1) is complete. Then, the residency director may ask you questions. Initial questions will be much like those asked for your pharmacy school interview, including why you want to add more years to your education in the form of a residency and why you are interested in their particular residency program.

They want to know why they should choose you among other applicants. Other questions they may ask could be general and personal, resembling questions you might be asked if interviewing for a job. For example, you may be asked about your best and worst attributes. Specific questions that have been asked of residency applications are presented below:

- "Tell me about yourself."
- "Can you summarize your accomplishments to date?"
- "What are your overarching professional goals?"
- "What do you like about our program?"
- "Evaluate your clinical abilities and tell me about your strengths and weaknesses."
- "Did you have specific academic difficulties as a student?"
- "What was your most/least favorite rotation?"
- "Have you performed any research or done any teaching?"
- "What do you seek in a residency experience?"
- "Why are you pursuing a residency in this area/this institution/this city/this state?"
- "What do you envision role will be as a resident here?"
- "What other residency programs are you considering?"
- "Why should we choose you over other applicants?"

Additional questions asked of interviewing residents involved actions and decisions related to patients. For instance, you may be asked what you would do given a patient with a particular health problem or who is taking a specific medication. You may be given chart or laboratory data and asked to identify drugs that need adjustment for that patient. You can be asked specifics about drugs and mechanisms of action. You can be queried on specific side effects and you may be required to explain a patient counseling decision or a physician consultation.

Finally, you can be quizzed about your ability to deal with change, conflict, trust, and shared decision making. The interviewer wants to learn as much as possible about you and to ensure that everyone gets the most from the opportunity. Knowing your philosophy about responsibility and patient care will go a long way toward measuring your "fitness" for that residency. Thus, you may be asked if you are a natural leader or whether you are more introverted.

The faculty interviewing you may have information about your skills or deficits as a student, and they may question particular difficulties you had with a preceptor, a patient, or any other professional on the healthcare team. You may be asked how you manage time and stress and how you cope when a treatment recommendation that you provide is dismissed. Some questions may require you to be longitudinally prepared. For example, if you can describe what you expect to be doing in your field in the next decade, you will be addressing where you think pharmacy is going in the future as a profession as well as suggesting what you really want from a particular residency program.

Never overlook residents themselves in your programs of interest. Ask them why *they* chose the residency in the first place. You may also wish to ask them what they like (or do not like) about their pathway. Perhaps they experienced a particular or unexpected challenge within the residency, and they can share this with you.

You may want to ask them if the size of their program had any influence on their choice, too. Perhaps there are aspects of their residency that they would change if they could. Answers to questions such as these can be very telling about resident happiness. For example, the residents may be presenting seminars frequently to different healthcare groups because their residency program is part of a major metropolitan healthcare center with many functioning parts. Residents in large programs with many students may gain precepting experience of their own, something that might be valuable to you.

THE PGY1 EXPERIENCE

Post-graduate residencies include areas of specialization recognized by the American Society of Health System Pharmacists.[222] In fact, some researchers predict that in the next 20 years, almost all pharmacists will possess some form of specialization.[223] Some PGY1 areas of emphasis offered in US pharmacy programs are depicted to the right, but this list is not completely inclusive:

A resident can elect to specialize in one of these areas, and then, for

Specialty Areas

- Adult Inpatient Medicine
- Ambulatory Care
- Cardiology
- Critical Care
- Emergency Medicine
- Hematology/Oncology
- Infectious Disease
- Investigational Drug Studies
- Management
- Medication Safety
- Oncology
- Pain Management
- Pediatrics
- Pharmacotherapy
- Pharmacy Administration
- Pharmacy Informatics
- Pharmacy Practice
- Quality Improvement

PGY2, the resident can narrow her focus within that area. For example, a Critical Care PGY1 focus can be further narrowed to intensive care areas such as general medicine, surgery and trauma, neuroscience, cardiothoracic, infectious diseases, and so on. Likewise, PGY1 residencies in oncology can be narrowed to areas of cancer care such as inpatient, ambulatory (outpatient), infusion therapy, gynecological, or pediatric subspecialties.

Students should remember that a unique residency experience may be found among US Veteran's Administration Medical Centers. Almost 90 of these accredited residency programs presently exist in the country's 155 Veteran's hospitals. Funding for these programs comes from the Veteran's central office in Washington DC. Thus, anyone with a passion for serving our military might welcome a residency in these well-run hospitals.

THE PGY2 EXPERIENCE

PGY2 training can extend first year post-graduate skills set and focus the PharmD's clinical interests even more. Board certification in particular specialty areas can be obtained after the PGY2 period as well. It may be obvious, but any accredited PGY2 residency is contingent on the completion of an accredited PGY1 residency. Because these are tied together this way, some PharmDs accept positions in the PGY2 program before entering the PGY1 experience, to ensure continual education at the same location.

Post-graduate areas of specialization may include managed care pharmacy systems, health administration pharmacy, ambulatory care, cardiology, critical care, drug information, emergency medicine, geriatric, HIV/infectious diseases, internal medicine, medication use safety, nephrology, nuclear, nutrition support, oncology, and palliative care/pain management.

Board certification, which is slightly different than a residency specialty, can be obtained in one of these nine specialties recognized by the Board of Pharmaceutical Specialties as depicted in the list below. Then, these credentials will appear on personal identification and in signature lines, along with the pharmacist's name and title.[222]

These board certifications may require not only a PharmD but also hours of training beyond the PGY1 or PGY2 experience, including an initial certification in another area prior to qualifying for eligibility. For example, the BCPS (AQC) requires BCPS certification first, and then the pharmacist can apply for additional certification (qualifications) in cardiology.

- BCACP: Board Certified Ambulatory Care Pharmacist
- BCPS (AQC): Board Certified Pharmacotherapy Specialist with Added Qualifications in Cardiology
- BCPS (AQ-ID): Board Certified Pharmacotherapy Specialist with Added Qualifications in Infectious Disease
- BCPS: Board Certified Pharmacotherapy Specialist

- BCNP: Board Certified Nuclear Pharmacist (BCNP)
- BCNSP: Board Certified Nutrition Support Pharmacist (BCNSP)
- BCOP: Board Certified Oncology Pharmacist
- BCPP: Board Certified Psychiatric Pharmacist

Additional multidisciplinary certifications are given below, along with the title information that will accompany the pharmacists' name if he completes one of these certification programs. The certifying bodies or organizations which provide these certificates to pharmacists may not be accredited, so if such accreditation is important to you, research your choices thoroughly.

- AAHIVE: HIV Expert
- AAHIVS: HIV Specialist
- AAPCC: Certified Specialist in Poison Information
- ACLS: Advanced Cardiovascular Life Support
- AE-C: Certified Asthma Educator
- AP: Accredited in Applied Pharmacology
- BC-ADM: Board Certified-Advanced Diabetes Management
- CACP: Certified Anticoagulation Care Provider
- CDE: Certified Diabetes Educator
- CGP: Certified Geriatric Pharmacist
- CLS: Clinical Lipid Specialist
- CNSC: Certified Nutrition Support Clinician
- CPEHR: Certified Professional in Electronic Health Records
- CPP: Credentialed Pain Practitioner
- DABT: Diplomat of the American Board of Applied Toxicology
- PALS: Pediatric Cardiovascular Life Support

STIPENDS

Pharmacy residents may be paid a stipend that varies by region. Typical annual stipend ranges are $40,000–60,000, and additional rewards may be given to residents such as retirement investment options, and multiple health insurance benefits (dental, medical, vision, etc.). Some residencies will even pay moving expenses for individual or family relocation, and some may advance a portion of the stipend to the resident to facilitate the transition.

Residencies may also include office space, malpractice insurance, spouse and family benefits, the opportunity to teach or train students, and paid vacation or sick leave. Some programs will fund travel to conferences or offer compensation to residents for educational opportunities. Library access and modest administrative assistance may be offered when needed as well. Residencies which offer these "perks" are more generous than most initial academic faculty positions, so consider yourself more than fortunate if you land such a coveted position.

CHAPTER 11

PUTTING YOUR DEGREE TO USE

CHANGING ROLES OF THE PHARMACIST

The role of the pharmacist is changing. Even as you read this sentence, the profession is undergoing a subtle metamorphosis as it embraces new responsibilities and privileges. In the past, patients did not view the community pharmacy as a "go to" site for health information but merely regarded the pharmacist as a "drug expert".[224]

This mindset is changing. Additional tasks are being extended to pharmacists because of the rising cost of healthcare, a growing lack of physician access, and significant economic and physical barriers to care. Such trends are driving increasing community pharmacy accessibility for the patient and greater importance and visibility for the pharmacist.[225-229]

Not all professional healthcare providers welcome these changes in the pharmacy profession. Physicians are reported to be notoriously resistant to change, and often they behave as if they have forgotten that their professional degree is virtually equivalent to the PharmD. Both the PharmD and the MD are first professional degrees of the same weight and length of initial training. Thus, new trends in healthcare may cause (for a short time, hopefully) mild infighting among healthcare team members. Such turf wars will resurface again as the roles of pharmacists expand beyond dispensing and advising patients about medications to include prescription writing in states where this is not already ongoing (see below).[230]

Interestingly, physicians or other healthcare professionals who are quick to condemn the idea of pharmacists independently prescribing drugs may be uninformed about the history of the profession. For example, traditionally, European chemists, druggists, and apothecaries performed quite similar tasks for patients. Only after apothecaries as a body of professionals departed from the chemist/druggist business to become general practitioners did the divergence of duties occur. Then, chemists and druggists merged into one profession that was distinct from the general practitioners. So, truthfully, pharmacists *began* their trade as prescription writers.[231-232]

At this time, prescribing privileges for pharmacists, specifically the ability to initiate and modify prescriptions when permitted, are usually carried out under protocols or collaborative drug therapy management agreements. These agreements are overseen by a physician or nurse practitioner. Currently, 25 states already allow pharmacists to prescribe from a narrow list of medications or formularies.[233] Additionally, 20 states are actively pursuing privileges for pharmacists that are similar to roles already enjoyed by nurse practitioners and physician assistants: nurse practitioners can prescribe in all US states, and physician assistants have prescriptive authority in 41 states.[233]

Battles for prescribing rights in the remaining five states will likely be lengthy and expensive as the American Medical Association lobbies state and federal legislatures against these attempts to, in their opinion, infringe on the professional territory of physicians.[234] Of course pharmacy organizations can return the favor and lobby *against* these narrow viewpoints.

Students who are active in undergraduate political organizations are shown to positively contribute to pharmacy-based legislative activities in their communities. So, encourage your class president and officers early and often to increase student awareness of (and perhaps actions to address) professional challenges that will eventually greet all pharmacy school graduates.[235] Remember, you are the face of your future profession, so be informed and be vocal.

Such political strategies by students and pharmacists alike may be the "prescription" for changing how healthcare operates. After all, the specter of prescribing pharmacists is such a perceived threat to some physicians that they will only refer to a pharmacist's legal prescriptive authority as "drug therapy management under protocol" to de-emphasize the importance of the pharmacist's role.[233] Many physicians expand this philosophy to a nihilistic point, suggesting that pharmacists actually endanger the lives of patients because they lack the necessary expertise in pharmacology to prescribe drugs (See **§Working with Other Healthcare Professionals**). Pharmacists must fight back against this misinformation.

The fact is that, presently, PharmDs trained in the US have more pharmacology and pharmacotherapy training than any other healthcare professional.[233] Thus, a PharmD will have clocked more hours in pharmacology than is offered to, or required for, future physicians during their medical college training. Furthermore, once in practice, physicians will probably reduce their prescribing range to 15–20 drugs that they routinely recommend for the patients in their area of specialization.

Thus, the pharmacist will utilize more diverse pharmacology over a career than a physician who sees hundreds of patients a week. It is wise to remember, too, that physicians may prescribe any drug off-label, meaning they can permit a drug to be used in a manner than is not approved by the FDA.[236-238] Off-label prescribing is a privilege of the medical physician and long understood to be a routine practice.

What patients may not know, and what a pharmacist may be able to provide in the form of counseling, is that often off-label prescriptions are based on no data, poor data, or word-of-mouth anecdotes from a pharmaceutical representative or a medical colleague.[239-241] Thus, the pharmacist has an important and everlasting role in patient (and physician!) education.[232, 242]

A recent experience of a pharmacy student gives credence to such interprofessional haranguing that has been referred to in the preceding paragraphs. This pharmacy student related a recent conversation he had with a medical student who glibly quipped to him, "You won't be needed soon. A kiosk that dispenses drugs based on patient input into a computer will replace pharmacists in the future."

The medical student's implication that the selection and dispensing of prescription medication approximates the skill involved in purchasing an airline ticket is an indictment of the medical student's lack of insight about the future of healthcare. Indeed, IBM's Watson (the computer/robot), which famously competed against and beat a *Jeopardy* contestant on television is presently analyzing Memorial Sloan-Kettering patient cases, learning to make diagnoses and treatment recommendations.[243]

Robots such as Watson are more accurate at diagnosing because physicians, as human beings, are inherently error-prone. Physicians have an "anchoring bias", which all people possess at various levels. However, for a physician, such bias is mightily consequential. For example, anchoring bias compels physicians to arrive at a diagnosis that is frequently based on a single data point that simply "stood out". Then, once the diagnosis is firm in the physician's mind, he may ignore the rest of the patient's story...information that might change the diagnostic decision. Robots have no such anchoring bias: they can rapidly filter through enormous volumes of data without preference.

Thus, the medical student *was* accurate in predicting the placement of technology or robotic entities in medicine, but he may be wrong about the *location* of those electronic helpers. Specifically, the co-founder of Sun Microsystems has stated that, in the future, "computers and robots would replace four out of five physicians in the US."[244] Compelling arguments for this arrangement abound. For example, telemedicine, phone- and computer-based applications now help patients manage diseases and vital signs and decrease physician visits. Such efficiencies mean that these advances are here to stay.

Also, the traditional medical visit is inherently inefficient: patients are often the sole symptom storytellers at the physician's office, and separate visits to two sites are still usually required to see a physician and to fill a prescription.[244] Thus, anything that increases healthcare effectiveness, such as the pharmacy being a one-stop shop for patients of the future, may be an intuitive mechanism for lowering healthcare costs and increasing patient satisfaction.

Along this theme, efforts to expand pharmacy education to include diagnostic skills such documenting patient histories, interpreting laboratory data, and making decisions based on medical records may ease the path for pharmacists to enjoy more expansive professional authority. Pharmacists already manage diabetic patients and give vaccines, so enlarging this scope of healthcare practice should be straightforward.[245-247] Finally, when pharmacists participate in collaborative care with prescribing privileges, studies show that the programs are cost-effective and have good patient outcomes.[248-250]

WHO'S THE BOSS?

Some students are surprised that pharmacists do not answer to the Food and Drug Administration (FDA) in their roles of dispensing medications to patients and providing drug advice. Rather, irrespective of whether a supervisor or chairman dictates the daily responsibilities of the pharmacist, all pharmacy professionals ultimately answer to their state board of pharmacy. Still, the reality for practicing, licensed retail pharmacists is that they may serve many masters. For example, a retail pharmacist may work for a chain store within a large corporation, answering to managers within the company in addition to the state board of pharmacy. A pharmacist in a hospital who has an appointment in an academic department may answer to a hospital pharmacy administrator as well as a departmental chairman, again, in addition to a state board of pharmacy.

State pharmacy boards guide the profession of pharmacy through unique continuing education demands and the imposition of diverse penalties for unprofessional behaviors. US boards of pharmacy are also responsible for pharmacy education, communication, legislation, regulation, and enforcement within the profession. Finally, state pharmacy boards control licensing and manage disciplinary matters when necessary. For example, they can suspend a license of a pharmacist if the situation warrants this action.

The FDA is involved in the business of pharmacy in a few, but important, occasions. When pharmacists compound drugs for patients, the FDA controls how much of these compounded medications can be created at once so that the pharmacist is not engaging in what the FDA considers "drug manufacturing". Also, the FDA participates in the pharmacy profession when drugs or medical devices are recalled or withdrawn from the market, and pharmacists (among other healthcare professionals) are instrumental in assisting with this process.

The FDA, as the US's oldest consumer protection body, chiefly exists to assure the safety of drugs on the market. Thus, the FDA is more collaborative than regulatory with respect to pharmacists and the practice of pharmacy. So, the pharmacist may, at the end of the day, report to a drug chain owner, clinic director, hospital administrator, or academic supervisor, but the pharmacist's duties are regulated by the state.

WORKING WITH THE PUBLIC

Pharmacists work closely with the public in both retail and hospital settings, and many freshly minted PharmDs find that "the public" is a strange and interesting beast. Working with populations not educated in healthcare—or not educated at all—can be shocking to many students who have existed in, what is for many students, a highly sheltered environment of college and pharmacy school...and these are indeed protected environments.

To explain, in both college and pharmacy school, you spend most of your time interacting with intelligent, well-groomed, well-spoken people who are gathered for similar purposes: to learn or to teach. Outside of this environment are people who may be so vastly different from you, your classmates, and your professors that you may wonder how you will ever be an effective healthcare provider for them.

For example, a few of your patients may be fundamentally illiterate, entirely lacking basic reading and writing skills. Perhaps they can only sign their name with an initial. Although the US boasts a literacy rate of 99%, illiteracy remains a real phenomenon, and other types of illiteracy are more prevalent in specific disadvantaged pockets of society.[251-254] For example, your patients may be visually illiterate (unable to understand graphs/visual information), computer illiterate (unable to navigate a computer), information illiterate (unable to obtain and apply any general information), or innumerate (unable to effectively use numbers). Some patients will have multiple literacy challenges.

Poor patients are disproportionately affected by educational deficits at many levels, and a patient's ability to read speaks directly to their ability to understand the purpose of their medication and follow the pharmacist's instructions when using it. Studies show that one-third or more of US adults cannot read a prescription label, and often patients perceive their prescription-deciphering ability as being much better than it really is.[255-256] Non-English speaking patients may have additional hurdles to understanding medication use.[257]

This sounds counter-intuitive to some people. If the patient can manage a doctor's appointment, then, how can this patient have trouble with medication compliance? Truthfully, even patients who can navigate the currently byzantine nature of medical care may be unable to simultaneously hold contrasting thoughts in their mind, or they may be unable to complete multiple mental step tasks. Students are often surprised to discover that patients need information to be repeated several times to comprehend it. Then, if the patient understands the information, they must be able to remember and apply it. Many cannot.

Another group of patients will have reasonable reading and comprehension skills but zero scientific literacy, and they will fall prey to marketing hype that they see on television and read in magazines or newspapers.[253, 258-260] This patient group may also mistrust modern medicine, spending hundreds of dollars on supplements and gimmicks that interfere with the drugs you are dispensing.

Pharmacists fight enduring battles against scientific misinformation and implausible rationales that patients present for their behaviors or inactions. Such intelligent people seem to be living contradictions because they may not follow your instructions or comply with medication regimens, worsening their illnesses or creating new ones. Because only 12% of the US population has sufficient health literacy, most of your patients may not seem to understand when they actually *do receive* appropriate medical treatment.[256, 261]

Because our world is more integrated and multiple ethnicities can share the same community, you may find that a patient's cultural customs or preferences are important for you to understand. In short, in addition to the pharmacy skills you already have, you need a healthy dose of cultural competence to manage most of your patients compassionately and safely. Patients may have rituals or activities that directly interfere with their care, but which they will not abandon due to religion, tradition, or heritage.[262] So, the public is a veritable stew of many types of people of various backgrounds with multiple motivations when they encounter a pharmacist. You must be able to creatively and carefully interact with every one of these personalities. After all, you probably will not be able to choose your patients!

WORKING WITH OTHER HEALTHCARE PROFESSIONALS

Another aspect of your profession could include interacting with other healthcare medical professionals. Trends in attitudes among professional school graduates suggest that tomorrow's new physicians are more willing to interact with pharmacists in a positive and collegial manner. This is in contrast to more senior physicians who can present significant obstacles to your provision of care.[263] Interestingly, pharmacists are also reported to have different responses to physicians that are based on the real or perceived age of each professional.

R̶x̶ 〝 *Physicians are increasing efforts to stem the number of providers who call themselves "Dr."...believe(ing) patients will be confused about provider roles. In fact, some states have adopted laws to prevent pharmacists from referring to themselves by their title....* 〞

These biases contribute to perceptions of power and social distance between the two occupations. Specifically, older pharmacists were reported to be less polite than younger pharmacy professionals in the context of recommending alternative drug recommendations to physicians.[264] Then, physicians can go so far as to actually represent significant barriers to patient care.[265] For example, older doctors may withhold essential patient information from the younger pharmacist, continually make themselves unavailable for phone calls, and even demand that a pharmacist cease "interfering in the medical care of patients".[229]

In fact, studies show that physicians of a certain vintage have actively chastened pharmacists for "scaring patients" and "practicing medicine without a license", or making "inappropriate comments" in the presence of patients.[266] Specifically, physicians have been documented to mistrust pharmacists' ability to help patients manage adverse drug reactions, suggest alternate drug regimens, or modify a dosage form to increase patient convenience.[263] It is easy to imagine that the mistrust and unprofessionalism of one group can precipitate the same behavior in another cohort, creating a circle of ineffectiveness.

Pharmacists may take comfort in the fact that they are not the only group targeted by physicians. In the scientific literature, the most frequently documented unprofessional behaviors seem to be directed from physicians to the nurses who work with them. In these descriptions, physicians are prominent sources of bullying and bad behavior.[267-270] Of course, nurses have been reported to engage in unethical personal behavior, too. Sadly, demeaning and intimidating other members of the healthcare team ultimately results in the patient not receiving optimal care, irrespective of who initiated the unbecoming professional conduct.

Professional hostility is simply unnecessary in this era of modern medicine. That practicing pharmacists need a PharmD reflects the increasing scope of professional practice and places emphasis on the equality pharmacists share with physicians and nurse practitioners, to name a few. All doctoral-level degrees in healthcare reflect that each profession is similarly credentialed. Even so, strong disagreement persists about the infrequently discussed concept of who should be actually called a "doctor" in the professional setting. Probably, most pharmacy students believe that they will be referred to with the appropriate honorific ("Dr.") after they receive their PharmD. This may not be true. Reports in the scientific literature address this aspect of interprofessional care:

"I've been in many situations where everyone calls the pharmacist by their first name and the nurse by their first name...which indicates a hierarchal system where the physician is deserving of more respect than anyone else."[271]

Physicians are increasing efforts to stem the number of providers who call themselves "Dr." because they are reported to believe patients will be confused about provider roles. In fact, some states have adopted laws to prevent pharmacists from referring to themselves by their title unless they immediately state their role.[272] A bill in the House of Representatives, sponsored by John Sullivan (Oklahoma) and co-sponsored by more than 60 other members of Congress, would prohibit any doctorate-holding medical professional (other than an MD) from using the title of "Dr." in a professional setting.[273] The American Medical Association has prepared campaign materials to lobby for this effort.[274] In their report, they state the following:

> "Confusion among Americans about who is and who is not qualified to provide specific patient care undermines the reliability of the health care system and can put patients at risk. People unqualified to perform health services can lead to medical errors and patient harm. The AMA urges lawmakers to take action to rectify this problem. To help ensure patients answer the simple question, "Who is a doctor?" the AMA believes that all health care professionals—physician and non-physicians—should be required to accurately and clearly disclose their training and qualifications to patients.

> Asking medical professions to display their credentials and their capabilities would allow Americans to make informed choices about their health care. In fact, 96% of patients believe that health care providers should be required to display their level of training and legal licensure. This includes full disclosure in all advertising and marketing materials. In addition, while some non-physicians call themselves "doctor" by virtue of a doctoral degree, nine out of ten patients believe only a medical doctor should be able to us the title "physician".[274]

Aside from the faulty logic that anyone who uses the title "Dr." is referring to themselves as a "physician", chances are good that no patient will be actually confused about the "Dr. Jones" who stands behind the pharmacy counter, helping patients with medications. The context of the pharmacy will inform the patient about who does what job. The idea that patients do not know the difference between the two roles could be insulting to many patients, some of whom are highly educated and who may be more degreed than their very healthcare providers. Physicians who oppose the title of "Dr." PharmD-titled pharmacists likely wish to stop the perceived erosion of their control over medicine.

Clearly, a physician perceives no confusion when he incorrectly asserts that he is a "physician-scientist" as many are prone to do. This is slightly more that inflated dishonesty and slightly less than fraud: a physician has zero training in science/as a scientist, and simply liking science or feeling a special affinity for science is not sufficient to adopt this professional title. Similar to pharmacists, a physician has studied a trade, learning the skill of caring for sick patients. He has not learned to produce research and has probably not contributed to the scientific enterprise, a requirement of all scientists.

As healthcare teams become the norm to control costs and reach more patients, the medical predominance of the physician will be wrested away naturally. Thus, someone who earns a doctorate is fully deserving of the title "Dr." Informed pharmacists can speak out publicly to decrease the influence of this restriction or they can mobilize other professionals to end it entirely. Consider this: if physicians are truly worried about unqualified health care being delivered to patients and causing them harm, they should probably cease allowing medical students (who are less trained than pharmacy professional "non-physicians") to literally "practice" on patients, effectively putting an end to the entire tradition of teaching hospitals.

MAJOR LAWS AND RULES GOVERNING HEALTHCARE

Because pharmacists primarily serve in healthcare-provider roles, particular laws and rules should be well understood. In fact, students interested in pharmacy careers would be well advised to know seminal and current events in healthcare legislation. Such knowledge can prevent students from violating the law at their place of employment or internship.

Also, now and then students infringe on patient rights during interviews for pharmacy school, repeating patient information to the faculty conducting the interview. Of course, these verbalizations can be (and often are) noted in the interview. Therefore, anyone on the admissions committee, if she felt strongly enough about the infraction, could recommend that such a chatty and indiscriminate applicant be rejected.

To edify any readers who do not regularly read the newspaper or consistently view the nightly news, an important healthcare law is described below. This law affects every action of the pharmacist and pharmacy personnel. Also, fundamental details of two popular government insurance programs are given. All pharmacy students should know the difference between the social insurance programs—and there are significant differences. The information below is just as integral to the practice of pharmacy and interacting with patients as knowing drug mechanisms of actions and first-line therapeutic choices.

- *HIPPA*

Every pharmacy student should understand one of the most significant laws in healthcare, the Health Insurance Portability and Accountability Act of 1996, or HIPPA. HIPPA establishes the definition of a patient's individual health information and sets standards for protection of this information. The second component of the law, the HIPPA Security Rule dictates how patient data can be shared while protecting the patient's confidentiality when they seek care, irrespective of the type of care, be it mental health visits to prescriptions for antibiotics.

HIPPA and the Security Rule apply to all health insurance plans and healthcare providers, from physicians to pharmacists. Any information that can be linked to a specific patient is protected and cannot be used unless the care provider is specifically using the information to implement care (or report violence or abuse, for example) or unless the patient requests that the information be shared. De-identified patient information can be shared in certain contexts; however, because such health data (by definition) have no linkages or references to a specific patient.

Where students can face significant trouble or even criminal sanctions with HIPPA is during rotations or IPPEs and APPEs. For instance, a student using a patient database in the hospital who takes a photo or prints patient information to take home for "working up a case" can violate this health care law and may be in additional trouble for theft of government documents, depending on what they were and where they were taken from.

Once a violation such as this is confirmed, a student may be banned from another rotation at that facility for the foreseeable future; the student may be barred from seeking employment at that site or any site in its network; or the entire pharmacy program may be "uninvited" from sending students to that site for a rotation. Thus, this can harm the student and the reputation of his professional program, and this harm may be permanent.

Next, most pharmacists will interact with patients who participate in a form of government-sponsored social insurance. Two such programs are Medicare and Medicaid. Each is a distinct entity with unique rules and patient criteria, and not all states offer the same benefits under these programs.

- *Medicare*

Medicare is a social insurance program that offers guaranteed benefits to older (65 years-of-age or older) individuals and disabled US citizens under the age of 65, as well as specific patients with kidney failure. Our taxes subsidize this insurance program. All people enrolled in Medicare receive the same benefits, unlike the private insurance market. Private insurance plans offer different benefits over unique tiers of purchased coverage. This sounds deceptively simple, so students may not know that Medicare has four components: A, B, D, and C.

Medicare part A is insurance for hospital, skilled nursing facility, and Hospice care, and there are limits to the length of care under this section of Medicare. Medicare Part B is general medical insurance, and it covers outpatient services such as medical equipment, tests, procedures, and any drugs given to the patient during an office visit. Part B is optional for those who have insurance through an employer.

Medicare Part D covers drug prescriptions, and this is a separate plan provided by a private insurance company with tiered care plans and unique coverage options. Part C, as it is named, gets attention in the press under the umbrella term, "Medicare Advantage Plans". Under Part C, Medicare recipients can obtain additional coverage through private insurers. Medicare C, when paired as a healthcare plan with Part D, is referred to as a "Medicare Advantage with Prescription Drug Plan".

Medicare and its Advantage extras are not necessarily attractive to healthcare providers who may refuse to take patients under these plans or restrict the number of patients they accept with Medicare plans. These payment plans, according to health professionals, grossly underpay for services. In fact, some medical offices see Medicare patients on one day of the week only, triple booking (scheduling three patients for the same office visit time) patients to make up for the lost revenue. Most Medicare recipients do not pay insurance premiums for Part A, and Part B premiums are deducted from social security checks. However, premiums are paid for Parts D and C.

- **Medicaid**

Medicaid is a social welfare program, not a social insurance program. It is funded primarily by the individual states which offer benefits to its citizens that include health and nursing home coverage. People who are eligible for Medicaid must meet certain financial criteria. Three different aspects of Medicaid exist: one is health insurance for low-income families with children and people with disabilities. Another component of Medicaid is the provision of long-term care for older US citizens and disabled people.

The last component of Medicaid is the supplemental coverage for low-income Medicare beneficiaries for items not covered by Medicare. Some patients can meet criteria for both Medicaid and Medicare, and are thus referred to as "dual eligible" patients. Assuming someone is a Medicaid or

Medicare patient by their skin color, dress, or demeanor is unprofessional and a form of social profiling that pharmacists (and other professionals) should avoid.[275-277] Your eyes cannot reliably tell you anything about a person's ability to afford healthcare.[278]

Now that you are apprised in the major insurance plans and health care laws that will influence every aspect of your day in the profession of pharmacy, you should know about the diverse roles of pharmacists in the workforce. You may be eligible for or interested in several of these options.

THE PHARMACY WORKFORCE

Jobs for pharmacists are as varied as the pharmacists' ever expanding skills set. Although the retail setting may be the most common visualization of a pharmacist at work, diverse jobs for pharmacists exist. Descriptions of such opportunities are presented below, along with relevant details about these unique positions.[279]

PharmDs-to-be should understand that in the pharmacy workforce, the economics of supply and demand are not always straightforward, meaning that not all graduates will find the job they wanted most in the area they wanted to live. The balance of these forces depends on national and regional needs and the age of the populations served by the pharmacist.

For example, the Department of Labor predicts that due to new drug products and an aging population, medications will be used more than ever. Increasing obesity and diabetes opens another population for therapeutic management, and these patients are unfortunately younger each year.[280-282] Nationwide insurance will certainly affect prescription medication usage, and drug therapy may increase in suddenly insured populations.[283-285] These changes suggest that the pharmacy workforce will have grown 25% during the decade between 2010 and 2020. This means that more than 300,000 pharmacists are estimated to be in the national workforce by 2020.[286]

The trends of demand described above are relevant, but they are merging with a potential oversupply of pharmacists. Even so, in the recent past, pharmacists have not been plentiful in areas of the greatest need, such as rural areas.[287] As more schools of pharmacy open, competition for applicants increases. Then, more students are eventually enrolled in colleges of pharmacy.[288]

Over time, this trend will result in more graduates competing for fewer choice employment slots in the best areas, especially as older pharmacists stay on the job to balance the latest economic downturn experienced across the nation. Increased competition for pharmacy jobs has multiple consequences, one being that, if a job can be found, it may be less desirable or the pay may be less than previous years.[287] Also, *having a job at all* may require a graduate to travel to another city because the job market where he lives is saturated.

Some students opt for a residency to "wait out" the time between graduation and employment. This is a wise choice for many students because a residency offers additional specialized training for pharmacists, and can increase the demand for that particular type of pharmacist (See **Chapter 10, §Post-Graduation**).[287] Because many US colleges of pharmacy are thought to do a poor job of educating students about the potential employment opportunities in the pharmacy field (only emphasizing the more traditional roles of retail and clinical pharmacy), some potential jobs for a new PharmD are described below.[279]

Salary ranges are given for the descriptions below, but remember that salaries for pharmacists cover a substantial range of incomes. These ranges may account for where the pharmacist lives and what type of practice he performs. National averages can be found that agree and disagree with the values represented below, but these may be reflective of several years on the job (may not reflect entry level salaries), additional responsibilities, or income supplements offered for sales bonuses, travel compensation, or inherent contractual limitations.[289-290] Salary ranges were obtained from online sources such as Glassdoor.com, Indeed.com, Salary.com, Simplyhired.com and individual job descriptions from human resources websites.[291-294]

- ***Retail Pharmacists***
  $ Salary range: $120,000–$140,000's

Retail work is probably the most common position for PharmDs, so it has the most generous description. Here, the pharmacist will validate prescriptions for correct dosage and for patient drug interactions and incompatibilities. Questions arising from a prescription may require calling the physician's office for clarifications or to recommend drug substitutions. Once the prescription is filled, the pharmacist may counsel the patient about the medication's use and some medication management strategies. There also may be third-party insurance forms and other paperwork that accompany each prescription in addition to responsibilities of ordering and stocking drugs.

Pharmacists may also field inquiries about health issues and disease symptoms. Retail pharmacists must always remain professional and keep patient information confidential. Challenges of retail pharmacy may include aggressive and angry patients, unprofessional treatment by staff in physicians' offices, and wearisome bureaucratic insurance companies. In busy retail stores, pharmacists may fill several hundred prescriptions each day, and filling quotas may be mandated by the pharmacy's corporate headquarters. Some days, a retail pharmacist will stand for 9–10 hours with little down time.

Creative aspects of retail pharmacy can be found in drug preparations: liquid medicines, ointments, powders, tablets and other medications may need formulating. Compounding of special prescription pharmaceutical products for unique patients may also be requested. Within the retail setting, the pharmacist may need to chemically preserve vaccines, sera, or drugs with limited shelf-lives. Retail pharmacists may also guide patients to specific medical (for diabetes, for instance) and surgical products (crutches, bandages, etc.).

Additionally, for this occupation, record keeping is essential, especially regarding the dispensing of controlled/scheduled drugs. Management of the pharmacy's financial records may be a component of the retail job, too. Finally, retail pharmacies stock and sell over the counter products, toiletries, groceries, and office supplies. Various employers of retail pharmacists include independent pharmacies, supermarket pharmacies, and various pharmacy chain stores.

- **Contract, Temporary, or Hourly Pharmacy Careers in Retail**
    $ Salary range: $140,000's

Non-permanent positions in retail might be best for a new graduate who is uncertain about where he might fit. Also, graduates who are eager to begin a family (or who are in the initial stages of starting one) might find contract or part-time work appealing and flexible. This type of work also permits graduates to pursue outside interests and a few may choose to work for two different employers at the same time. Because a licensed pharmacist must be present in every pharmacy that is conducting business, part-time work may be very easy to acquire in many desirable locations.

- **Clinical Pharmacist**
    $ Salary range: $100, 000–110,000

The clinical pharmacist has multiple roles to ensure the safe and effective use of medications by patients and hospital staff. They may provide medication order verification, monitor, optimal drug selection and recommend dosage regimens as they provide patient care. Clinical pharmacists may participate in hospital rounds with other clinical staff as an integral member of the clinical team. Interestingly, some pharmacists insist that all pharmacists are "clinical" pharmacists...if they are excellent at what they do.[295]

Challenges for a clinical pharmacist might include resolving issues for diseases for which no therapeutic exists, recommending care for patients given the wrong medication or the wrong amount of drug. Clinical pharmacists may have a role in verifying patient medication orders for accuracy and they may be required to document clinical interventions. In the setting of clinical pharmacy, the pharmacist may interact with patients, too. Therefore, the right "personality" is needed to properly care for patients who may range in health from the very ill and uncommunicative to the ambulatory and conversant.

Because the pharmacist is the drug expert, clinical staff will call upon the pharmacist to provide appropriate, comprehensive, and timely responses to drug information requests. If the clinical pharmacist is within a teaching hospital, training students or taking on residents may also be required.

Clinical pharmacists are needed in hospitals (affiliated with a university or not), Veteran's Administration hospitals, and within specialized outpatient clinics (ex. geriatric care centers). In these jobs, a clinical pharmacist can take many roles at multiple levels, from specializing in a particular area of pharmacy to directing the hospital pharmacy and supervising its employees.

- *Academic Pharmacists*
  $ Salary range: $90,000–100,000

These positions in universities may not require a license if the position does not involve providing medical services or patient care.[296] These jobs can Include research, publication of scholarly work, and teaching pharmacy, medical, or other health professional students, depending upon the faculty's area of expertise. Academic pharmacists may also conduct research, publish articles about this work, and attend scientific meetings to share research findings. Academic positions for pharmacists tend to have lower salary ranges than typical pharmacy careers. However, the freedom of an academic environment is a trade-off many pharmacists are willing to make. Another aspect of academia is being surrounded by basic scientists, who can become excellent resources for research assistance and mentoring.

- *Drug Information Specialist/Drug Safety Expert*
  $ Salary range: $50,000–70,000

This position relies on a keen ability to research the scientific literature for answers to drug information questions. Perhaps from this research, this specialist will develop medication-use policies for institutions or improve a healthcare system's adverse-drug-reaction reporting, such as working within a medication safety office. As long as dispensing drugs is not a component of the job description, a pharmacy license is not required.[296-297]

- ***Medical Writer***
  - $ Salary range: $40,000–60,000

Medical or scientific writers work for research universities, pharmaceutical companies, medical device manufacturers, and science or medicine publishing companies.[296, 298-299] Medical or scientific writers must have a mastery of the fundamental aspects of most basic sciences and a significant expertise in the language of clinical medicine. This position usually includes on-the-job training with more experienced and board-certified editors or writers. Juggling multiple deadlines, attention to minute details, and a working knowledge of journal or research proposal guidelines are necessary for this type of work.

- ***Poison Control Pharmacist***
  - $ Salary range: $70,000's

Typically, a positing within a government-funded poison control center requires additional certification above the PharmD, such as board recognition as a Diplomat of the American Board of Toxicologists (DABT). Because toxicology as a discrete subject is not common in pharmacy school programs, this certification would assure the pharmacist of accurate and timely toxicity information about drug and non-drug compounds such as plants, animal venoms, pesticides, and other chemicals people may encounter.[300-301]

Also, and perhaps less well known is that a pharmacist may find employment in an animal poison control center. These may not be entirely funded by the government and they may charge people a small fee for calling and seeking assistance. Again, a firm grasp of toxicology is a must to be competitive and successful in such a unique position. A pharmacy license may also be required.[296, 300-301]

- ***Military Pharmacists***
  - $ Salary range: Various

Pharmacy school graduates are often surprised to learn that the US military needs pharmacists, too.[302] In this special role, the PharmD who is a US citizen will provide pharmacy services in the army, navy, marines, or coast guard to name a few areas. The job may involve dispensing medication, caring for patients in the context of drug therapy management, surveillance and control of scheduled drugs, and pharmacy research.[296, 303-304] Pay for a military pharmacist is highly variable, depending on the branch and what type of duty is performed in addition to the pharmacy aspect. The salary may consist of a starting base pay that increases over time. Also, military pharmacists may receive signing bonuses, retention bonuses, and other increases for special continuing educational achievements.

- **Pharmacist Positions with the FDA**

  $ Salary range: $40,000–95,000

Food and Drug Administration (FDA) pharmacists play important roles in getting drugs to the US market. They may evaluate new drug applications submitted by pharmaceutical companies and participate in decisions for new drug indications. They may work alongside pharmacologists (PhD) to research pharmacokinetics of new drugs and prepare study documents.[296] Pay in the FDA, like other government jobs, is tied to a general schedule (GS) system. This system determines pay ranges based on education and experience. For example, FDA pharmacists enter the job around the GS-9 to GS-13 level of pay and can have salary increases within these grades based on years of service in that schedule. Pay adjustments may be made based on location of the position, as well.

- **FDA Consumer Safety Officer**

  $ Salary range: $60,000–90,000

Also within the FDA, pharmacists are needed to serve as consumer safety officers. In this capacity, the pharmacist will hold a role as a regulatory expert on a team of reviewers. They may contribute to the regulatory requirements of a pharmaceutical company or healthcare center. Safety officers may investigate injury or illness reports arising from an FDA-regulated product. In this job, a pharmacist may advise industry, state, and local leaders or consumers about product safety enforcement policies.

Pharmacists who are well organized and adept at working as a team member on large projects are especially suited for this position. Safety officers holding advanced degrees such as a PharmD will enter the workforce at a higher GS level (GS-11 to GS-13), but they may work alongside employees who are significantly lower in the GS rankings (GS-5 and up), so pay may vary according to education and experience

- **Medication Therapy Management Specialist**

  $ Salary range: $110,000–120,000

With fewer primary healthcare providers specializing in family medicine and geriatric care, along with the scarcity of healthcare resources in rural areas of the US, the pharmacist will be called upon to take more responsibility in delivering patient care.[305] Medication management (MM) is one such responsibility. In this role, the pharmacist can use excellent interpersonal skills to assist patients with medication instructions and compliance.[306-307]

Reimbursement for such important MM services is a popular topic in the healthcare and insurance industry.[308-309] Thus, being vocal in your community about fees for MM services can improve the financial security of members of your profession. MM may evolve as internet-based healthcare becomes more ubiquitous; the pharmacist may conduct telemedicine-type counseling (video over computer) sessions for remote patients who cannot be physically present for the MM consult.[310-311]

- ## Nuclear Pharmacists
     $ Salary range: $100,000–$120,000

Nuclear pharmacists assist with measuring and delivering the diagnostic radioactive or radio-contrast agents used in magnetic resonance imaging, computed tomography, positron emission tomography, and other medical digital imaging techniques.[312] They may also prepare, assure quality of, and distribute specific radioactive cancer ablation products, such as radioactive prostate cancer pellets.[313] Special skills are required for handling biohazards, and this knowledge might be obtained in pharmacy school in the form of an elective course.[314]

- ## Long-term Care/Hospice Pharmacists
     $ Salary range: $70,000–125,000

Often overlooked, assisted living or long-term care facilities for patients who require help with tasks of daily living require pharmacists.[315-316] Pharmacists in these roles may not directly interact with the patients; skilled nurses may instead deliver medications to the patients and assist with MM.[317] The pharmacist dispenses drugs, maintains the formulary for the long-term care center and the pharmacist may be "on call" or required to be available by text or phone for patient emergencies. Also, pharmacists in this setting may develop drug storage and handling policies and may offer patient education.[318]

Hospice, in contrast, is a care system for patients who have been diagnosed as having a potential survival of 6 months or less. This end-of-life care is especially important for maintaining patient dignity and final wishes.[319] A pharmacist can play a monumental role in helping with the last days of a patient in Hospice, recommending therapeutic options that increase patient comfort and peace of mind.[315, 320-321] Students may not know that Hospice organizations train pharmacy students. If this interests you, inquire with your pharmacy program director.[322]

- ### Cancer Center/Chemotherapy Pharmacists
  $ Salary range: $50,000–60,000

Pharmacists who work in cancer centers assist with the delivery of chemotherapy for patients.[323-324] They may prepare the chemotherapy drugs and recommend additional therapeutic options, taking care to monitor drug-drug and drug-illness interactions. Pharmacists are experts in the often-needed parenteral nutrition for cancer patients who cannot tolerate solid foods.[325] They also can contribute to recommending therapeutic strategies that increase patient comfort and reduce the psychical and psychic burden of chemotherapy.[326]

- ### Infusion Therapy Pharmacists
  $ Salary range: $100,000–110,000

Pharmacists specialized infusion therapy may travel to patient homes to administer intravenous drugs such as antibiotics, or they may work within healthcare clinics.[327] Such jobs require additional training to become familiar with the specific products used in infusion therapy.[328] Pharmacists who provide this service enjoy meeting new patients and traveling to different areas to cover their patient base.

- ### Pharmacy Benefit Managers
  $ Salary range: $60,000–80,000

Benefit managers have an unusual but important role in the delivery of healthcare.[329-330] They operate between the employer and the insurance company with respect to coverage and reimbursement amounts for drugs allowed on various employee health plans. At this time, pharmacy benefit managers are networked with more than 200 million patients in the US and to every retail pharmacy in the nation.[331] Benefit managers are seeing increasing participation in resolving drug shortage problems because of their large dispensing operations.[331] A license is not required but a foundation in health insurance is essential. Health plans vary by state and by employer, so responsibilities will vary within this type of job.

- ### Healthcare Information Technology
  $ Salary range: $60,000–95,000

The government mandate for all healthcare providers to have electronic medical records is driving the force of hiring in Healthcare Information Technology (IT).[332-333] A PharmD who elects to pursue a career in IT must have expertise in computer and internet-ready digital devices as well as the infrastructure of the hospital, clinic, or medical office where the IT is required. Also, a thorough knowledge of HIPPA regulations will be part of the

PharmD's professional arsenal when seeking a position in this area which is instrumental in delivering timely patient information.

- **Medical Recruiting/"Headhunter"**

    $ Salary range: $40,000–90,000

Recruiting for medical or pharmaceutical companies is a form of a sales job. You will spend most of the work day on the phone, talking to potential hires for corporations or institutions and negotiating meetings and conferences so that the employer can meet potential employees who may be scientists, nurses, physicians, or other healthcare professionals. Patience, persistence, and an unflappable professional demeanor are absolutely required for a job such as this, and the high turnover rate within the field may suggest that this is not an appropriate job for every type of personality.

- **The Pharmaceutical Industry Workforce**

Within the pharmaceutical or medical industry, PharmDs can find jobs that ultimately provide a product or service to hospitals, clinicians, or other medical providers or facilities.[334-335] These products may include drugs, medical devices and supplies, or medical or clinical software. A PharmD may begin at an entry-level position but management careers are possible.[336] A position within the pharmaceutical industry may include marketing, research, product development, quality control, sales (or directing the sales force), and company administration. Here, the graduate with a dual PharmD/MBA may be a perfect fit for such employment.[296, 337-339]

- **Industry: Pharmaceutical Liaison**

    $ Salary range: 95,000–110,000 with opportunities for bonuses

Within the pharmaceutical industry are medical science liaisons. These people may hold a PhD or a PharmD. Their purpose within the company is to educate physicians, nurses, and perhaps the pharmaceutical company's sales representatives about the drugs and devices made by the company. Some travel may be required for visiting and speaking with healthcare professionals or training drug representatives.

- **Industry: Pharmaco-economist**

    $ Salary range: $100,000–125,000

Pharmaco-economics is an essential area of interest for pharmaceutical companies. PharmDs who aspire to hold positions in this area may conduct research to identify, measure, and compare data for pharmaceutical products and services. They may conduct cost-benefit analyses to assess new medicines against their expected benefits. Pharmaco-economists or health/medical economists, as they are also called, usually have a PhD or a PharmD, with some type of training with an economic focus, depending on the level of specialization within the field.

- *Industry: Pharmaceutical Sales/Medical Device Representative*
  - $ Salary range: $40,000–70,000

Pharmaceutical sales representation ("drug rep") does not necessarily require an advanced degree, and many sales representatives may only have a Bachelor's degree. Again, this position requires stamina and strong salesmanship skills, especially with the changing environment of pharmaceutical sales and healthcare. Increasingly, laws are emerging that restrict the privileges of sales representatives with respect to contacting and interacting with healthcare professionals. Also, travel is a certainty, although some representatives can request to work a specific "territory" to minimize driving time. Naturally, this position requires that the representative have excruciatingly accurate and intimate knowledge about the drug or device they are promoting.

CHAPTER 12

IN THE TRENCHES

COMMENTS FROM CURRENT PHARMACISTS

Even if you are committed to a pharmacy program and an eventual PharmD, obtaining additional input from unique sources can be either helpful or scarily insightful. Frequently, the advice you receive about the pharmacy profession is given in a well-meaning and highly positive manner. So, less attractive aspects of the job might not be discussed at all. After all, few people are willing to re-hash details of truly bad days and unruly patients.

Thus, to fill in the potential informational gaps in this area, comments are presented below from current pharmacists who host online postings and discussions (weblogs) about their profession. These comments have been chosen for diversity of viewpoint. When profanity or denigrating language was to describe patients or the profession, such comments have been edited to decrease the offensive nature of the commentary, while preserving the author's tone.

> R℞ **" *I realized that all of us who work with the public are in the same boat. We deal with the same (censored) the same impatient (censored), the same (censored) who (censored) that their prescription isn't ready yet....* "**

Blog citations are given for each commentary piece as appropriate. * Keep in mind that even professionals are more prone to speak out/blog when they are unhappy. Complaints simply get more vocalizations. Oddly, when people are content with a process or situation, they make fewer remarks. Therefore, remember that when viewing statements made by current pharmacists, they are voicing frustrations for your edification *and entertainment*. They likely also have wonderful, fulfilling experiences as pharmacists, which simply do not make the blog because they are "less interesting" or less humorous.

Here they are:

"At work, I have to constantly defer to other people. Corporate makes a new policy, and I'm expected to carry it out. There's no room for argument, no room for disagreement."[340]

"I once had a lady ask me, 'Are the drugs fresh?' As if pharmaceuticals were poultry. 'Ma'am," I replied, 'you will expire before these drugs will.' Didn't get fired. True story."[341]

"...Community pharmacy pushes pharmacists away from our instinctive patient-care thought processes. We simply aren't judged by our work as much as we're held accountable for the performance of a store or geographical area."[342]

"I did have a position at a regional grocery chain (where we filled 120-180 scripts/day) where I was able to talk to my patients. I got to know my patients and their families. And when warranted, I would be blunt with them. They understood that it was coming from somebody who cared for them and wanted to see them healthy. It has been 3 years since I left that position and I still get stopped at football games and

---

Statements presented in this chapter do not represent the thoughts or opinions of the author or the author's employer.

swim meets by my former patients who thank me for how I helped them with their medical conditions."[343]

"I am struggling with (the fact that) a former classmate in pharmacy school... made a deal in pleading guilty in a case that I have had a hard time understanding. (He) was the type of student in our class who was a man of character...one of the good guys....He has had some legal trouble in which there was some sort of federal charge brought against him for distributing (Oxycontin) from his pharmacy...(he) is going to likely go to prison for around five years or so, and my heart breaks for him."[295]

"I can always tell when a patient of mine works with the public. They are pretty nice, easy going, and realize that sometimes (censored) happens. They patiently wait for their prescription, and use the foreign words we never hear like 'please' and 'thank you'. They are mindful of our time and actually show appreciation to the service that we give them. How foreign is that in a pharmacy?"[342]

"As pharmacists, we're told that we have to be constantly vigilant for signs of drug abuse and misuse...our license could be on the line if we don't document that we at least tried to verify any suspicious prescriptions. However, prescribers have free reign to allow patients to basically write their own prescriptions for narcotics."[340]

"This profession has fallen so far that its (sic) not recognizable to what it was when I started. Patient care has been replaced with performance goals for Script counts, labor models, inventory limits, and vaccination quotas."[344]

"I realized that all of us who work with the public are in the same boat. We deal with the same (censored) the same impatient (censored), the same (censored) who (censored) that their prescription isn't ready yet...."[342]

"...Most patients pay for prescription medications using some sort of complicated third party insurance and you have a recipe for further confusion. Patients simply don't understand drug prices."[342]

"With customers, I'm either the drug expert who dispenses medical advice, or I'm the customer service representative who has to basically kiss (censored). There's not a whole lot of genuine back and forth. The customers don't challenge my knowledge, and I can't challenge them when I think they're being stupid."[340]

"...The most important aspect of retail pharmacy isn't all the drug-drug interactions, the kinetics...knowing the pharmacology of benzodiazepines, or even the rationale behind giving someone an ACE-I in CHF; its dealing with the unwashed masses."[342]

"Your techs and your clerks are your work-family. Unless you want to be counting out everything, ringing up people yourself, and screening all your own phone-calls yourself, treat them with respect and kindness."[342]

"My manager was nearly 1/3rd my age...out of pharmacy school for only a year. She was nice, but had no idea how to be a leader, talk to customers, or manage employees. She was offended when older people wanted to talk to me. She treated me like an old codger."[344]

"Many new pharmacists are far from humble about their newly minted abilities. I speak from experience: Pending passing of my state board and law exam, I bought myself a 1972 Corvette as a graduation present. It matched my attitude perfectly. I was downright brash about my skills. I was good, but nowhere near as good as I am today. Eighteen years of clinical experience have taught me as much as my education of my beloved (deleted text) did."[341]

"The company rules were oppressive...a long list of tasks to do, reports to keep, forms to fill out each day-week-month, and insufficient time to do it. Tho *(sic)* it was officially against the rules to work off the clock, they knew we had to do it to keep up with their requirements...."[344]

"I don't LOVE most people anymore. I am pretty sure it has been beaten out of me after 26 years of retail pharmacy."[344]

"The annual Gallup survey of professional honesty and ethics for 2012 was released this month. This survey shows pharmacists scoring their highest score ever. In fact, 75% of respondents rated the honesty and ethical standards of pharmacists either highly or very highly. During the 3 decades Gallup has conducted this poll, pharmacists have routinely ranked near the top."[345]

CONCLUSION

The career trajectory to a job in pharmacy is not often clear or straightforward. Having the right information at the correct time is an enormous advantage. The most prepared students are those who plan well in advance, perhaps before college. This enables the student to enroll in the necessary prerequisites and apply for a college of pharmacy that is the best fits and offers the most desirable choices to the student.

Judicious study habits and professional behavior ensure that a student graduates with excellent letters of recommendations from his faculty and a sense of pride and belonging to that school of pharmacy. As an alumnus, the new pharmacy professional will have a lifetime connection to his college as he embarks on a new role in his community, serving patients as a valuable and visible member of the healthcare team.

BIBLIOGRAPHY

1. Kinnard WJ. American Schools of Pharmacy: Their Organization & Administration. American Journal of Pharmaceutical Education 1980.

2. Popovich NG, Boh LE. A Review of the Externship Experience in Pharmacy Education. American Journal of Pharmaceutical Education 1991.

3. Robers PA. The Externship Experience: A Comparison of Externs' & Preceptors' Beliefs about Professionalism. American Journal of Pharmaceutical Education 1989.

4. Friesner D, Scott D. Identifying characteristics that allow pharmacy technicians to assume unconventional roles in the pharmacy. Journal of the American Pharmacists Association 2010;50:686.

5. Kalman MK, Witkowski DE, Ogawa GS. Increasing pharmacy productivity by expanding the role of pharmacy technicians. American Journal of Hospital Pharmacy 1992;49:84-9.

6. Skrocki R. Pharmacy computerization: a rational step forward. Computing & Healthcare 1983;4:28, 32.

7. Jaschik S. Hope on PhD Attrition Rates: Except in Humanities. Washington DC; 2007 December 7, 2007.

8. Shannon SB, Bradley-Baker LR, Truong HA. Pharmacy residencies & dual degrees as complementary or competitive advanced training opportunities. American Journal of Pharmacy Education;76:145.

9. Chumney EC, Ragucci KR, Jones KJ. Impact of a dual PharmD/MBA degree on graduates' academic performance, career opportunities, & earning potential. American Journal of Pharmacy Education 2008;72:26.

10. Matzke GR. Regarding "Status of PharmD/PhD programs in colleges of pharmacy". American Journal of Pharmacy Education 2006;70:93; author reply

11. Filerman GL, Komaridis KL. The pharmacy leadership competency gap: diagnosis & prescription. The Journal of Health Administration Education 2007;24:117-34.

12. Gourley DR, Rowell C, Wingate L, et al. Status of PharmD/PhD programs in colleges of pharmacy: the University of Tennessee dual PharmD/PhD program. American Journal of Pharmacy Education 2006;70:44.

13. Chumney EC, Ragucci KR. Student satisfaction & academic performance in a dual PharmD/MBA degree program. American Journal of Pharmacy Education 2006;70:29.

14. Senft SL, Thompson C, Blumenschein K. Dual degree programs at the University of Kentucky College of Pharmacy. American Journal of Pharmacy Education 2008;72:12.

15. Academic Pharmacy's Vital Statistics. 2012. (Accessed on March 1, 2013, at *http://www.aacp.org/about/pages/vitalstats.aspx.*)

16. Compare US Pharmacy Programs. 2013. (Accessed on March 25, 2013 at http://www.aacp.org/resources/student/pharmacyforyou/admissions/Pages/compareuspharmacyprograms.aspx.)

17. National Institutes of Health. NIH Ranking of Schools of Pharmacy; 2012.

18. US News & World Report. Pharmacy Rankings; 2012.

19. Texas Tech University Health Sciences Center School of Pharmacy 2013. (Accessed at *http://schoolpages.pharmcas.org/publishedsurvey/503.*)

20. Beca JP, Browne F, Valdebenito C, Bataszew A, Martinez MJ. [Student patient relationship from the patient's point of view]. Revista medica de Chile 2006;134:955-9.

21. Gilbert HC, Rich BA, Fine P. Quality of care, teaching responsibilities, & patients' preferences. Pain medicine (Malden, Mass 2004;5:206-11.

22. Cohen DL, McCullough LB, Kessel RW, Apostolides AY, Heiderich KJ, Alden ER. A national survey concerning the ethical aspects of informed consent & role of medical students. Journal of medical education 1988;63:821-9.

23. Cohen DL, McCullough LB, Kessel RW, Apostolides AY, Alden ER, Heiderich KJ. Informed consent policies governing medical students' interactions with patients. Journal of medical education 1987;62:789-98.

24. McGrath SH, Snyder ME, Duenas GG, Pringle JL, Smith RB, McGivney MS. Physician perceptions of pharmacist-provided medication therapy management: qualitative analysis. Journal of the American Pharmacy Association (2003) 2010;50:67-71.

25. Taylor DA, Taylor JN. The pharmacy student population: applications received 2010-11, degrees conferred 2010-11, fall 2011 enrollments. American Journal of Pharmacy Education;76:S2.

26. Taylor DA, Patton JM. The pharmacy student population: applications received 2009-10, degrees conferred 2009-10, fall 2010 enrollments. American Journal of Pharmacy Education;75:S3.

27. Taylor DA, Patton JM. The pharmacy student population: applications received 2008-09, degrees conferred 2008-09, fall 2009 enrollments. American Journal of Pharmacy Education;74:S2.

28. Taylor DA, Patton JM. The pharmacy student population: applications received 2007-08, degrees conferred 2007-08, fall 2008 enrollments. American Journal of Pharmacy Education 2009;73 Suppl:S2.

29. Patton JM. The pharmacy student population: applications received 2004-05, degrees conferred 2004-05, fall 2005 enrollments. American Journal of Pharmacy Education 2006;70:S04.

30. Kirk KW. Women in male-dominated professions. American Journal of Hospital Pharmacy 1982;39:2089-93.

31. Lavallee D. URI pharmacy student is grandfather, full-time EMT. In. Kingston, RI: University of Rhode Island; 2006.

32. Pharmacy School Admissions Requirements. A Partner Site of The Student Doctor Network: http://pharmapplicants.com/, 2010. (Accessed May 2013 at http://pharmapplicants.com/Detailed_Pharmacy_ School_Information.pdf.)

33. American Association of Colleges of Pharmacy. Pharmacy School Admission Requirements 2011-2012; 2013.

34. Plan of Study for the Prepharmacy Program at Valparaiso University. 2013. (Accessed May 2013 at http://www.pharmacy.purdue.edu/academics /prepharm/off-campus/Valpo.pdf.)

35. Rogers J. Plan of Study for the Prepharmacy Program at Wabash College. 2013.

36. Chatterjee A, Talwalkar JS. An innovative medical Spanish curriculum for resident doctors. Medical Education;46:521-2.

37. Copeland H, Jones M, Duran MA, et al. Teaching medical Spanish on the surgery clerkship: a response to the increased demand for Spanish proficiency among physicians. The American surgeon;77:1715-7.

38. Reuland DS, Slatt LM, Aleman MA, Fernandez A, Dewalt D. Effect of Spanish language immersion rotations on medical student Spanish fluency. Family Medicine;44:110-6.

39. Frick LJ, Frick JL, Coffman RE, Dey S. Student stress in a three-year doctor of pharmacy program using a mastery learning educational model. American Journal of Pharmacy Education 2011;75:64.

40. Ramirez E. More High School Kids Take College Classes. US News & World Report: Education 2008 June 26, 2008.

41. Clark K. Community Colleges: Cheaper but Not Necessarily Better. US News & World Report: Education 2009 January 9, 2012.

42. Barnett E, Hughes K. Community College & High School Partnerships; 2009.

43. Olson A. PCAT Basics: Purpose, Structure, & Administration. Bloomington, MN: NCS Pearson; 2012.

44. Meagher DG, Lin A, Perez CD. Predicting pharmacy students' performance from PCAT scores: a further analysis of predictive validity study data. American Journal of Pharmacy Education 2007;71:101.

45. Meagher DG, Pan T, Perez CD. Predicting performance in the first-year of pharmacy school. American Journal of Pharmacy Education 2011;75:81.

46. Wallman A, Vaudan C, Sporrong SK. Communications training in pharmacy education, 1995-2010. American Journal of Pharmacy Education 2013;77:36.

47. Conway JM, Ahmed GF. A pharmacotherapy capstone course to advance pharmacy students' clinical documentation skills. American Journal of Pharmacy Education 2012;76:134.

48. Lonie JM, Rahim H. Does the addition of writing into a pharmacy communication skills course significantly impact student communicative learning outcomes? A pilot study. Journal of Pharmacy Practice 2010;23:525-30.

49. Johnston P, Afflerbach P. Centrality & Reading Comprehension Test Questions; 1982.

50. Schilling GV. Test Questions Employed by Science Teachers in Public Junior High & Middle Schools of Louisiana; 1972.

51. Lei SA, Bartlett KA, Gorney SE, Herschbach TR. Resistance to Reading Compliance among College Students: Instructors' Perspectives. College Student Journal.

52.   Damashek R. Six Step Process to Helping Students Produce Quality Writing; 2003.

53.   PharmCAS frequently asked questions. 2013. (Accessed May 2013 at https://portal.pharmcas.org/applicants2013/faq/pcas_faqs.shtml.)

54.   Foster AL. Plagiarism-Detection Tool Creates Legal Quandary. Chronicle of Higher Education 2002.

55.   Atkins T, Nelson G. Plagiarism & the Internet: Turning the Tables. English Journal 2001.

56.   Grand Canyon University. Turnitin: Making Intelligent Decisions about Students' Originality Reports; 2011.

57.   Kiersma ME, Plake KS, Mason HL. Relationship between admission data & pharmacy student involvement in extracurricular activities. American Journal of Pharmacy Education 2011;75:155.

58.   Doutre WH, Buesing AS, Ingrim NB, Guernsey BG, Hokanson JA, Galvan E. Behaviorally anchored ranking scale versus letters of recommendation for evaluating residency candidates. American Journal of Hospital Pharmacy 1984;41:2367-70.

59.   —. Scott v. Savers Property & Casualty Insurance Company. In: 663 NW 2d 715. Wisconsin; 2003.

60.   Sain v. Cedar Rapids Community School District 626. In: NW 2d 115 Iowa; 2011.

61.   Van Dusen V. Liability & litigation risks for colleges & schools of pharmacy. American Journal of Pharmacy Education 2011;75:52.

62.   Duncan-Hewitt WC. Designing Admissions Criteria: A Framework. American Journal of Pharmaceutical Education 1996.

63.   Fjortoft NF. College Student Employment: Opportunity or Deterrent?; 1995.

64.   Zorek JA, Sprague JE, Popovich NG. Bulimic learning. American Journal of Pharmacy Education 2010;74:157.

65.   Hidayat L, Vansal S, Kim E, Sullivan M, Salbu R. Pharmacy student absenteeism & academic performance. American Journal of Pharmacy Education 2012;76:8.

66.   Davenport WS. A Study of the Relationship between Attendance & Grades of Three Business Law Classes at Broome Community College; 1990.

67. van Schalkwyk S, Menkveld H, Ruiters J. What's the Story with Class Attendance? First-Year Students: Statistics & Perspectives. South African Journal of Higher Education.

68. Buxton EC, De Muth JE. Pharmacists' perceptions of a live continuing education program comparing distance learning versus local learning. Research in Social & Administrative Pharmacy 2013;9:230-5.

69. Ried LD. A distance education course in statistics. American Journal of Pharmacy Education 2010;74:172.

70. Lenz TL, Monaghan MS, Wilson AF, Tilleman JA, Jones RM, Hayes MM. Using performance-based assessments to evaluate parity between a campus & distance education pathway. American Journal of Pharmacy Education 2006;70:90.

71. Steinberg M, Morin AK. Academic performance in a pharmacotherapeutics course sequence taught synchronously on two campuses using distance education technology. American Journal of Pharmacy Education 2011;75:150.

72. Zapantis A, Maniscalco-Feichtl M. Teaching in a distance education program. American Journal of Health System Pharmacists 2008;65:912-20.

73. Ward B. The Best of Both Worlds: A Hybrid Statistics Course. Journal of Statistics Education 2004.

74. Congdon HB, Nutter DA, Charneski L, Butko P. Impact of hybrid delivery of education on student academic performance & the student experience. American Journal of Pharmacy Education 2009;73:121.

75. Adams J, Defleur M. The Acceptability of Online Degrees Earned as a Credential for Obtaining Employment. Communication Education 2006;55.

76. Wellen A. Degrees of Acceptance The New York Times 2006 July 30, 2006.

77. PharmD Distance Pathway. 2012. (Accessed May 2013 at http://spahp.creighton.edu/admission/pharmacy/pharmd-distance-pathway.)

78. Stolte SK, Richard C, Rahman A, Kidd RS. Student pharmacists' use & perceived impact of educational technologies. American Journal of Pharmacy Education 2011;75:92.

79. Larkin HE. "But They Won't Come to Lectures..." The Impact of Audio Recorded Lectures on Student Experience & Attendance. Australasian Journal of Educational Technology.

80. Yoon C, Sneddon J. Student Perceptions of Effective Use of Tablet PC Recorded Lectures in Undergraduate Mathematics Courses. International Journal of Mathematical Education in Science & Technology.

81. Catanese V, Aronson P. A case of student cheating. Virtual Mentor 2005;7.

82. Chaput de Saintonge DM, Pavlovic A. Cheating. Medical Education 2004;38:8-9.

83. Chiodo GT, Tolle SW. Student cheating: ethical issues. Dentistry (American Student Dental Association) 1994;14:21-6.

84. Chambers DW. Evil games. The Journal of the American College of Dentists 2010;77:35-43.

85. Saulsbury MD, Brown UJ, 3rd, Heyliger SO, Beale RL. Effect of dispositional traits on pharmacy students' attitude toward cheating. American Journal of Pharmacy Education;75:69.

86. Neville L. Do economic equality & generalized trust inhibit academic dishonesty? Evidence from state-level search-engine queries. Psychological science;23:339-45.

87. Harding TS, Carpenter DD, Finelli CJ, Passow HJ. Does academic dishonesty relate to unethical behavior in professional practice? An exploratory study. Science & engineering ethics 2004;10:311-24.

88. Harper MG. High tech cheating. Nurse Education in Practice 2006;6:364-71.

89. Karlins M, Hargis E, Balfour A. Student ethics in an era of personal entitlement. Psychological Reports 2012;110:144-8.

90. Sierles FS, Kushner BD, Krause PB. A controlled experiment with a medical student honor system. Journal of medical education 1988;63:705-12.

91. Finn G, Sawdon M, Clipsham L, McLachlan J. Peer estimation of lack of professionalism correlates with low Conscientiousness Index scores. Medical Education 2009;43:960-7.

92. Coulehan J, Williams PC, McCrary SV, Belling C. The best lack all conviction: biomedical ethics, professionalism, & social responsibility. Camb Q Healthc Ethics 2003;12:21-38.

93. Patient: missing link to professionalism. Hospitals 1971;45:93-102 passim.

94. Ricker RH. Chain drugstores & professionalism. American Journal of Hospital Pharmacy 1977;34:232.

95. Smith A. The Cost of Professionalism. Journal of the Oklahoma State Medical Assocation 1964;57:399-403.

96. Ahmadi K, Ahmad Hassali MA. Professionalism in pharmacy: a continual societal & intellectual challenge. American Journal of Pharmacy Education 2012;76:72.

97. Carr D, Davies T, Lavin A. The Effect of Business Faculty Attire on Student Perceptions of the Quality of Instruction & Program Quality. College Student Journal 2009.

98. Khanfar NM, Zapantis A, Alkhateeb FM, Clauson KA, Beckey C. Patient Attitudes Toward Community Pharmacist Attire. Journal of Pharmacy Practice 2012.

99. Bentley JP, Stroup LJ, Wilkin NE, Bouldin AS. Patient evaluations of pharmacist performance with variations in attire & communication levels. Journal of the American Pharmacy Association (2003) 2005;45:600-7.

100. Khanfar NM, Zapantis A, Alkhateeb FM, Clauson KA, Beckey C. Patient Attitudes Toward Community Pharmacist Attire. Journal of Pharmacy Practice.

101. Cain J, Scott DR, Akers P. Pharmacy students' Facebook activity & opinions regarding accountability & e-professionalism. American Journal of Pharmacy Education 2009;73:104.

102. Cain J, Scott DR, Smith K. Use of social media by residency program directors for resident selection. American Journal of Health System Pharmacists 2010;67:1635-9.

103. Rutter PM, Duncan G. Pharmacy professionalism & the digital age. International Journal of Pharmacy Practice 2011;19:431-4.

104. Metzger AH, Finley KN, Ulbrich TR, McAuley JW. Pharmacy faculty members' perspectives on the student/faculty relationship in online social networks. American Journal of Pharmacy Education 2010;74:188.

105. Mattingly TJ, 2nd, Cain J, Fink JL, 3rd. Pharmacists on Facebook: online social networking & the profession. Journal of the American Pharmacy Association (2003) 2010;50:424-7.

106. Bongartz J, Vang C, Havrda D, Fravel M, McDanel D, Farris KB. Student pharmacist, pharmacy resident, & graduate student perceptions of social interactions with faculty members. American Journal of Pharmacy Education 2011;75:180.

107. Fingerman KL, Cheng Y-P, Wesselmann ED, Zarit S, Furstenberg F, Birditt KS. Helicopter Parents & Landing Pad Kids: Intense Parental Support of Grown Children. Journal of Marriage & Family.

108. Pricer WF. At Issue: Helicopter Parents & Millennial Students, an Annotated Bibliography. Community College Enterprise 2008.

109. Lum L. Handling "Helicopter Parents". Diverse: Issues in Higher Education 2006.

110. Lippmann S, Bulanda RE, Wagenaar TC. Student Entitlement: Issues & Strategies for Confronting Entitlement in the Classroom & Beyond. College Teaching 2009.

111. Buckley MR, Novicevic MM, Halbesleben JRB, Harvey M. Course Management & Students' Expectations: Theory-Based Considerations. International Journal of Educational Management 2004.

112. Markoe M. A Renaissance of Rudeness. The Wall Street Journal 2011 May 11, 2011.

113. Broekemier GM. A Comparison of Two-Year & Four-Year Adult Students: Motivations To Attend College & the Importance of Choice Criteria. Journal of Marketing for Higher Education 2002.

114. Swenson C. Customers & Markets: The Cuss Words of Academe. Change 1998.

115. Rayburn W, Shain R. Ownership of Course Materials as a Tool in Faculty Recruitment; 2000.

116. Achacoso MV. What do you mean my grade is not an A?" An investigation of academic entitlement, causal attributions, & self-regulation in college students. Austin, Texas: The University of Texas at Austin; 2002.

117. Doyle R. Dumbing down. Scientific American 2006;295:32.

118. Horseman RE. Dumbing down of America. Journal of the California Dental Association 2002;30:946, 5.

119. Mowa R, Alcolado J. Medical degrees with honours; the 'dumbing down' of undergraduate examinations? Clinical Medicine (London, England) 2004;4:381-3.

120. Warren JR. Grade inflation. Science New York, NY 1976;191:340c.

121. Howland HC. Grade inflation. Science New York, NY 1976;191:340.

122. Pear JJ. Grade inflation. Science New York, NY 1976;191:340c.

123. Shearin KK. Grade inflation. Science New York, NY 1976;191:340b.

124. Fighting grade inflation. Science New York, NY 1994;264:1255.

125. Shoemaker JK, DeVos M. Are we a gift shop? A perspective on grade inflation. The Journal of nursing education 1999;38:394-8; discussion 8-9.

126. Denison RF. Grade inflation: students seek it, funders reward it. Nature 2004;432:549.

127. Rojstaczer S. Grade inflation keeps the customers happy. Nature 2004;432:549.

128. Scanlan JM, Care WD. Grade inflation: should we be concerned? The Journal of Nursing Education 2004;43:475-8.

129. Hill WT, Jr., McClain PR. Education needs of the black pharmacy student. Journal of the American Pharmacy Association 1973;13:80-2.

130. Eichorn L. Reasonable Accommodations & Awkward Compromises: Issues Concerning Learning Disabled Students & Professional Schools in the Law School Context. Journal of Law & Education 1997.

131. Getzel EEE, Wehman PE. Going to College: Expanding Opportunities for People with Disabilities. Brookes Publishing Company 2005.

132. Walhof R. The Blind in Medical Professions. Future Reflections 1985 July-Sept 1985.

133. Gave K. Blind Pharmacist is Poison Specialist. The Times-News 1983 March 26, 1983.

134. Pitts L. Don't Lower the Bar on Education Standards. The Miami Herald 2012 November 24, 2012.

135. Barrett DJ. The evolving organizational structure of academic health centers: the case of the University of Florida. Academic Medicine 2008;83:804-8.

136. Spahlinger DA, Pai CW, Waldinger MB, Billi JE, Wicha MS. New organizational & funds flow models for an academic cancer center. Academic Medicine 2004;79:623-7.

137. Ovseiko PV, Davies SM, Buchan AM. Organizational models of emerging academic health science centers in England. Academic Medicine 2010;85:1282-9.

138. Newhouse RP. Expert opinion: challenges & opportunities for academic & organizational partnership in evidence-based nursing practice. Journal of Nursing Administration 2006;36:441-5.

139. Lobas JG. Leadership in academic medicine: capabilities & conditions for organizational success. The American Journal of Medicine 2006;119:617-21.

140. Wilkes MS, Srinivasan M, Flamholtz E. Effective organizational control: implications for academic medicine. Academic Medicine 2005;80:1054-63.

141. Ohvall RA. Pharmacy faculty with nonpharmacy backgrounds: academic employment opportunities. American Journal of Pharmacy Education 1977;41:389-91.

142. Tobin GA, Weinberg AK. Volume II: Religious beliefs & behavior of college faculty. Institute for Jewish & Community Research; 2007.

143. The Pew Research Center. Scientific achievements less prominent than a decade ago. public praises science; scientists faculty public, Media; 2009.

144. Paik C, Broedel-Zaugg K. Pharmacy students' opinions on civility & preferences regarding professors. American Journal of Pharmacy Education 2006;70:88.

145. Boaz M. Faculty Tenure: To hold or not to hold. Educational Research Quarterly 1985.

146. Baez B. Affirmative action, hate speech, & tenure: narratives about race, law, & the Academy; 2002.

147. Hamilton NW. Peer Review: The linchpin of academic freedom & tenure. Academe 1997.

148. Jaschik S. The new class monitors. Inside Higher Education 2006 January 18, 2006

149. Holman J. University reacts to controversial video of professor. Daily Trojan 2013.

150. The Associated Press. Columbia professor strips, shows 9/11 tape during class. The Associate Press 2013 February 19, 2013.

151. Jane Doe v. Norwalk Community College. 248 FRD 372 In. Connecticut; 2007.

152. Foral PA, Turner PD, Monaghan MS, et al. Faculty & student expectations & perceptions of e-mail communication in a campus & distance doctor of pharmacy program. American Journal of Pharmacy Education 2010;74:191.

153. Kelly PJ. Age of entitlement: How does physician assistant education change to accommodate the generation Y student? J Physician Assist Educ 2010;21:47-51.

154. Latif DA, Alkhateeb FM. Pharmacy faculty retirement at colleges & schools of pharmacy in the United States & Canada. American Journal of Pharmacy Education 2012;76:4.

155. Amato D, Quirt I. Lecture handouts of projected slides in a medical course. Medical Teacher 1991.

156. Brook C. Immediacy of Course Materials. Teaching at a Distance 1979.

157. Hofstad ME. Enhancing Student Learning in Online Courses; 2003.

158. Carle AC, Jaffee D, Miller D. Engaging College Science Students & Changing Academic Achievement with Technology: A Quasi-Experimental Preliminary Investigation. Computers & Education 2009.

159. Young JR. Caught (Unfortunately) on Tape. Chronicle of Higher Education 2009.

160. Gwinn JF, Beal LF. On-Line Computer Testing: Implementation & Endorsement. Journal of Educational Technology Systems 1988.

161. Hong H, Kinshuk, He X, Patel A, Jesshope C. Trends in web-based learning environments. Distance Education Report 2001.

162. Clay B. Is this a trick question? a short guide to writing effective test questions. Kansas Curriculum Center; 2001.

163. Varma S. Preliminary Item statistics using point-biserial correlation & p-values. Morgan Hill, CA; —.

164. Cain J, Romanelli F, Smith KM. Academic entitlement in pharmacy education. American Journal of Pharmacy Education 2012;76:189.

165. Rosovsky H, Hartley M. Evaluation & the academy: are we doing the right thing? grade inflation & letters of recommendation; 2002.

166. Johnson V. Grade Inflation: A Crisis in College Education. New York, New York: Springer; 2003.

167. Against grade inflation. Nature 2004;431:723.

168. Rakoczy K. Academy Report Reveals Grade Inflation Nationwide. The Harvard Crimson 2002 February 01, 2002.

169. Johnson V. Teacher course evaluations & student grades: an academic tango. Chance 2002;15:9-16.

170. Michalowsky A. Computer science students successfully boycott class final The Johns Hopkins News-letter 2013 January 31, 2013

171. Marklein MB. A call for an end to grade inflation. USA Today 2002.

172. Osborn E. Should you offer extra credit. The Chronicle of Higher Education 2011.

173. The University of Michigan F. Surviving college; 2007.

174. A Journey through My Life's Goal of being a Legal Drug Dealer. 2011. (Accessed May 2013 at *http://www.iwanttobeapharmacist.com/*.)

175. The Pharamcy Student Blog. 2013. (Accessed May 2013 at *http://pharmacyschoolforums.com/blog/*.)

176. Year One of UCSF Pharmacy School. 2007. (Accessed May 2013 at *http://ucsfpharmacy.blogspot.com/*.)

177. RX to life at PSCP. 2013. (Accessed May 2013 at http://rxtolifeatpcsp.blogspot.com/2013/05/first-year-of-pharmacy-school.html.)

178. Godog Blog: University of Minnesota College of Pharmacy Blog. 2013. (Accessed May 2013 at *http://godogblog.net/page/2/*.)

179. Godog Blog: University of Minnesota College of Pharmacy Blog. 2013. (Accessed May 2013 at *http://godogblog.net/page/2/*.)

180. Restless until I Rest in Thee. 2012. (Accessed May 2013 at http://agnes1990.blogspot.com/2012/01/little-bit-about-my-pharmacy-school.html.)

181. Self-Assigned Seating. 2013. (Accessed May 2013 at http://connect.ashp.org/Blogs/ViewBlogs/?BlogKey=9db9323d-8e0a-4938-a736-66a42189117b.)

182. Kiersma ME, Plake KS, Mason HL. Relationship between admission data & pharmacy student involvement in extracurricular activities. American Journal of Pharmacy Education;75:155.

183. Kiersma ME, Plake KS, Newton GD, Mason HL. Factors affecting prepharmacy students' perceptions of the professional role of pharmacists. American Journal of Pharmacy Education;74:161.

184. Jacobs TF, Manor SM. Effect of a seminar on pharmacy student attitudes toward residency training. American Journal of Health System Pharmacists 2008;65:1358-62.

185. Brown DL, Ferrill MJ, Pankaskie MC. White coat ceremonies in US schools of pharmacy. Ann Pharmacother 2003;37:1414-9.

186. Chen JJ. The white coat. American Journal of Health System Pharmacists 2003;60:611.

187. Nahata MC. Reflections shared at white coat ceremonies. Ann Pharmacother;46:1430-1.

188. Rapport F, Doel MA, Hutchings HA, et al. Eleven themes of patient-centred professionalism in community pharmacy: innovative approaches to consulting. Int Journal of Pharmacy Practice 2010;18:260-8.

189. RX to life at PSCP. 2013. (Accessed May 2013 at http://rxtolifeatpcsp. blogspot.com/2013/05/first-year-of-pharmacy-school.html.)

190. Lasts & Firsts. 2013. (Accessed May 2013 at http://connect.ashp. org/Blogs/ViewBlogs/?BlogKey=9db9323d-8e0a-4938-a736-66a42189117b.)

191. Life as a Pharmacy Student. 2013. (Accessed May 2013 at http://audiblerx.blogspot.com/2013/06/life-as-pharmacy-student.html?utm_source=feedburner&utm_medium=feed&utm_campaign=Feed%3A+audiblerx+%28AuibleRx%2C+Medication+information+you+listen+to.%29.)

192. Skrabal MZ, Jones RM, Nemire RE, et al. National survey of volunteer pharmacy preceptors. American Journal of Pharmacy Education 2008;72:112.

193. Skrabal MZ, Jones RM, Walters RW, et al. National survey of volunteer pharmacy preceptors: effects of region, practice setting, & population density on responses. Journal of Pharmacy Practice 2010;23:265-72.

194. Skrabal MZ, Kahaleh AA, Nemire RE, et al. Preceptors' perspectives on benefits of precepting student pharmacists to students, preceptors, & the profession. Journal of the American Pharmacy Association (2003) 2006;46:605-12.

195. Truong C, Wyllie A, Bailie T, Austin Z. A needs assessment study of hospital pharmacy residency preceptors. Can J Hospital Pharmacy 2012;65:202-8.

196. Teagarden JR. When preceptors fail their students. American Journal of Pharmacy Education 2010;74:176e.

197. Tofade T, Chou S, Foushee L, Caiola SM, Eckel S. Continuing professional development training program among pharmacist preceptors & nonpreceptors. Journal of the American Pharmacy Association (2003) 2010;50:730-5.

198. Smith KM, Phelps PK, Mazur JE, May JR. Relationships between colleges of pharmacy & academic medical centers. American Journal of Health System Pharmacists 2008;65:1750-4.

199. Investigational Drug Services Rotation. 2013. (Accessed May 2013 at http://connect.ashp.org/Blogs/ViewBlogs/?BlogKey=2826fd00-e32b-45a4-951a-ebe2691e45cd.)

200. NAPLEX Blueprint. 2013. (Accessed May 2013 at *http://www.nabp.net/programs/examination/naplex/naplex-blueprint.*)

201. Residency Directory. 2013. (Accessed May 2013 at *www.ashp.org/ResidencyDirectory (http://www.ashp.org/menu/Accreditation/ResidencyDirectory.aspx).*)

202. Residency & Fellowship Directory. 2013. (Accessed June 2013 at *www.accp.com/resandfel/.*)

203. American College of Clinical Pharmacy. Value of Conducting Pharmacy Residency Training—The Organizational Perspective; 2010.

204. Speedie MK. Should residencies be required by 2020? The argument against. American Journal of Pharmacy Education 2007;71:56.

205. Wiser TH. The University of Maryland Primary Care Residency Program. American Pharmacy 1983;NS23:20-3.

206. American Pharmacists Association. 2010-11 Postgraduate year one community residency program directory. *http://www.pharmacist.com/AM/Template.cfm?Section=Home2&TEMPLATE=/CM/ContentDisplay.cfm&CONTENTID=21849.* Accessed August 11, 2011.

207. Schommer J, Bonnarens J, Brown L, Goode J. Value of community pharmacy residency programs: college of pharmacy & practice site perspectives. Journal of the American Pharmacy Association 2010;50:72-88.

208. PGY1 community pharmacy residency open forum. American Society of Health-System Pharmacists. (Accessed April 30, 2013, at *http://www.ashp.org/DocLibrary/Accreditation/PRC2011/Actual-Expansion-Community.aspx.*)

209. Bucci KK, Knapp KK, Ohri LK, Brooks PJ. Factors motivating pharmacy students to pursue residency & fellowship training. American Journal of Health System Pharmacists 1995;52:2696-701.

210. Shord SS, Schwinghammer TL, Badowski M, et al. Desired professional development pathways for clinical pharmacists. Pharmacotherapy 2013;33:e34-42.

211. Flaherty JF, Jr., Boucher BA, Bahal-O'Mara N, Hutchinson RA. Recruitment & funding for clinical pharmacy residency & fellowship programs. Pharmacotherapy 1996;16:271-9.

212. Knapp KK, Letendre DE. Educational differentiation of the pharmacy work force. American Journal of Hospital Pharmacy 1989;46:2476-82.

213. 1996 ASHP National Residency Preceptors Conference: structuring residencies to meet the challenge of changes in contemporary pharmacy practice. American Journal of Health System Pharmacists 1997;54:2110-14.

214. Shapiro L. Foundation dedicates $1.5 million in grants for pharmacy residencies; 2010.

215. Scott S, Constantine LM. Community pharmacy residency programs lend a fresh perspective to practice. Journal of the American Pharmacy Association (Wash) 1999;39:750-1.

216. Song A. SOAP note: Why I want to complete a pharmacy practice residency. American Journal of Health System Pharmacists 2005;62:2041-2.

217. Fit KE, Padiyara RS, Rabi SM, Burkiewicz JS. Factors influencing pursuit of residency training. American Journal of Health System Pharmacists 2005;62:2226, 35.

218. —. Definitions of pharmacy residencies & fellowships. American Journal of Hospital Pharmacy 1987;44:1142-4.

219. Nahata MC. Fellowship & residency distinctions. Drug Intell Clin Pharm 1986;20:625.

220. Crannage AJ, Drew AM, Pritchard LM, Murphy JA. Managing the residency scramble. American Journal of Health System Pharmacists 2011;68:110-4.

221. May JR, Chan J, Choudhary K, et al. Coping with the residency scramble: the need for national guidelines. American Journal of Health System Pharmacists 2012;69:253-5.

222. Specialty Certifications. 2013. (Accessed June 2013 at *http://www.ashp.org/menu/Education/Certifications.aspx.*)

223. Saseen JJ, Grady SE, Hansen LB, et al. Future clinical pharmacy practitioners should be board-certified specialists. Pharmacotherapy 2006;26:1816-25.

224. Anderson C, Blenkinsopp A, Armstrong M. Feedback from community pharmacy users on the contribution of community pharmacy to improving the public's health: a systematic review of the peer reviewed & non-peer reviewed literature 1990-2002. Health Expect 2004;7:191-202.

225. Fevang L. Changing role of pharmacists. Canadian Medical Association Journal 1994;151:909, 12.

226. Fink JL, 3rd. Liability & the changing role of pharmacists. American Pharmacy 1995;NS35:34-5.

227. Muijrers PE, Knottnerus JA, Sijbrandij J, Janknegt R, Grol RP. Changing relationships: attitudes & opinions of general practitioners & pharmacists regarding the role of the community pharmacist. Pharmacy & World Science 2003;25:235-41.

228. Tully MP, Latif S, Cantrill JA, Parker D. Pharmacists' changing views of their supplementary prescribing authority. Pharmacy & World Science 2007;29:628-34.

229. Cowen DL. Changing relationship between pharmacists & physicians. American Journal of Hospital Pharmacy 1992;49:2715-21.

230. Conlan M. Pharmacist prescribing Coming on Strong. Drug Topics 1997;15:62-4,7.

231. Nissen L. Pharmacist prescribing: what are the next steps? American Journal of Health System Pharmacists 2011;68:2357-61.

232. Malleck DJ. Professionalism & the boundaries of control: pharmacists, physicians & dangerous substances in Canada, 1840-1908. Medical History 2004;48:175-98.

233. Koch K. Trends in collaborative drug therapy management 2000.

234. Keely JL. Pharmacist scope of practice. Annals of Internal Medicine 2002;136:79-85.

235. Blake EW, Powell PH. A pharmacy political advocacy elective course. American Journal of Pharmacy Education 2011;75:137.

236. Tabarrok A. From off-label prescribing towards a new FDA. Medical hypotheses 2009;72:11-3.

237. Bright JL. Positive outcomes through the appropriate use of off-label prescribing. Archives of Internal Medicine 2006;166:2554-5; author reply 5.

238. Monestime-Williams N, Dickerson LM, Basco WT, Jr. Off-label prescribing of medications for children. Journal of the South Carolina Medical Association (1975) 2007;103:130-3.

239. Dresser R, Frader J. Off-label prescribing: a call for heightened professional & government oversight. J Law Med Ethics 2009;37:476-86, 396.

240. Hill P. Off licence & off label prescribing in children: litigation fears for physicians. Archives of disease in childhood 2005;90 Suppl 1:i17-8.

241. Radley DC, Finkelstein SN, Stafford RS. Off-label prescribing among office-based physicians. Archives of Internal Medicine 2006;166:1021-6.

242. Sanazaro PJ. Medicine & pharmacy: our once & future status as professions. American Journal of Hospital Pharmacy 1987;44:521-4.

243. Cohn J. The Robot Will See You Now. The Atlantic 2013 February 20, 2013.

244. Khosla V. Do We Need Doctors Or Algorithms? In: TechCrunch. San Francisco, CA: AOL, Inc; 2012.

245. Barbero Gonzalez A, Alvarez de Toledo Saavedra F, Esteban Fernandez J, et al. [Management of vaccinations & prophylaxis of international travellers from community pharmacy (VINTAF study)]. Atencion primaria / Sociedad Espanola de Medicina de Familia y Comunitaria 2003;32:276-81.

246. Steyer TE, Ragucci KR, Pearson WS, Mainous AG, 3rd. The role of pharmacists in the delivery of influenza vaccinations. Vaccine 2004;22:1001-6.

247. Ragland D, Payakachat N, Hays EB, Banken J, Dajani NK, Ott RE. Depression & diabetes: Establishing the pharmacist's role in detecting comorbidity in pregnant women. Journal of the American Pharmacy Association (2003);50:195-9.

248. Fuller TS, Christensen DB, Williams DH. Satisfaction with prescriptive authority protocols. Journal of the American Pharmacy Association (Wash) 1996;NS36:739-45.

249. Furmaga EM. Pharmacist management of a hyperlipidemia clinic. American Journal of Hospital Pharmacy 1993;50:91-5.

250. Glasier A, Baird D. The effects of self-administering emergency contraception. The New England Journal of Medicine 1998;339:1-4.

251. Dropkin R. Illiterate patients. Physician Assistant 1981;5:71-3.

252. Sorensen JC, Neely PH. Teaching illiterate patients to read. Hospital & Community Psychiatry 1966;17:248-9.

253. Orr V. Are We a Nation of Scientific Illiterates? American Education 1983.

254. Hofstadter DR. Number numbness, or why innumeracy may be just as dangerous as illiteracy. Scientific American 1982.

255. Stewart JE, Martin JL. Correlates of patients' perceived & real knowledge of prescription directions. Contemporary pharmacy practice 1979;2:144-8.

256. Institute of Medicine (U.S.). Roundtable on Health Literacy., Hernandez LM, Institute of Medicine (U.S.). Board on Population Health & Public Health Practice. Standardizing medication labels : confusing patients less : workshop summary. Washington, D.C.: National Academies Press; 2008.

257. Julia AM, Garcia SV, Breckinridge MF. Spanish labeling guide. Drug Intelligence in Clinical Pharmacy 1983;17:580-90.

258. Morrow J. Is There a Cure for Scientific Illiteracy? Media & Methods 1980.

259. Worthy W. AAAS Offers Guidelines to Combat Scientific Illiteracy Problem. Chemical & Engineering News 1989.

260. Pool R. Science Literacy: The Enemy Is Us. Science 1991.

261. Kutner M, Greenberg E, Jin Y, Paulsen C. The Health Literacy of America's Adults: Results From the 2003 National Assessment of Adult Literacy (NCES 2006-483). Washington, DC; 2006.

262. Chavunduka D, Dzimwasha M, Madondo F, Mafana E, Mbewe A, Nyazema NZ. Drug information for patients in the community. World Health Forum 1991;12:29-33.

263. Bradshaw SJ, Doucette WR. Community pharmacists as patient advocates: physician attitudes. Journal of the American Pharmacy Association (Wash) 1998;38:598-602.

264. Lambert BL. Face & politeness in pharmacist-physician interaction. Soc Sci Med 1996;43:1189-98.

265. Raisch DW. Barriers to providing cognitive services. American Pharmacy 1993;NS33:54-8.

266. Ranelli PL, Biss J. Physicians' perceptions of communication with & responsibilities of pharmacists. Journal of the American Pharmacy Association (Wash) 2000;40:625-30.

267. Hottin S. Abusive physicians: violence is not "part of the job". Journal of Emergency Nursing 2004;30:7.

268. Armstrong H. Fear & denial: grappling with the reality of abusive physicians. Canadian Medical Association Journal 1995;153:177-9.

269. Hutchinson M, Vickers MH, Jackson D, Wilkes L. 'They stand you in a corner; you are not to speak': nurses tell of abusive indoctrination in work teams dominated by bullies. Contemporary nurse 2006;21:228-38.

270. O'Garr B. Abusive docs drive out nurses. Hospitals & Health Networks / AHA 2004;78:10.

271. Macdonald MB, Bally JM, Ferguson LM, Lee Murray B, Fowler-Kerry SE, Anonson JM. Knowledge of the professional role of others: a key interprofessional competency. Nurse Education in Practice;10:238-42.

272. Harris G. When the nurse wants to be called 'doctor'. New York Times 2011 October 1, 2011.

273. Healthcare Truth & Transparency Act of 2011. In: HR 451. January 26, 2011 ed; 2011.

274. American Medical Association ARC. Truth in Advertising Campaign; 2010 May 2010.

275. van Ryn M, Burke J. The effect of patient race & socio-economic status on physicians' perceptions of patients. Soc Sci Med 2000;50:813-28.

276. Jones C. The impact of racism on health. Ethn Dis 2002;12:S2-10-3.

277. Jones CP. Invited commentary: "race," racism, & the practice of epidemiology. Americal Journal of Epidemiology 2001;154:299-304; discussion 5-6.

278. Acquaviva KD, Mintz M. Perspective: are we teaching racial profiling? The dangers of subjective determinations of race & ethnicity in case presentations. Academic Medicine 2010;85:702-5.

279. Svensson CK, Ascione FJ, Bauman JL, et al. Are we producing innovators & leaders or change resisters & followers? American Journal of Pharmacy Education;76:124.

280. Lee JM, Pilli S, Gebremariam A, et al. Getting heavier, younger: trajectories of obesity over the life course. International Journal of Obesity (2005);34:614-23.

281. Ciampa PJ, Kumar D, Barkin SL, et al. Interventions aimed at decreasing obesity in children younger than 2 years: a systematic review. Archives of Pediatrics & Adolescent Medicine 2011;164:1098-104.

282. Maalouf-Manasseh Z, Metallinos-Katsaras E, Dewey KG. Obesity in preschool children is more prevalent & identified at a younger age when WHO growth charts are used compared with CDC charts. The Journal of Nutrition;141:1154-8.

283. Klein J. Obamacare vs. Medicare: meshing the two plans could lead to better care & savings for taxpayers. Time;180:27.

284. Faria MA. ObamaCare: Another step toward corporate socialized medicine in the US. Surgical Neurology International;3:71.

285. Pollack R. Why Obamacare is good for seniors & America. Caring;31:34.

286. US Department of Labor. US Bureau of Labor Statistics, Employment Projections Program; 2013.

287. Ryssdal K. An overdose of pharmacy students. In: Farmer B, ed. Marketplace for Monday, May 21, 2012: American Public Media; 2012.

288. Expansion of Pharmacy Education: Time for Reconsideration. 2010. (Accessed 2013, at www.pharmacist.com/Content/ContentFolders3/NewsReleases/2010/OctDec/WP_Concerns_about_the_Accelerating_Expansion_of_Pharmacy_Education_FINAL.pdf.)

289. Pham K. Pharmacist Salary for Academia, Clinical Pharmacy, Retail, Pharmaceutical Industry, & Pharmacy Owner; 2013.

290. Salary Data. 2013. (Accessed March 1, 2013, at http://www.aacp.org/career/salarydata/pages/default.aspx.)

291. An Inside Look at Jobs & Companies. 2013. (Accessed June 2013 at http://www.glassdoor.com/index.htm.)

292. You Are More than Just a Salary. 2013. (Accessed June 2013 at *http://www.salary.com/.*)

293. One Search. All Jobs. 2013. (Accessed June 2013 at *http://www.indeed.com/.*)

294. Simply Hired. 2013. (Accessed June 2013 at *http://www.simplyhired.com/.*)

295. The Blonde Pharmacist. 2013. (Accessed June 2013 at http://theblondepharmacist.com/2013/01/18/when-people-fail/.)

296. Hans R. Pharmacy Jobs without License Requirements; 2012.

297. Hermansen-Kobulnicky CJ, Wiederholt JB, Chewning B. Adverse effect monitoring: opportunity for patient care & pharmacy practice. Journal of the American Pharmacy Association (2003) 2004;44:75-86; quiz 7-8.

298. Falletta JM. Physicians as science writers. North Carolina Medical Journal 1987;48:41-3.

299. Blakeslee A. Scientists & science writers. Cancer Investigation 1985;3:189-91.

300. Trudeau T. How our pharmacists act as poison control specialists. Pharmacy Times 1982;48:34-9.

301. Rodman MJ. Pharmacists' role in poison control. Hospital Progress 1959;40:103-4 passim.

302. Young D. Military reserve pharmacists provide vital services. American Journal of Health System Pharmacists 2003;60:420-1.

303. Petoletti AR. Military pharmacists establish. Surveillance of controlled drugs. Journal of the American Pharmacy Association 1975;15:84-5.

304. Timberlake CV, Kaplan MR. The military pharmacists' responsibility in the quality control of drugs. Military Medicine 1965;130:570-7.

305. Houle SK, Chuck AW, Tsuyuki RT. Blood pressure kiosks for medication therapy management programs: business opportunity for pharmacists. Journal of the American Pharmacy Association (2003);52:188-94.

306. Isetts BJ, Buffington DE. CPT code-change proposal: National data on pharmacists' medication therapy management services. Journal of the American Pharmacy Association (2003) 2007;47:491-5.

307. Pinto SL, Morgan EE. Preparing pharmacists for medication therapy management services: designing lementing pharmacist-run diabetes management program in a community setting. Managment Care Interface 2007;20:52-6.

308. Gruber J. Medication therapy management: a challenge for pharmacists. Consulting Pharmacy;27:782-96.

309. Wang J, Hong SH. Contingent valuation & pharmacists' acceptable levels of compensation for medication therapy management services. Research in Social & Administrative Pharmacy.

310. Battaglia JN, Kieser MA, Bruskiewitz RH, Pitterle ME, Thorpe JM. An online virtual-patient program to teach pharmacists & pharmacy students how to provide diabetes-specific medication therapy management. American Journal of Pharmacy Education;76:131.

311. McFarland M, Davis K, Wallace J, et al. Use of home telehealth monitoring with active medication therapy management by clinical pharmacists in veterans with poorly controlled type 2 diabetes mellitus. Pharmacotherapy;32:420-6.

312. Callahan RJ, Dragotakes SC. The role of the practice of nuclear pharmacy in positron emission tomography. Clinical Positron Imaging 1999;2:211-6.

313. Kawada TK, Tubis M, Ebenkamp T, Wolf W. Review of nuclear pharmacy practice in hospitals. American Journal of Hospital Pharmacy 1982;39:266-74.

314. Cazin JL, Gosselin P. Implementing a multiple-isolator unit for centralized preparation of cytotoxic drugs in a cancer center pharmacy. Pharmacy World Science 1999;21:177-83.

315. Whigham WD, Jr., Roberts KB. Considerations when proposing consultant pharmacist services to hospice programs. Contemporary Pharmacy Practice 1982;5:239-45.

316. Podell LB. Medicare coverage of hospice care. American Journal of Hospital Pharmacy 1984;41:942-4.

317. Sylvester RK, Roberg J, Roden W, Smithson K. A hospice-based advanced pharmacy experience. American Journal of Pharmacy Education 2009;73:44.

318. Berry JI, Pulliam CC, Caiola SM, Eckel FM. Pharmaceutical services in hospices. American Journal of Hospital Pharmacy 1981;38:1010-4.

319. Cramer R. Opportunities for pharmacists in hospice organizations. American Journal of Hospital Pharmacy 1988;45:76.

320. Timmons ED. How pharmacists provide useful Rx services to hospice patients. Pharmacy times 1987;53:88, 91, 6.

321. Nnadi-Okolo EE. Euthanasia & the healthcare professional. Hospital Pharmacy 1995;30:208-10, 13, 20.

322. Herndon CM, Fike DS, Anderson AC, Dole EJ. Pharmacy student training in United States hospices. Am J Hosp Palliat Care 2001;18:181-6.

323. Ohya M, Gohda Y, Sato S, Makishima K, Murakami M. [Role of pharmacists on the safety management of ambulatory cancer chemotherapy]. Gan to kagaku ryoho 2009;36 Suppl 1:57-9.

324. Atayee RS, Best BM, Daniels CE. Development of an ambulatory palliative care pharmacist practice. Journal of palliative medicine 2008;11:1077-82.

325. Muller RJ, Hoffman DM, Mulligan RM. Parenteral nutrition program in a major cancer center. Hospital Pharmacy 1981;16:54-66.

326. Hudzinski DM. An algorithmic approach to cancer pain management. The Nursing Clinics of North America 1995;30:711-23.

327. Rich D. Physicians, pharmacists, & home infusion antibiotic therapy. The American Journal of Medicine 1994;97:3-8.

328. Kwan JW, Anderson RW. Pharmacists' knowledge of infusion devices. American Journal of Hospital Pharmacy 1991;48:S52-3.

329. Shrank WH, Porter ME, Jain SH, Choudhry NK. A blueprint for pharmacy benefit managers to increase value. The American Journal of Managed Care 2009;15:87-93.

330. Seay M, Lee LL. Pharmaceuticals: Pharmacy Benefit Managers (PBMs). Issue brief (Health Policy Tracking Service) 2007:1-14.

331. Teagarden JR, Epstein RS. Pharmacy benefit managers & their obligations during serious prescription drug shortages. Clinical Pharmacology & Therapeutics;93:143-5.

332. Spiro RF, Gagnon JP, Knutson AR. Role of health information technology in optimizing pharmacists' patient care services. Journal of the American Pharmacy Association (2003);50:4-8.

333. Fuji KT, Galt KA. Pharmacists & health information technology: emerging issues in patient safety. HEC Forum 2008;20:259-75.

334. Lucisano LJ. Spurring pharmacists to industry. American Pharmacy 1988;NS28:22-4.

335. Johnson JB. Transitions: exploring career options. Pharmacists in industry. Topics in hospital pharmacy management/Aspen Systems Corporation 1986;6:28-31.

336. Walker SE, Schafermeyer KW, Rickert DR, Hurd PD. Opportunities for pharmacists as managers: perceptions of senior executives in the pharmaceutical industry. Journal of the American Pharmacy Association (Wash) 1999;39:41-4.

337. Farthing-Papineau EC, Peak AS. Pharmacists' perceptions of the pharmaceutical industry. American Journal of Health System Pharmacists 2005;62:2401-9.

338. Lear JS, Kirk KW. Women pharmacists in the pharmaceutical industry. Their preparation, satisfaction, & outlook. American Pharmacy 1987;NS27:34-9.

339. Faust RE. Opportunities in industry for graduate-degreed pharmacists. American Pharmacy 1984;NS24:74-8.

340. Retail Pharmacy, Life, & General Lunacy. 2011. (Accessed May 2013 at *http://pharmacymike.blogspot.com/*.)

341. The Lighter Side of Pharmacy. 2012. (Accessed May 2013 at http://www.pharmacytimes.com/blogs/piller-of-the-community/1212/The-Lighter-Side-of-Pharmacy.)

342. —. The Redheaded Pharmacist: Rants & Musings of a Retail Pharmacist; 2013.

343. Even if the Truth Hurts. 2011. (Accessed May 2013 at http://www.pharmacytimes.com/blogs/eric-blog/1011/Even-If-the-Truth-Hurts.)

344. "Chick". The Pharmacy Chick: Flying the Coop In Retail. 2013.

345. Gallup survey finds public confidence in pharmacists at a record high. 2012. (Accessed May 2013 at http://www.pharmacytimes.com/blogs/reinvented-pharmacist/1212/Gallup-Survey-Finds-Public-Confidence-in-Pharmacists-at-a-Record-High.)

INDEX

Activities in the First Year
  Class Officers, 117
  Pharmacy Organizations, 118
Activities in the Fourth Year
  Applying for Licensure, 142
  NaPLEX Practice Questions, 140
  The MPJE, 142
    Cost, 142
    Not Required, 142
    Number of Questions, 142
    Test Content, 142
  The Naplex, 139
    Questions, 140
  The NaPlex
    Number of Questions, 142
  The NaPLEX
    Cost, 140
    Test Duration, 140
Activities in the Second Year
  Summer Opportunities
    Community Pharmacy IPPE
    Duration, 127
Activities in the Third Year
  Preceptors, 133
Appendix I
  Geographical Locations of
    Colleges of Pharmacy, 216,
    224
Appendix III
  Professional Organizations for
    Pharmacy Students
    Academy of Student
    Pharmacists, 232
    American Association of
    Colleges of Pharmacy, 232
    American Association of
    Pharmaceutical Scientists, 232
    American College of Clinical
    Pharmacy, 232

American Society of Consultant
  Pharmacists, 233
American Society of Health-
  System Pharmacists, 233
Christian Pharmacists
  Fellowship International, 233
College of Psychiatric and
  Neurologic Pharmacists, 233
Hematology/Oncology
  Pharmacy Association, 233
Kappa Epsilon, 234
Kappa Psi, 234
National Academy of Managed
  Care Pharmacy, 234
National Community
  Pharmacists Association, 234
National Pharmaceutical
  Association, 234
Pediatric Pharmacy Advocacy
  Group, 234
Phi Delta Chi, 235
Pi Lambda Sigma, 235
Rho Chi, 235
Social Organizations for
  Pharmacy Students, 232
Society of Critical Care
  Medicine, 235
Society of Infectious Diseases
  Pharmacists, 235
Student National
  Pharmaceutical Association, 236
Appendix IV
  Answers to Practice Questions,
    238
Appendix V
  Top 200 Drugs by Prescription
    Sales, 240
Areas of Specialization, 150
  Board Certification, 151
Attrition

Causes, 109

Measures to Stop, 109

Audience Response Systems

Cost, 94

Exams

Mis-keying Answers, 94

System Errors, 95

Between Years

Summer Opportunities

Community Pharmacy IPPE, 119

Duration, 119

Hospital Pharmacy IPPE

Duration, 119

IPPE

Hours Needed for Internship, 120

Licensure Requirements, 120

Skills Required, 119

Changing Roles of the Pharmacist

Collaborative Care

Role of the Pharmacist, 157

Pharmacists

Robots, 156

Physicians

Diagnostic Bias, 157

Robots, 157

Prescription Authority, 155

Physician Antagonism, 155

Physician Off-label Prescribing, 156

Chapters

Chapter 1, 1

Chapter 10, 145

Chapter 11, 154

Chapter 12, 176

Chapter 2, 21

Chapter 3, 41

Chapter 4, 69

Chapter 5, 90

Chapter 6, 110

Chapter 7, 122

Chapter 8, 128

Chapter 9:, 135

Choosing a Program

Schools of Pharmacy

Number of Programs, 12

Private School, 13

Public School, 13

Class Structure

Faculty Language Barriers, 81

Effects on Students, 82

Teaching in Teams, 81

Communication with Faculty

Educational Media, 75

Email, 75

Office Appointments, 75

Conclusion, 181

Contemplating a Career in Pharmacy, 1

Course Descriptions

Table 1—Potential Courses for the First Year, 111

Table 1—Potential Courses for the Second Year, 123

Table 1—Potential Courses for the Third Year, 129

Course Descriptions in the First Year, 111

Course Descriptions in the Fourth Year

Travel Required, 136

Course Descriptions in the Second Year, 123

Electives, 125

Patient Interactions, 125

Course Descriptions in the Third Year, 129

Course Materials

Course Notes, 87

Course Objectives, 86

Course Packets, 87

Course Study Guides, 87
Course Syllabi, 86
Instructors
   Course Authority, 87
Lecture Recordings, 88
Coursework
   Bulimic Learning, 46
   Common Curriculum, 46
   Little Flexibility, 45
   Memorization, 46
   Skipping Courses, 46
   Student Disabilities, 46
Creating Student Advantages
   Community Colleges for Pre-requisites, 25
   Pre-requisites
      Rigor, 26
   The PCAT, 27
      Not Required, 27
Criteria for Going
   GPA, 24
      Cumulative, 24
      Forgiveness, 25
      Key, 24
      Normalized, 24
      Recalculation, 25
      Retention, 24
      Science, 24
      Subject, 25
      Weighting, 24
   Helpful Courses, 23
   Pre-Pharmacy Advisory Track, 22
   Program Duration, 23
Degree Details
   "First Professional Degree", 9
   "PharmD Candidate", 10
   Candidate
      Graduate School, 10
      Professional School, 10
   Figure 1—Degree Tree, 9

Graduate Degrees, 9
Oral Candidacy Exam
   Graduate School, 10
PharmD Candidate
   Usage of Term, 9
Professional Degrees, 9
Professional *vs.* Graduate School, 9
The NaPLEX
   Licensure Requirement, 10
The PCAT
   Admissions Requirement, 10
Written Candidacy Exam
   Graduate School, 10
Distance Education
   Global University, 49
   Khan Academy, 49
   Main Campus, 49
   Online Degrees, 50
   Remote Campuses, 49
   Satellite Campuses, 49
During Lecture
   Changes over Time, 48
   Seat Time, 48
   Videos and Lecture Recordings, 47
Educating the Pharmacist
   Changes, 8
   Honorifics/Titles, 9
   PharmD First Declared, 8
   Stratification of US Degrees, 8
Exams and Student Evaluation Tools
   Exam Behavior, 91
   Online Exams, 91
      Browser Lockdown Mechanisms, 92
      Security, 92
      Software, 92
   Paper Exams, 90
   Randomization of Questions/Answers, 91

Test Review, 91

Test Versions, 91

Expectations in the First Year

Future Colleagues, 116

Student Voices, 116

Testing, 115

Expectations in the Fourth Year

Advanced Practice Pharmacy Experiences, 136

Medication Management, 138

Residency Letters of Recommendation, 143

Rotations

Choices, 138

Hours Required, 136

Major Medical Centers, 136

Patient Diversity, 139

Patient Workup, 138

Patients and Diseases, 139

Student Voices, 137

Supporting Therapy Recommendations, 139

Transcripts for Residency, 144

Expectations in the Second Year

Helping Underclassmen, 125

Pre-residency Experiences, 126

Expectations in the Third Year

Student Voices, 129

Faculty Duties

Availability for Students, 78

Contractual Obligations, 78

Free Time, 77

Integrity and Honesty, 78

Lecture Delivery, 77

Failing

Academic Probation, 108

Causes, 107

Repeating Coursework, 108

Summer School, 108

Figures

Figure 1—Degree Tree, 9

Figure 1—Test Statistics, 101

Figure 2—Distribution of US Schools of Pharmacy, 11

Figure 3—US Pharmacy School Tuition, 13

Grade Modifications

Curving Scores, 104

Normal *vs.* Skewed Grade Curves, 103

Point Adjustments, 103

Honor

Cheating, 53

Mechanisms, 54

Future Professional Ramifications, 54

Honor Codes, 53

Student Choice in Obeyance, 54

Student Integrity, 54

Student Trust, 53

How to Obtain a Residency

American College of Clinical Pharmacy Residency and Fellowship Directory, 143

American Society of Hospital Pharmacists Residency Directory, 143

In the Know

Newspapers, 45

In the Trenches

Comments from Current Pharmacists, 176

Introduction and Purpose, i

Disclaimer, i

Inside Information, i

Lecture Recordings

Attendance, 52

Student Performance, 52

Letters of Recommendation

Favorable Letters, 36

Good Choices, 35

Poor Choices, 35

Unfavorable Letters, 36

Major Laws and Rules Governing
Healthcare, 164

    Health Insurance Portability and
        Accountability Act of 1996

    HIPPA, 163

    Violations, 163

    Medicare

    Medicaid

        Medicare and Medicaid"Dual
        Eligible", 165

        Social Welfare, 165

    Part A, 165

    Part B, 165

    Part C

        Advantage Plan, 165

    Part D, 165

        Advantage with Drug Plans,
        165

Making it through the Professional
Program

    Coursework

        Test Strategies, 46

    Student Expectations, 41

Making the Grade

    Requesting Grade Changes, 102

Motivation

    "Helping People", 2

    "Liking Science", 2

    Innovative Responses, 2

    Questions to Consider, 3

        Difficult Questions, 3

    Easy Questions, 3

Personal Statement/Essay

    Grammar, Syntax, Diction, 37

    Strategies, 36

PharmD Plus One

    Dual-degree Programs, 11

    Figure 2—Distribution of US
        Schools of Pharmacy, 11

PharmD/MBA, 11

PharmD/MHA, 11

PharmD/MPH, 12

PharmD/MSCR, 12

PharmD/Other Degree
    Combinations, 12

PharmD/PhD, 11

Potential Classmates

    Average Student Age, 19

    Average Student Maturity, 19

    Gender Composition, 19

    Racial Composition, 19

    Young Students, 19

Pre-professional Experience

    Paid Employment, 7

    Pharmacy Career Considerations,
        5

    Pharmacy Technician, 5

        Duties, 6

        Duty Limitations, 6

    Shadowing, 7

    Speaking to Pharmacists, 7

Professionalism

    Different Definitions, 55

    Professioanl Dress, 58

    Professional Dress

        Body Art and Piercings, 58

        Females, 58

        Males, 58

    Professionalism Committee, 55

    Unprofessional Conduct, 56

        Examples, 56

Program Tuition and Fees

    Building Fees, 15

    Educational Technology Fees, 15

    Figure 3—US Pharmacy School
        Tuition, 13

    Laboratory Fees, 15

    Matriculation Fees, 14

    Seat Fees, 14

Student Activity Fees, 15
Tuition, 13
 In-State, 14
 Out-of-State, 14
White Coat Fees, 15
Pure Performance
 Effects of Extra Credit, 107
Resolving Problems
 Final Decisions, 80
  Undemocratic, 80
 Initial Contacts, 79
 Secondary Contacts, 80
Rotations
 Academic, 131
 Clinical, 131
Self-Awareness
 Academic Entitlement Issues, 64
 Academic Entitlement Origins, 64
 Academic Entitlement Scale, 63
  Beliefs and Actions, 63
  Narcissism, 63
Stipends
 Other Benefits, 153
 Residency Pay, 152
Student Abilities
 Disabilities, 65
 Disability Accomodation, 65
 Grade Inflation, 65
 Lack of Rigor, 65
Student Disabilities
 Americans with Disabilities Act, 66
 Blind Pharmacist, 66
 Leonard Pitts, 68
 Opinion Piece, 67
 Section 504 of the Rehabilitation
  Act of 1973, 66
 Unpreparedness, 67
Student Entitlement
 Consumerism, 61

Course Materials and Intellectual
 Property, 62
Examples, 61
Problems, 61
Tables
 Table 1—4.0 Grading Scale, 24
 Table 1—Potential Courses for the
  First Year, 111
 Table 1—Potential Courses for the
  Second Year, 123
 Table 1—Potential Courses for the
  Third Year, 129
Test Review
 Confidentiality, 98
Testing Preparedness
 Appropriate Queries about Tests,
  95
 Arriving Late for Tests, 97
 Focus on Grades, 95
 In-appropriate Queries about
  Tests, 96
 Missing A Test, 97
Testing the Test
 Appropriate Student Test
  Question Challenges, 102
 Bi-serial Values, 99
 Figure 1, 101
 Grade Distribution, 98
 Student Performance, 98
 Test Creation, 101
 Test Reliability, 99
 Test Statistics, 99
 What Tests Measure, 99
Textbooks
 Electronic Textbooks, 42
 Laptops and Tablets, 43
 Required *vs.* Suggested, 42
The Acceptance Process
 Late Student Data, 39
 Letter Cycles, 39
 Special Admittances, 40

The Best Students, 39
    Wait Lists, 40
The Application Process, 30
    Turnitin Software, 30
The Inner Workings of the Professional Pharmacy Program, 69
The Internet and Social Media
    Facebook, 59
    Friending Faculty, 59
    Permanence, 60
The Interview
    Bad Ideas, 30
    Common Questions, 31
    Faculty Obligations, 32
    Good Ideas, 31
    Guests, 31
    Pointers, 31
    Student and Faculty Conduct, 33
    Student Obligations, 31
The PCAT
    Composite Scores, 29
    Correlation with Success, 29
    Percentiles, 28
    Performance, 28
    Reading Comprehension Section, 28
    Science Sections, 28
    The First Test, 28
    The Writing Sample, 29
The PGY1 Experience
    Community Pharmacy Residency, 147
    Health System, 147
    Residency Funding Mechanisms, 147
    Residency Interview Questions, 148
    Residency Match and Scramble, 148
The PGY2 Experience

Veteran's Administration Medical Center Residency, 151
The Pharmacy Workforce
    Academic Pharmacists, 169
      Freedoms, 169
      Salary, 169
    Cancer Chemotherapy Pharmacist, 173
      Salary, 173
    Clinical Pharmacist, 168
      Challenges, 169
      Salary, 169
      The Right Personality for the Job, 169
    Competition
      Pharmacy Jobs, 166
    Contract, Temporary, or Hourly Pharmacy Careers, 168
      Salary, 168
    Drug Information Specialist, 169
      Salary, 170
    FDA Consumer Safety Officer, 171
      Salary, 171
    Glassdoor.com, 167
    Healthcare Information Technology, 173
      Salary, 174
    Indeed.com, 167
    Infusion Therapy Pharmacist, 173
      Salary, 173
    Long-term Care/Hospice Pharmacists, 172
      Salary, 172
    Medical Recruiting, 174
      Salary, 174
      The Right Personality for the Job, 174
    Medical Writer, 170
      Salary, 170
    Medication Therapy Management Specialist, 171

Salary, 172
Telemedicine, 172
Military Pharmacists, 170
Salary, 171
Nuclear Pharmacists, 172
Salary, 172
Pharmaceutical Industry Liaison, 174
Pharmaceutical Industry Pharmacist, 174
Salary, 174
Pharmaceutical Industry Pharmaco-economist, 174
Salary, 175
Pharmaceutical Industry Sales or Medical Device Representative, 175
Salary, 175
Pharmaceutical Industry/Pharmaceutical Liaison
Salary, 174
Pharmacist Positions with the FDA, 171
Salary, 171
Pharmacy Benefit Manager, 173
Salary, 173
Pharmacy Residency
Employment Opportunities, 167
Poison Control Pharmacist, 170
Animal Services, 170
Salary, 170
Toxicology Certification, 170
Retail Pharmacists, 167
Retail Pharmacy
Challenges, 167
Opportunities for Creativity, 168
Salary, 167
Salary Ranges, 167
Salary.com, 167
Simplyhired.com, 167

Supply and Demand of Pharmacists, 166
The Players in Pharmacy
Board of Trustees, 71
Chairmen/women, 71
Deans, 70
Executive, 71
Other Positions, 70
Departments and Divisions, 72
Faculty, 72
General Faculty Characteristics, 73
Free Speech, 74
Political, 74
Religious, 73
Roles of Individuals, 73
Staff, 71
Teaching Positions, 72
The Significance of the White Coat Ceremony, 121
Pharmacists as Public Figures, 121
Pharmacists' Coat, 120
Top of the Heap
"Intellectual Inbreeding", 16
Associations with Teaching Hospitals, 18
Student Advantages, 18
Choosing the Best School, 15
Patient Interactions, 18
School Hiring Trends, 16
School Rankings
National Institutes of Health, 15
Top Ten Schools for NIH Funding, 16
US News and World Report, 17
Top Ten—US News and World, 18
Who's the Boss?
FDA
Regulation of Pharmacy Practice, 158

State Boards of Pharmacy
  Regulation of Pharmacy
  Practice, 158
  Supervisors, 158
Why Choose a Residency
  In Contrast with Fellowships, 147
  Mandatory Training, 146, 147
Working
  Faculty Attitudes, 44
  Grades, 43
  Strategies, 44
Working with Other Healthcare
Professionals
  Interprofessionalism
    Attitudes, 162
  Pharmacists
    Rights of Title, 163

Physicians
  Working Relationships, 161
Professionalism
  Nurses, 161
  Physicians, 161
Working with the Public
  Cultural Competence, 160
Literacy
  Patient Health Literacy, 159
Medical Myths
  Patient Health Literacy, 160
Patient Compliance, 160
  Comprehension Skills, 159
  Cultural Attitudes, 160
Patient Education, 159
Working with Laypeople, 158

APPENDIX I: US COLLEGES OF PHARMACY

State	School	City	Univ.
AL	Harrison Sch. of Pharm.	Auburn	Auburn Univ.
	McWhorter Sch. of Pharm.	Birmingham	Samford Univ.
AZ	Coll. of Pharm.-Glendale	Glendale	Midwestern Univ.
	Coll. of Pharm.	Tucson	Univ. of Arizona
AR	Coll. of Pharm.	Searcy	Harding Univ.
	Coll. of Pharm.	Little Rock	Univ. of Arkansas for Medical Sciences
CA	Sch. of Pharm.	Clovis	California Health Sciences Univ.
	Coll. of Pharm.	Rancho Cordova	California Northstate Univ.
	Sch. of Pharm.	Claremont	Keck Graduate Institute
	Sch. of Pharm.	Loma Linda	Loma Linda Univ.
	Coll. of Pharm.	Vallejo	Touro Univ.
	Skaggs Sch. of Pharm. & Pharmaceutical Sciences	La Jolla	Univ. of California-San Diego
	Sch. of Pharm.	San Francisco	Univ. of California-San Francisco
	Thomas J. Long Sch. of Pharm. & Health Science	Stockton	Univ. of the Pacific
	Sch. of Pharm.	Los Angeles	Univ. of Southern California
	Coll. of Pharm.	Los Angeles	West Coast Univ.
	Coll. of Pharm.	Pomona	Western Univ. of Health Sciences
CO	Rueckert-Hartman College for Health Professions	Denver	Regis Univ.
	Skaggs Sch. of Pharm. and Pharmaceutical Sciences	Aurora	Univ. of Colorado Denver
CT	Sch. of Pharm.	Hartford	Saint Joseph Univ.
	Sch. of Pharm.	Storrs	Univ. of Connecticut

State	School	City	Univ.
DC	Coll. of Pharm.	Washington, DC	Howard Univ.
FL	Coll. of Pharm. and Pharmaceutical Sciences	Tallahassee	Florida Agricultural and Mechanical Univ.
	LECOM Sch. of Pharm. Bradenton Campus	Bradenton	Lake Erie College of Osteopathic Medicine
	Coll. of Pharm.	Fort Lauderdale	Nova Southeastern Univ.
	Lloyd L. Gregory Sch. of Pharm.	West Palm Beach	Palm Beach Atlantic Univ.
	Coll. of Pharm.	Gainesville	Univ. of Florida
	Coll. of Pharm.	Tampa	Univ. of South Florida
GA	Coll. of Pharm. and Health Sciences	Atlanta	Mercer Univ.
	Sch. of Pharm.–Georgia Campus	Suwanee	Philadelphia College of Osteopathic Medicine
	Sch. of Pharm.	Savannah	South Univ.
	Coll. of Pharm.	Athens	Univ. of Georgia
HI	Daniel K. Inouye Coll. of Pharm.	Hilo	Univ. of Hawaii at Hilo
ID	Coll. of Pharm.	Pocatello	Idaho State Univ.
IL	Coll. of Pharm.	Chicago	Chicago State Univ.
	Chicago Coll. of Pharm.	Downers Grove	Midwestern Univ.
	Coll. of Pharm.	Schaumburg	Roosevelt Univ.
	Coll. of Pharm.	North Chicago	Rosalind Franklin Univ. of Medicine and Science
	Sch. of Pharm.	Edwardsville	Southern Illinois Univ. Edwardsville
	Coll. of Pharm.	Chicago	Univ. of Illinois at Chicago
IN	Coll. of Pharm. and Health Sciences	Indianapolis	Butler Univ.
	Coll. of Pharm.	Fort Wayne	Manchester Univ.
	Coll. of Pharm.	West	Purdue Univ.

State	School	City	Univ.
		Lafayette	
IA	Coll. of Pharm. and Health Sciences	Des Moines	Drake Univ.
	Coll. of Pharm.	Iowa City	Univ. of Iowa
KS	Sch. of Pharm.	Lawrence	Univ. of Kansas
KY	Coll. of Pharm.	Louisville	Sullivan Univ.
	Coll. of Pharm.	Lexington	Univ. of Kentucky
LA	Coll. of Pharm.	Monroe	Univ. of Louisiana at Monroe
	Coll. of Pharm.	New Orleans	Xavier Univ. of Louisiana
ME	Sch. of Pharm.	Bangor	Husson Univ.
	Sch. of Pharm.	Portland	Univ. of New England
MD	Sch. of Pharm.	Baltimore	Univ. of Maryland
	Sch. of Pharm.	Baltimore	Notre Dame of Maryland Univ.
	Sch. of Pharm.	Princess Anne	Univ. of Maryland Eastern Shore
MA	Sch. of Pharm.-Boston	Boston	Massachusetts Coll. of Pharm. and Health Sciences
	Sch. of Pharm.–Worcester/Manchester	Worcester	Massachusetts Coll. of Pharm. and Health Sciences
	Sch. of Pharm.	Boston	Northeastern Univ.
	Sch. of Pharm.	Springfield	Western New England Univ.
MI	Coll. of Pharm.	Big Rapids	Ferris State Univ.
	Coll. of Pharm.	Ann Arbor	Univ. of Michigan
	Eugene Applebaum Coll. of Pharm. and Health Sciences	Detroit	Wayne State Univ.
MN	Coll. of Pharm.	Minneapolis	Univ. of Minnesota
	Coll. of Pharm.	Duluth	Univ. of Minnesota Duluth

State	School	City	Univ.
MS	Coll. of Pharm.	Univ.	Univ. of Mississippi
MO	—	St. Louis	St. Louis Coll. of Pharm.
	Sch. of Pharm.	Kansas City	Univ. of Missouri–Kansas City
MT	Skaggs Sch. of Pharm.	Missoula	Univ. of Montana
NE	Sch. of Pharm. and Health Professions	Omaha	Creighton Univ.
	Coll. of Pharm.	Omaha	Univ. of Nebraska Medical Center
NV	Coll. of Pharm.	Henderson	Roseman Univ. of Health Sciences
NJ	Sch. of Pharm.	Florham Park	Fairleigh Dickinson Univ.
	Ernest Mario Sch. of Pharm.	Piscataway	Rutgers, The State Univ. of New Jersey
NM	Coll. of Pharm.	Albuquerque	Univ. of New Mexico
NY	Albany Coll. of Pharm.	Albany	Albany Coll. of Pharm. and Health Sciences
	Sch. of Pharm.	Buffalo	D'Youville College
	Arnold & Marie Schwartz Coll. of Pharm. and Health Sciences	Brooklyn	Long Island Univ.
	Coll. of Pharm. and Health Professions	Queens	St. John's Univ.
	Wegmans Sch. of Pharm.	Rochester	St. John Fisher College
	–	New York	Touro Coll. of Pharm.
	Sch. of Pharm. and Pharmaceutical Sciences	Buffalo	Univ. at Buffalo, The State Univ. of New York
NC	Coll. of Pharm. & Health Sciences	Buies Creek	Campbell Univ.
	Sch. of Pharm.	High Point	High Point Univ.
	Eshelman Sch. of Pharm.	Chapel Hill	Univ. of North Carolina at Chapel Hill
	Sch. of Pharm.	Wingate	Wingate Univ.
ND	Coll. of Pharm., Nursing, and Allied Sciences	Fargo	North Dakota State Univ.

State	School	City	Univ.
	Sch. of Pharm.	Cedarville	Cedarville Univ.
	Coll. of Pharm.	Rootstown	Northeast Ohio Medical Univ.
	Raabe Coll. of Pharm.	Ada	Ohio Northern Univ.
OH	Coll. of Pharm.	Columbus	Ohio State Univ.
	James L. Winkle Coll. of Pharm.	Cincinnati	Univ. of Cincinnati
	Coll. of Pharm.	Findlay	Univ. of Findlay
	Coll. of Pharm. & Pharmaceutical Sciences	Toledo	Univ. of Toledo
OK	Coll. of Pharm.	Weatherford	Southwestern Oklahoma State Univ.
	Coll. of Pharm.	Oklahoma City	Univ. of Oklahoma
OR	Coll. of Pharm.	Corvallis	Oregon State Univ.
	Coll. of Pharm.	Hillsboro	Pacific Univ. Oregon
	Mylan Sch. of Pharm.	Pittsburgh	Duquesne Univ.
	LECOM Sch. of Pharm. Erie Campus	Erie	Lake Erie College of Osteopathic Medicine
PA	Sch. of Pharm.	Philadelphia	Temple Univ.
	Jefferson Sch. of Pharm.	Philadelphia	Thomas Jefferson Univ.
	Philadelphia Coll. of Pharm.	Philadelphia	Univ. of the Sciences
	Sch. of Pharm.	Pittsburgh	Univ. of Pittsburgh
	Nesbitt Sch. of Pharm.	Wilkes-Barre	Wilkes Univ.
RI	Coll. of Pharm.	Kingston	Univ. of Rhode Island
	Coll. of Pharm.	Charleston	Medical Univ. of South Carolina
SC	Sch. of Pharm.	Clinton	Presbyterian College
	Sch. of Pharm.	Columbia	South Univ.
	Coll. of Pharm.	Columbia	Univ. of South Carolina
	Coll. of Pharm.	Nashville	Belmont Univ.
TN	Bill Gatton Coll. of Pharm.	Johnson City	East Tennessee State Univ.

State	School	City	Univ.
	Coll. of Pharm.	Nashville	Lipscomb Univ.
	Sch. of Pharm.	Knoxville	South College
	Sch. of Pharm.	Jackson	Union Univ.
	Coll. of Pharm.	Memphis	Univ. of Tennessee
TX	Irma Lerma Rangel Coll. of Pharm.	Kingsville	Texas A&M Health Science Center
	Coll. of Pharm. and Health Sciences	Houston	Texas Southern Univ.
	Sch. of Pharm.	Amarillo	Texas Tech Univ. Health Sciences Center
	Coll. of Pharm.	Houston	Univ. of Houston
	Coll. of Pharm.	Austin	Univ. of Texas at Austin
	Feik Sch. of Pharm.	San Antonio	Univ. of the Incarnate Word
	UNT System Coll. of Pharm.	Fort Worth	Univ. of North Texas Health Science Center
UT	Coll. of Pharm.	Henderson	Roseman Univ. of Health Sciences
	Coll. of Pharm.	Salt Lake City	Univ. of Utah
VA	Coll. of Pharm.	Oakwood	Appalachian Coll. of Pharm.
	Sch. of Pharm.	Hampton	Hampton Univ.
	Bernard J. Dunn Sch. of Pharm.	Winchester	Shenandoah Univ.
	Sch. of Pharm.	Richmond	Virginia Commonwealth Univ.
VT	Albany Coll. of Pharm.	Colchester	Albany Coll. of Pharm. and Health Sciences
WA	Sch. of Pharm.	Seattle	Univ. of Washington
	Coll. of Pharm.	Pullman	Washington State Univ.
WV	Sch. of Pharm.	Huntington	Marshall Univ.
	Sch. of Pharm.	Charleston	Univ. of Charleston
	Sch. of Pharm.	Morgantown	West Virginia Univ.
WI	Sch. of Pharm.	Mequon	Concordia Univ.

State	School	City	Univ.
			Wisconsin
	Sch. of Pharm.	Madison	Univ. of Wisconsin–Madison
WY	Sch. of Pharm.	Laramie	Univ. of Wyoming
PR[*]	Sch. of Pharm.	San Juan	Univ. of Puerto Rico

*PR: Puerto Rico

APPENDIX II: PRE-REQUISITES FOR US COLLEGES OF PHARMACY

Table footnotes: A&P: anatomy and physiology IM immunology; MC: microbiology; BC: biochemistry; CA: calculus; ST: statistics; PI/PII: physics I and II. CR: conditional requirement; R2: two units required; R3: three units required; R*: may have additional requirements within the course; S: suggested or recommended; S*: suggested and may have additional recommended components. ** No requirement for biology I and II; ***No requirement for biology II; ^ no requirement for organic I and II.

	School	Affiliation	AP	IM	MC	BC	CA	ST	PI/II
AL	Harrison	Auburn Univ.	R*	R	R	R	R	R	R
	McWhorter Sch. of Pharm..**	Samford Univ.**	R2		R		R	R	
AR	Coll. of Pharm.	Univ. of Arkansas for Medical Sciences	CR		R	CR	R		R/CR
AZ	Coll. of Pharm.	Harding Univ.	R2		R	R	R	R	R
	Coll. of Pharm.	Univ. of Arizona	R2		R		R	R	R
	Coll. of Pharm.— Glendale	Midwestern Univ. Glendale	R				R	R	R*
CA	Sch. of Pharm.	Keck Graduate Institute	R2		R	R	R	R	R
	Coll. of Pharm.	California Northstate	R2		R	CR	R	R	R
	Sch. of Pharm.	Univ. of San Diego					R*		R*
	Sch. of Pharm.	Univ. of San Francisco	R4 6				R2		R*/ R*
	Coll. of Pharm.	California Health Sciences University	R2		R	CR	R		
	Skaggs Sch. of Pharm. & Pharmaceutical Sciences	Chapman University	R		R		R	R	R
	Sch. of Pharm.	Loma Linda Univ.	R		R	R	R*		R/R
	Thomas J. Long Sch. of Pharm. &	Univ. of the Pacific			R		R		R

	School	Affiliation	AP	IM	MC	BC	CA	ST	PI/II
	Health Science								
	Sch. of Pharm.	Pacific Univ. Oregon	R2		R		R		R
	Coll. of Pharm.	Univ. of Southern California	R		R	R	R*	R*	R*
	Coll. of Pharm.**	Touro Univ.	R		R		R		
	Rueckert-Hartman College for Health Professions	West Coast University	R2				R	R	R
	Skaggs Sch. of Pharm. and Pharmaceutical Sciences**	Western Univ.	R2		R7	R2	R		
CO	Sch. of Pharm.	Colorado Denver, Univ. of	R2		R	R	R		R
	Sch. of Pharm.	Regis Univ.	R2		R		R		
CT	Coll. of Pharm.	Connecticut, Univ. of	R2		R	R	R		R
	Coll. of Pharm. and Pharmaceutical Sciences**	Saint Joseph, Univ.	R2	CR	R	CR	R*	R	R
DC	LECOM Sch. of Pharm. Bradenton Campus	Howard Univ.	R2		R	R	R		R/R
FL	Coll. of Pharm.	Florida, Univ. of	R2		R	R	R*	R	R/R
	Lloyd L. Gregory Sch. of Pharm.	Florida A&M Univ.	R2				R		R/R
	Coll. of Pharm.	Nova Southeastern Univ.	R2		CR	CR	R		R
	Coll. of Pharm.	Palm Beach Atlantic Univ.	R2		R	R	R	R	
	Coll. of Pharm.	Univ. of South	R2		R	R	R	R	R

	School	Affiliation	AP	IM	MC	BC	CA	ST	PI/II
	and Health Sciences	Florida							
GA	Sch. of Pharm.–Georgia Campus	Georgia, Univ. of	R2		R	R	R*	R	
	Sch. of Pharm.	Mercer Univ.	R3		R	R	R	R	R
	Coll. of Pharm.	Philadelphia College of Osteopathic Medicine					R	R	R
	Daniel K. Inouye Coll. of Pharm.	South Univ.	R2				R		R
HI	Coll. of Pharm.	Hawaii-Hilo, Univ. of	R2		R		R		
IA	Coll. of Pharm.	Drake Univ.			R		R	R	
	Chicago Coll. of Pharm.	Iowa, Univ. of	R2		R	R	R	R	CR
ID	Coll. of Pharm.	Idaho State Univ.	R2		R	R	R	R	R
IL	Coll. of Pharm.	Chicago State Univ.	R				R*	R	R*
	Sch. of Pharm.	Univ. of Illinois Chicago	R				R*		R/R
	Coll. of Pharm.	Midwestern Univ (Chicago)	R				R*	R	R*
	Coll. of Pharm. and Health Sciences	Roosevelt Univ.	R2		R		R	R	R
	Coll. of Pharm.	Rosalind Franklin Univ.	R				R		R/R
	Coll. of Pharm.	Southern Illinois Univ. Edwardsville IL	R2				R		R/R
IN	Coll. of Pharm. and Health Sciences	Butler Univ.	R2		R		R*		
	Coll. of Pharm.	Manchester Univ.	CR		R		R	R	R
	Sch. of Pharm.	Purdue Univ.	R2	R	R	R	R2	R	R

	School	Affiliation	AP	IM	MC	BC	CA	ST	PI/II
KS	Coll. of Pharm.**	Kansas, Univ.	R3		R		R	R	CR
KY	Sch. of Pharm.	Univ. of Kentucky	R		R		R*	R	R/R
	Coll. of Pharm.	Sullivan Univ.	R		R		R	R	R
LA	Coll. of Pharm.**	Louisiana at Monroe, Univ.	R2		R	R	R	R	R
	Coll. of Pharm.	Xavier Univ.			R		R	R*	R
	Sch. of Pharm.	Massachusetts-Boston			R		R2	R	R
MA	Sch. of Pharm.	Massachusetts-Worcester/Manchester			R		R	R	R
	Sch. of Pharm.	Northeastern Univ.	R2			R	R		R
	Sch. of Pharm.	Western New England Univ.	R2		R		R	R	R
	Sch. of Pharm.	Univ. of Maryland	R2		R		R	R	R/R
MD	Sch. of Pharm.-Boston	Univ. of Maryland Eastern Shore	R2		R		R	R	R
	Sch. of Pharm.–Worcester/Manchester	Notre Dame of Maryland Univ.	R2		R		R	R	R
ME	Sch. of Pharm.	Husson Univ.	R2				R	R	
	Sch. of Pharm.	Univ. of New England	R2				R	R	R
	Coll. of Pharm.	Ferris State Univ.	R2		R	R	R*	R	R
MI	Coll. of Pharm.	Michigan, Univ. of	R2		R	R	R	R	R2
	Eugene Applebaum Coll. of Pharm. and Health Sciences***	Wayne State Univ.	R2		R		R		R

	School	Affiliation	AP	IM	MC	BC	CA	ST	PI/II
MN	Coll. of Pharm.	Minnesota, Univ. of	R2		R		R	R	R/R
MO	Coll. of Pharm.	Missouri—Kansas City, Univ. of	R		R		R*		R
	Coll. of Pharm.	St. Louis	R2				R		R/R
MS	—	Mississippi, Univ. of	R41	R	R7	R	R	R	R/R
MT	Sch. of Pharm.**	Montana, Univ. of	R2				R	R	R
	Skaggs Sch. of Pharm.	Campbell Univ.	S*	S*	S*	S*	R*		R
NC	Sch. of Pharm. and Health Professions	North Carolina Chapel Hill, Univ. of	R		R	CR	R	R	R/R
	Coll. of Pharm.	Wingate Univ.	R2		R		R	R	R
ND	Coll. of Pharm.	North Dakota State Univ.	R2		R2	R2	R	R	R
	Sch. of Pharm.	Creighton Univ.	R*				R		
NE	Ernest Mario Sch. of Pharm.***	Univ. of Nebraska Medical Center	R2				R	R	R/R
NJ	Coll. of Pharm.	Fairleigh Dickinson University	R2			R	R	R	R/R
	Albany Coll. of Pharm.	Rutgers	R42				R	R	R/R
NM	Sch. of Pharm.**	Univ. of New Mexico	R2		R		R	R	R/R
NV	Arnold & Marie Schwartz Coll. of Pharm. and Health Sciences**	Roseman Univ. of Health Sciences	R2		R		R		
NY	Coll. of Pharm. and Health Professions	Albany Coll. of Pharm.	CR		R	CR	R	R	R/R
	Wegmans Sch. of Pharm.	Buffalo The SUNY, Univ. at	R3		R	R	R2	R	R

	School	Affiliation	AP	IM	MC	BC	CA	ST	PI/II
	–	D'Youville College	CR		CR		R	R	R/R
	Sch. of Pharm. and Pharmaceutical Sciences	Long Island Univ.	R				R		R
	Coll. of Pharm. & Health Sciences	St. John Fisher College	CR				R	R	R
	Sch. of Pharm.**^	St. John's Univ.							
	Eshelman Sch. of Pharm.	Touro College	R2		R	R	R		
	Sch. of Pharm.	Cedarville Univ.	R2	R	R		R	R	R
	Coll. of Pharm., Nursing, and Allied Sciences	Univ. of Cincinnati			R		R2	R	R/R
OH	Sch. of Pharm.**	Findlay, Univ. of	R2				R2	R	R
	Coll. of Pharm.	Northeast Ohio				R2	R	R	R/R
	Raabe Coll. of Pharm.**	Ohio Northern Univ.							
	Coll. of Pharm.***	Ohio State Univ.	R		R		R	R	R/R
	James L. Winkle Coll. of Pharm.	Toledo, Univ. of	R2*				R2		R
OK	Coll. of Pharm.	Univ. of Oklahoma			R		R		R
	Coll. of Pharm. & Pharmaceutical Sciences***	Southwestern Oklahoma State	R		R		R		R
OR	Coll. of Pharm.	Oregon State Univ.	R3		R	R	R	R	R/R
PA	Coll. of Pharm.	Duquesne Univ.					R	R	R
	Coll. of Pharm.	Philadelphia, Univ. of the Sciences in	R2		R		R		R/R
	Coll. of Pharm.	Univ. of Pittsburgh					R	R	
	Mylan Sch. of Pharm.	Temple Univ.	R2				R	R	R/R
	LECOM Sch. of Pharm. Erie Campus	Thomas Jefferson Univ.	R2		R		R		R/R

	School	Affiliation	AP	IM	MC	BC	CA	ST	PI/II
RI	Sch. of Pharm.	Wilkes Univ.					R	R	R
	Jefferson Sch. of Pharm.	LECOM					R	R	R
	Nesbitt Sch. of Pharm.**	Rhode Island, Univ.							
SC	Coll. of Pharm.	Presbyterian College	R2		R		R	R	R
	Coll. of Pharm.	South Carolina COP	R2				R	R	R/R
	Coll. of Pharm.	Medical Univ. of South Carolina	R2				R	R	R/R
SD	Sch. of Pharm.	South Dakota State Univ.	R2		R		R		
TN	Sch. of Pharm.	Belmont Univ.	CR				R	R	R
	Coll. of Pharm.	East Tennessee State Univ.	CR		R	CR	R	R	R
	Coll. of Pharm.	Lipscomb Univ.					R*	R	R
	Bill Gatton Coll. of Pharm.	South College	R2		R		R	R	R
	Coll. of Pharm.	Univ. of Tennessee	R2		R	R2	R	R	
	Sch. of Pharm.	Union Univ.	R2		R		R	R	R
TX	Sch. of Pharm.	Univ. of Houston			R		R	R	R
	Coll. of Pharm.	Univ. of the Incarnate Word	R2		R		R	R	R
	Irma Lerma Rangel Coll. of Pharm.	Univ. of North Texas	R		R		R	R	R
	Coll. of Pharm. and Health Sciences	Texas A&M Univ.			R		R	R	R
	Sch. of Pharm.	Texas Southern Univ.	CR 2				R	R	R
	Coll. of Pharm.	Texas Tech Univ.			R		R	R	R
	Coll. of Pharm.***	Texas-Austin, Univ.	CR		R			R	

	School	Affiliation	AP	IM	MC	BC	CA	ST	PI/II
UT	Feik Sch. of Pharm.**	Univ. of Utah	R2		R		R2	R	R
	UNT System Coll. of Pharm.	Appalachian Coll. of Pharm.	R2		R		R	R	R/R
	Coll. of Pharm.	Hampton Univ.					R		R/R
VA	Coll. of Pharm.	Shenandoah Univ.	R2		R	CR	R		R
	Coll. of Pharm.	Virginia Commonwealth Univ.	R2		R	R	R	R	R
VT	Sch. of Pharm.	Albany Coll. of Pharm.	CR		R	CR	R	R	R/R
WA	Bernard J. Dunn Sch. of Pharm.	Univ. of Washington			R	R	R	R	
	Sch. of Pharm.	Washington State Univ.	R2		R	R	R	R	
WI	Albany Coll. of Pharm.	Concordia University					CR	R	R/R
	Sch. of Pharm.	Wisconsin, Univ. of			R		R	R	R/R
WV	Coll. of Pharm.	Marshall University	R2		R		R*	R	R2
	Sch. of Pharm.	Charleston, Univ. of	R2		R		R	R	R
	Sch. of Pharm.	West Virginia Univ.			R	R	R	R	R/R
WY	Sch. of Pharm.	Univ. of Wyoming	R2		R*		R	R	
PR	Sch. of Pharm.	Univ. of Puerto Rico	R2				R		R/R

APPENDIX III: PROFESSIONAL ORGANIZATIONS FOR PHARMACY STUDENTS

- **Academy of Student Pharmacists (APhA-ASP)**

APhA-ASP is the student body component of the APhA (see below). APhA-ASP represents student pharmacists in all US colleges of pharmacy (and Puerto Rico).

  - Website: www.pharmacist.com/apha-asp

- **American Association of Colleges of Pharmacy (AACP)**

The ACCP leads through member partnerships to advance pharmacy education, research, scholarship, practice, and service to improve societal health. They offer networking and professional development, faculty support services, and a sounding board for professional curriculum improvements.

  - Website: http://www.aacp.org

- **American Association of Pharmaceutical Scientists (AAPS)**

AAPS supports scientists (and student scientists-to-be) who are "dedicated to the discovery, development, and manufacture of pharmaceutical products and therapies through advances in science and technology." AAPS emphasizes scientific data exchange to enhance health contributions. Scientific programs, continuing education, networking, and professional development opportunities are offered, too).

  - Website: http://www.aapspharmaceutica.com/

- **American College of Clinical Pharmacy (ACCP)**

ACCP exists to advance human health and quality of life by helping pharmacists expand practice and research through leadership, education, advocacy, and resource provision. These tools will enable pharmacists to advance drug therapy.

  - Website: http://www.accp.com

- **American Pharmacists Association (APhA)**

The APhA was the first national professional pharmacist society (and was previously known as the American Pharmaceutical Association). Representing the largest association of US pharmacists, practicing pharmacists, pharmaceutical scientists, student pharmacists, and pharmacy technicians, this organization advances the profession of pharmacy through diverse activities.

- Website: http://www.pharmacist.com

- *American Society of Consultant Pharmacists (ASCP)*

ASCP is an international professional association providing leadership, education, advocacy, and resources to advance consultant and senior care pharmacy.

  - Website: http://www.ascp.com/

- *American Society of Health-System Pharmacists (ASHP)*

ASHP is a national professional association representing pharmacists who practice in hospitals, health maintenance organizations, long-term care facilities, home care, and other health care systems. ASHP is a "collective voice" on issues related to medication use and public health. A student branch of this society, the Student Society of Health-System Pharmacists (SSHP) focuses on the interests of hospital and allied health professionals.

  - Website: http://www.ashp.org/
  - Website: Student Affiliation
    (*http://www.ashp.org/Import/MEMBERCENTER*
    /StudentForum/StudentSocieties/BecomeanSSHP.aspx)

- *Christian Pharmacists Fellowship International (CPFI)*

CPFI is a worldwide, interdenominational ministry of pharmacy students and pharmacists who serve every area of pharmaceutical service and practice, emphasizing the Christian principles of ethics and spirituality.

  - Website: http://www.cpfi.org/

- *College of Psychiatric and Neurologic Pharmacists (CPNP)*

CPNP promotes excellence in pharmacy practice, education, and research by optimizing psychiatric and neurologic patient treatment outcomes. They possess and share expertise in pharmacotherapy and patient care and provide community support.

  - Website: http://cpnp.org/

- *Hematology/Oncology Pharmacy Association (HOPA)*

HOPA supports hematology/oncology pharmacy practitioners in optimizing the care of patients with cancer. This group's mission is to reduce the cancer burden on society and promote optimal, cost-effective care for people affected by cancer.

  - Website: https://www.hoparx.org

- *Kappa Epsilon (KE)*

Kappa Epsilon, founded in 1921, is a professional pharmacy fraternity emphasizing personal and professional fulfillment through continuing education, providing networking opportunities, promoting pharmacy as a career and by participating in national projects.

- Website: http://www.kappaepsilon.org/

- *Kappa Psi (KΨ)*

Kappa Psi is the world's oldest and largest co-educational pharmaceutical fraternity, founded in 1879. Fraternity goals include fellowship, industry, fostering high ideals, scholarship, and pharmaceutical research. Kappa Psi represents every critical segment of the pharmacy profession and includes many of the most distinguished names in the annals of American pharmacy.

- Website: https://www.kappapsi.org/

- **National Academy of Managed Care Pharmacy (AMCP)**

AMCP is a professional association of individual pharmacists who use managed care techniques in pharmacy practice. They offer conferences, online learning opportunities, and leadership development seminars.

- Website: http://www.amcp.org/home

- **National Community Pharmacists Association (NCPA)**

NCPA is a national organization that represents the interests of independent and private practice pharmacists (owners, managers, and employees from more than 23,000 independent US community pharmacies).

- Website: http://www.ncpanet.org/

- **National Pharmaceutical Association (NPhA)**

NPhA is dedicated to representing the views and ideals of minority pharmacists on critical issues affecting health care and pharmacy, as well as advancing the standards of pharmaceutical care among all practitioners.

- Website: http://nationalpharmaceuticalassociation.org/

- **Pediatric Pharmacy Advocacy Group (PPAG)**

PPAG is an international, nonprofit, professional association representing the interests of pediatric pharmacists and their patients. They promote safe and effective medication use in children through communication, education, and research.

- Website: http://www.ppag.org/

- *Phi Delta Chi (ΠΔΧ)*

This is the first pharmacy fraternity established to advance the science of pharmacy and its allied interests, and to foster and promote a fraternal spirit among its "brothers" which now includes men and women.

- Website: http://www.phideltachi.org/

- *Phi Lambda Sigma (ΠΛΣ)*

Phi Lambda Sigma is a national pharmacy leadership honor society that exists to increase awareness of the continuing need for pharmacy leaders. To accomplish this goal, they promote opportunities and rewards for leadership in the profession of pharmacy and motivate students to accept these visible roles.

- Website: http://www.philambdasigma.org/PLS/Mission.aspx

- *Rho Chi Society (PX)*

Rho Chi is an honorary organization for the profession of pharmacy. Membership is by invitation and is based on high academic achievement in the professional curriculum. Rho Chi recognizes excellence in intellectual achievement and advocates critical inquiry in all aspects of pharmacy while encouraging high standards of conduct and character, fostering fellowship among its members.

- Website: http://www.rhochi.org/

- **Society of Critical Care Medicine (SCCM)**

SCCM is the largest multi-professional organization dedicated to excellence in critical care for ill and injured patients by emphasizing integrated healthcare team approaches. The mission of SCCM is to incorporate knowledge, technology, and patient compassion to provide prompt and effective care

- Website: http://www.sccm.org

- **Society of Infectious Diseases Pharmacists (SIDP)**

SIDP is a dynamic association of diverse health professionals committed to promoting antimicrobial education through the provision of educational programs about infectious disease treatment. SIDP is comprised of pharmacists and other professionals from all areas of healthcare.

- Website: http://www.sidp.org/

- **Student National Pharmaceutical Association (SNPhA)**

SNPhA was founded in 1972 as an affiliate of the National Pharmaceutical Association (NPhA). This group is an educational and service association of students who are concerned about pharmacy issues, professional development, and the lack of minority representation in pharmacy and other health-related professions. Chapters can be found nationwide except for Arizona, Washington, Utah, and Colorado, states which do not have student chapters at this time.

- Website: http://www.snpha.org/

APPENDIX IV: ANSWERS TO PRACTICE QUESTIONS

The following information addresses the answers to the previous practice questions offered in Chapter 10, beginning on page 121. Answers are accompanied by explanations.

- Answer to Question 1: D, Tablet lubricant

Magnesium stearate is used as a tablet lubricant in tablet formulation (others: calcium stearate, mineral oil, and zinc stearate) to reduce friction during tablet compression. Tablet disintegrants (i.e., alginic acid, carboxymethylcellulose calcium, and microcrystalline cellulose) promote the breaking apart of solid dosage forms into smaller particles that can be more readily dispersed. Tablet glidants (cornstarch and talc) improve the flow properties of powder mixtures. Tablet opaquants (titanium dioxide) decrease the transparency of tablet coatings and may be used with colorants. Tablet polishing agents (white wax, carnauba wax) give coated tablets a pharmaceutically elegant sheen.

- Answer to Question 2: B, Elixir

Elixirs by definition are sweetened hydro-alcoholic solutions, and alcohol content varies widely among different elixirs. Medications with an alcohol content greater than 10–12% usually do not require antimicrobials for preservation; they are self-preserving. Most elixirs also contain flavoring and coloring agents to enhance taste and appearance.

- Answer to Question 3: A, Non-alcoholic mouthwash.

Mouthwashes are helpful for the management of dry mouth, but they should be alcohol-free. Alcohol may increase oral dryness. Mild flavorings are preferred in mouthwashes, too because strong flavors may exacerbate oral irritation. Chewing gums and mints may help with dry mouth, but they should be sugar-free to minimize dental caries.

- Answer to Question 4: C, The drug has a low molecular weight

Low molecular drugs will likely across the placenta. In general, compounds with lower molecular weights (250–500 kDa) will cross the placenta easily. Medications with molecular weights of 500–1,000 kDa do not cross easily, and those with molecular weights greater than 1,000 kDa cross the placenta poorly.

- Answer to Question 5: D, Hydroxylation

Only "hydroxylation" is a chemical reaction

- Answer to Question 6: D, Docusate

Docusate is a surfactant that reduces surface tension and increases the water solubility of organic compounds.

- Answer to Question 7: C, Doxazosin

This is a direct recall question. You simply must know this fact.

- Answer to Question 8: E, Tramadol

This is a direct recall question. See above.

APPENDIX V: TOP 200 DRUGS BY PRESCRIPTION SALES

Generic	Trade Name	Indication
levothyroxine	Synthroid	Thyroid Hormone
hydrocodone/APAP, II	Generic Only	Pain Relief
amoxicillin	Amoxil	Antibiotic
lisinopril	Prinivil	ACE Inhibitor
esomeprazole	Nexium	GERD
atorvastatin	Lipitor	Cholesterol
simvastatin	Zocor	Cholesterol
clopidogrel	Plavix	Anti-Platelet
montelukast	Singulair	Asthma
rosuvastatin	Crestor	Cholesterol
metoprolol	Lopressor	Beta Blocker
escitalopram	Lexapro	Anti-Depressant
azithromycin	Zithromax	Antibiotic
albuterol	ProAir HFA	Asthma Inhaler
hydrochlorothiazide	HCTZ	Diuretic
metformin	Glucophage	Anti-Diabetic
sertraline	Zoloft	Anti-Depressant
ibuprofen	Advil	NSAID
zolpidem, iv	Ambien	Insomnia
furosemide	Lasix	Diuretic
omeprazole	Prilosec	GERD
trazodone	Desyrel	Anti-Depressant
valsartan	Diovan	ARB
tramadol	Ultram	Pain Relief
duloxetine	Cymbalta	Anti-Depressant
warfarin	Coumadin	Blood Thinner
amlodipine	Norvasc	CCB
oxycodone/APAP, II	Percocet	Pain Relief
quetiapine	Seroquel	Anti-Psychotic
promethazine	Phenergan	Anti-Histamine
fluticasone	Flonase	Allergies -
alprazolam, IV	Xanax	Anti-Anxiety
clonazepam, IV	Klonopin	Anti-Anxiety
benazepril	Lotensin	ACE Inhibitor
meloxicam	Mobic	NSAID (Arthritis)
citalopram	Celexa	Anti-Depressant
cephalexin	Keflex	Antibiotic
tiotropium	Spiriva	COPD
gabapentin	Neurontin	Anti-Epileptic
aripiprazole	Abilify	Anti-Depressant
potassium	K-Tab	Electrolyte

Generic	Trade Name	Indication
cyclobenzaprine	Flexeril	Muscle Relaxer
methylprednisolone	Medrol	Corticosteroid
methylphenidate, II	Concerta	ADHD
fexofenadine	Allegra	Allergies
carvedilol	Coreg	CHF
carisoprodol, IV	Soma	Muscle Relaxer
digoxin	Lanoxin	CHF
memantine	Namenda	Alzheimer's
atenolol	Tenormin	Beta Blocker
diazepam, IV	Valium	Anti-Anxiety
oxycodone, II	OxyContin	Pain Relief
risedronate	Actonel	Osteoporosis
folic acid	Folvite	Supplement
olmesartan	Benicar	ARB
prednisone	Deltasone	Anti-Inflammatory
doxycycline	Vibramycin	Antibiotic
alendronate	Fosamax	Osteoporosis
pantoprazole	Protonix	GERD
tamsulosin	Flomax	Frequent Urination
triamterene/HCTZ	Dyazide	Diuretic Combo
paroxetine	Paxil	Anti-Depressant
buprenorphine, III	Suboxone	Opiate Addiction
enalapril	Vasotec	ACE Inhibitor
lovastatin	Mevacor	Cholesterol
pioglitazone	Actos	Diabetes
pravastatin	Pravachol	Cholesterol
fluoxetine	Prozac	Anti-Depressant
insulin detemir	Levemir	Long-Acting Insulin
fluconazole	Diflucan	Anti-Fungal
levofloxacin	Levaquin	Antibiotic
rivaroxaban	Xarelto	Blood Thinner
celecoxib	Celebrex	NSAID
codeine/APAP, III	Tylenol #2	Pain Relief
mometasone	Nasonex	Allergies
ciprofloxacin	Cipro	Antibiotic
pregabalin	Lyrica	Anti-convulsant
insulin aspart	Novolog	Rapid-Acting Insulin
venlafaxine	Effexor	Anti-Depressant
lorazepam, IV	Ativan	Anti-Anxiety
ezetimibe	Zetia	Cholesterol
estrogen	Premarin	Menopause
allopurinol	Zyloprim	Anti-gout
penicillin	Pen VK	Antibiotic

Generic	Trade Name	Indication
sitagliptin	Januvia	Diabetes
amitriptyline	Elavil	Anti-Depressant
clonidine	Catapres	Hypertension
latanoprost	Xalatan	Glaucoma
lisdexamfetamine, II	Vyvanse	ADHD
niacin	Niaspan	Cholesterol
naproxen	Aleve	NSAID
dexlansoprazole	Dexilant	GERD
glyburide	Diabeta	Diabetes
olanzapine	Zyprexa	Anti-Psychotic
tolterodine	Detrol	Incontinence
ranitidine	Zantac	GERD
famotidine	Pepcid	GERD
diltiazem	Cardizem	Hypertension
insulin glargine	Lantus	Long-Acting Insulin
thyroid	Armour Thyroid	Thyroid Hormone
bupropion	Wellbutrin	Antidepressant
cetirizine	Zyrtec	Allergies
topiramate	Topamax	Antiepileptic
valacyclovir	Valtrex	Herpes Mgmt
eszopiclone, IV	Lunesta	Sleep Aid
acyclovir	Zovirax	Herpes Mgmt
cefdinir	Omnicef	Antibiotic
clindamycin	Cleocin	Antibiotic
colchicine	Colcrys	Gout
gemfibrozil	Lopid	Cholesterol
guaifenesin	Robitussin	Expectorant
glipizide	Glucotrol	Diabetes(II)
irbesartan	Avapro	ARB
metoclopramide	Reglan	GERD
losartan	Cozaar	Hypertension
meclizine	Dramamine	Antiemetic
metronidazole	Flagyl	Antibiotic
vitamin D	Caltrate	Supplement
testosterone, III	AndroGel	Low T
ropinirole	Requip	Parkinson's
risperidone	Risperdal	Antipsychotic
olopatadine	Patanol	Antihistamine
moxifloxacin	Avelox	Antibacterial
dexmethylphenidate, II	Focalin	ADHD
enoxaparin	Lovenox	Anti-coagulant
fentanyl, II	Duragesic	Narcotic Analgesic
dicyclomine	Bentyl	IBS

Generic	Trade Name	Indication
bisoprolol	Zebeta	Beta Blocker
atomoxetine	Strattera	ADHD
ramipril	Altace	Hypertension
temazepam, IV	Restoril	Sleep Aid
phentermine, IV	Adipex P	Weight Loss
quinapril	Accupril	ACE Inhibitor
sildenafil	Viagra	Impotence
ondansetron	Zofran	Antiemetic
oseltamivir	Tamiflu	Antiviral (Flu)
methotrexate	Rheumatrex	Rheum arthritis
dabigatran	Pradaxa	Anticoagulant
budesonide	Uceris	Ulcerative colitis
doxazosin	Cardura	Freq Urination
desvenlafaxine	Pristiq	Anti-depressant
insulin lispro	Humalog	Rapid-Acting Insulin
clarithromycin	Biaxin	Antibiotic
buspirone	Buspar	Anti-anxiety
finasteride	Proscar	BPH
ketoconazole	Nizoral	Antifungal
solifenacin	VESIcare	Overactive Bladder
methadone, II	Dolophine	Anti-addictive
minocycline	Minocin	Antibiotic
phenazopyridine	Pyridium	UTI
spironolactone	Aldactone	Diuretic
vardenafil	Levitra	Impotence
clobetasol	Clovate	Corticosteroid
benzonatate	Tessalon	Antitussive
divalproex	Depakote	Antiepileptic
dutasteride	Avodart	BPH
febuxostat	Uloric	Gout
lamotrigine	Lamictal	Antiepileptic
nortriptyline	Pamelor	Antidepressant
roflumilast	Daliresp	COPD
rabeprazole	Aciphex	GERD
etanercept	Enbrel	Anti-Arthritis
nebivolol	Bystolic	Beta Blocker
nabumetone	Relafen	NSAID
nifedipine	Procardia	CCB
nitrofurantoin	Macrobid	Antibiotic
nitroglycerine	NitroStat SL	Angina
oxybutynin	Ditropan	Incontinence
tadalafil	Cialis	Impotence
triamcinolone	Kenalog	Corticosteroid

Generic	Trade Name	Indication
rivastigmine	Exelon	Dementia
lansoprazole	Prevacid	GERD
cefuroxime	Ceftin	Antibiotic
methocarbamol	Robaxin	Muscle Relaxer
travoprost	Travatan	Ocular Hypertension
lurasidone	Latuda	Antipsychotic
terazosin	Hytrin	BPH
sumatriptan	Imitrex	Migraine
raloxifene	Evista	Osteoporosis
mirtazepine	Remeron	Antidepressant
adalimumab	Humira	Anti-inflammatory
benztropine	Cogentin	Parkinson's
baclofen	Gablofen	Muscle Relaxer
hydralazine	Apresoline	Hypertension
mupirocin	Bactroban	Antibacterial
propranolol	Inderal	Hypertension
varenicline	Chantix	Smoking addiction
verapamil	Verelan	CCB
clotrimazole	Lotrimin	Antifungal
phenytoin	Dilantin	Anticonvulsant
pramipexole	Mirapex	Parkinson's
liraglutide	Victoza	Anti-Diabetic
ticagrelor	Brilinta	Heart Disease
diclofenac	Voltaren	NSAID Gel
saxagliptin	Onglyza	Anti-Diabetic
lomitapide	Juxtapid	Cholesterol
tizanidine	Zanaflex	Muscle Relaxer
amphetamine /dextro-amphetamine, II	Adderall	Stimulant ADHD/Narcolepsy
zoster vaccine	Zostavax	Shingles Vaccine
ezetimibe/ simvastatin	Vytorin	Cholesterol

AUTHOR INFORMATION

I wrote this book with several unique pharmacy/pharmacist experiences in mind. Most of these are wonderful memories. Oddly, the one experience that was terrible may have been the most important for the lesson I learned from it.

First, my earliest memory of interacting with a pharmacist was when I was around the age of eight. My five-year-old sister and I wanted a surprise birthday present for my mother. Considering the places we could go to find a perfect gift, we realized with sadness and anxiety that we were too small to walk anywhere except a new family-owned pharmacy which was slightly beyond our neighborhood. We walked down our long street, hand in hand, and crossed a dusty and worn foot path that would connect us to a small empty lot behind the pharmacy.

My sister and I entered the small, clean-smelling shop and browsed the retail items that might make a great gift. We settled on a ceramic Mary Poppins figurine for our mother. It was perfect, and the doll had red hair, just like Mom. We approached the counter to pay, and the pharmacist, Dr. Toni Bari, peered over his counter at our two filthy faces. I handed over the Mary Poppins along with my sweaty clutch of money. I had no idea what the object cost or whether I had enough money. I had never previously purchased anything all by myself.

Dr. Bari rang up the figurine and counted out our money, pressing each paper bill onto the counter and arranging them in a tiny stack. He said, "Well, we have this Mary Poppins, which is on sale, and then we have the Gibson family pharmacy discount, of course, and well...that comes to a little under what you have. Is this for someone special?" We told him that it was a birthday present for our mother. He nodded and smiled, wrapped the figurine, and handed us some small coins for change. We were gleeful all the way home.

Mom opened her present that afternoon and was amazed that we had procured it in such an independent fashion. She was more surprised that we could pay for it. After all, the figurine had not been on sale (as the price tag tackily left on the present indicated) and we did not have any such discount. Dr. Bari had fudged the numbers a little to enable me and my sister to perform a miracle of kindness that my mother will tell you never happened again in her house.

So, my first pharmacist interaction was one of kindness and compassion.

The next pharmacist experience was an interaction that could be collectively described as hostile. If you prefer *proper* language: one pharmacist was a jerk.

The interaction was precipitated by the fact that I had a new prescription for a chronic condition, and I had no job to pay for the drugs. I was in my first year of college (1988), so I needed to obtain my drugs cheaply and easily. I thought I might call a few pharmacies to ask about the price of the drugs, aspiring to get the best deal.

I was so delighted with my plan that I phoned the first three pharmacies in the Jonesboro Southwestern Bell telephone book. All three pharmacies were independent, family-owned stores. Retail pharmacies did not exist in my hometown. When I thought of retail pharmacies, I pictured the gargantuan Duane Reed in Manhattan. You needed a map to get around that place.

When the first pharmacist I called heard my question about drug pricing, he hung up on me. The next pharmacist put the phone down and walked off, forcing *me* to hang up on *him*. The last pharmacist I called paused when I asked how much he charged for my medication.

He was gathering his breath for what would come next.

He yelled, "I WILL NOT PLAY THIS GAME. HOW DARE YOU ASK ME SUCH A THING! WHAT KIND OF PERSON ARE YOU?"

Big mistake.

Who knew that consumer pricing and cost transparency would arrive almost 30 years *after* my little inquiry? Let's just say I was way ahead of my time, and that will let me sleep at night. By the way, when you are ahead of your time, you don't know it. You just feel stupid, like you are naked at a picnic.

Another idea that helps me sleep at night is knowing that this guy was out of business after Medicare Part D was enacted. This new re-imbursement schedule put a lot of family-owned pharmacies into bankruptcy, which is terrible and a sign of what the government can do to free enterprise. Still, I wondered how such a jerk would treat patients if he was working for someone other than himself.

My final actual memory of interacting with a pharmacist changed my opinion about the role of pharmacists in healthcare. In my final year of college in Batesville, AR (1992), I began inexplicably coughing every hour of every day for about 10 days. I could not stop. My parents noticed this annoying and persistent hacking when I called home. Thus, my mom drove the hour or so to my college to check on me that January, and immediately packed me into the car after seeing how ill I was. We headed to the ER where I was diagnosed with double pneumonia.

The ER physician who treated me prescribed a liquid preparation that would treat my problem. Then, Mom and I found a pharmacy by the ER to fill the prescription. The pharmacist looked over the prescription and then looked me over. He went into the back and bumped around for a minute, emerging with a phone receiver pressed to his ear. We heard him say into the phone, "Hey, did you know that this prescription is probably not right for this patient? The formulation of this medication changed recently. She should not have this drug as written, so can we change this?"

We could.

He then explained that taking the drug as prescribed meant I would be taking twice the dose needed to treat my illness. Thus, he had phoned the ER to tell them about this error and request an adjustment.

Would I have died from this error?

No.

Was I impressed that the pharmacist was willing to make this correction for me, and that he was not afraid to correct the ER physician, too?

You bet.

So, these experiences (minus the jerk, of course) were on my mind when I began teaching pharmacy students, which was to be my most recent unique experience with this field. At the time, I had presumed that the education we provided was somehow transformative, morphing indifferent college students into kind, caring, smart professionals.

I was completely wrong.

Now, I know that those kind, caring, and smart students *were that way all along*. We just helped them obtain a PharmD so that they could share their special brand of beneficence with the rest of us.

CPSIA information can be obtained
at www.ICGtesting.com
Printed in the USA
LVHW081325250619
622302LV00029B/351/P